Digitization of Healthcare Data Using Blockchain

Scrivener Publishing
100 Cummings Center, Suite 541J
Beverly, MA 01915-6106

Next-Generation Computing and Communication Engineering

Series Editors: Dr. G. R. Kanagachidambaresan and Dr. Kolla Bhanu Prakash

Developments in articial intelligence are made more challenging because the involvement of multi-domain technology creates new problems for researchers. Therefore, in order to help meet the challenge, this book series concentrates on next generation computing and communication methodologies involving smart and ambient environment design. It is an effective publishing platform for monographs, handbooks, and edited volumes on Industry 4.0, agriculture, smart city development, new computing and communication paradigms. Although the series mainly focuses on design, it also addresses analytics and investigation of industry-related real-time problems.

Publishers at Scrivener
Martin Scrivener (martin@scrivenerpublishing.com)
Phillip Carmical (pcarmical@scrivenerpublishing.com)

Digitization of Healthcare Data Using Blockchain

Edited by
T. Poongodi
D. Sumathi
B. Balamurugan
and
K. S. Savita

Scrivener
Publishing

This edition first published 2022 by John Wiley & Sons, Inc., 111 River Street, Hoboken, NJ 07030, USA and Scrivener Publishing LLC, 100 Cummings Center, Suite 541J, Beverly, MA 01915, USA
© 2022 Scrivener Publishing LLC
For more information about Scrivener publications please visit www.scrivenerpublishing.com.

Wiley Global Headquarters
111 River Street, Hoboken, NJ 07030, USA

For details of our global editorial offices, customer services, and more information about Wiley products visit us at www.wiley.com.

Limit of Liability/Disclaimer of Warranty
While the publisher and authors have used their best efforts in preparing this work, they make no representations or warranties with respect to the accuracy or completeness of the contents of this work and specifically disclaim all warranties, including without limitation any implied warranties of merchantability or fitness for a particular purpose. No warranty may be created or extended by sales representatives, written sales materials, or promotional statements for this work. The fact that an organization, website, or product is referred to in this work as a citation and/or potential source of further information does not mean that the publisher and authors endorse the information or services the organization, website, or product may provide or recommendations it may make. This work is sold with the understanding that the publisher is not engaged in rendering professional services. The advice and strategies contained herein may not be suitable for your situation. You should consult with a specialist where appropriate. Neither the publisher nor authors shall be liable for any loss of profit or any other commercial damages, including but not limited to special, incidental, consequential, or other damages. Further, readers should be aware that websites listed in this work may have changed or disappeared between when this work was written and when it is read.

Library of Congress Cataloging-in-Publication Data

ISBN 978-1-119-79185-0

Cover image: Pixabay.Com
Cover design by Russell Richardson

Set in size of 11pt and Minion Pro by Manila Typesetting Company, Makati, Philippines

Printed in the USA

10 9 8 7 6 5 4 3 2 1

Contents

Preface

The revolutionary changes taking place in healthcare domains have attracted the attention of various researchers. Accessing effective, affordable and innovative healthcare is considered to be one of the necessities of modern life. Hence, the need has arisen to empower the digitization of health data in order to make healthcare systems more efficient. By implementing an electronic health record (EHR), progress has been seen in terms of the quality of healthcare. Based on this observation, blockchain technology has gained momentum by gathering all stakeholders in the healthcare sector to solve prevailing challenges. Thus, all of the above factors have driven the editors to propose this book with the goal of enhancing the knowledge of researchers in this state-of-the-art technology and facilitate learning by exposing students, professionals and research scholars in various domains to the information provided by several contributors who are specialists in their areas. This specialized information associated with the incorporation of IoT and blockchain might motivate readers to develop various frameworks along with applications for solving the challenges in various sectors associated with the healthcare domains. Toward this end, a brief description of the information contained in the 12 chapters of this book is presented below.

- Chapter 1 provides a comprehensive review of current research topics, challenges and future prospects in blockchain technology. It also presents various use cases of blockchain technology.
- Chapter 2 explores the intervention of geospatial blockchain analysis in the healthcare industry and also presents policies associated with information security and privacy protection.
- Chapter 3 presents a thorough study of current state-of-the-art technologies by applying blockchain in healthcare domains.

- Chapter 4 deals with the implementation of smart contract and distributed ledger in healthcare informatics.
- Chapter 5 highlights the deployment of consensus algorithms in healthcare domains.
- Chapter 6 investigates the integration of Industry 4.0 with blockchain from the viewpoint of several applications.
- Chapter 7 discusses the utilization of blockchain technology for solving issues in electronic health records.
- Chapter 8 emphasizes the incorporation of IoT and blockchain for the next-generation healthcare services.
- Chapter 9 proposes algorithms for disease prediction with the help of machine learning algorithms.
- Chapter 10 analyzes the impact of blockchain and machine learning in healthcare services.
- Chapter 11 furnishes the advancement techniques in deep learning and blockchain technology in the health informatics field.
- Chapter 12 equips researchers with applications, such as data management, storage and security, in the field of the Internet of Medical Things (IoMT). Apart from that, a review is presented on future prospects in other domains like claims, bill management and drug delivery.

We thank all contributors for their excellent contributions.

The Editors
May 2022

1

Evolution of Blockchain Technologies and its Fundamental Characteristics

Aradhna Saini[1]*, R. Gopal[2], S. Suganthi[3] and T. Poongodi[4]

[1]Department of Computer Science and Engineering, Noida Institute of Engineering and Technology, Greater Noida, Uttar Pradesh, India
[2]Information and Communication Engineering, College of Engineering, University of Buraimi, Al Buraimi, Oman
[3]Department of Computer Science, Cauvery College for Women, Tiruchirapalli, Tamilnadu, India
[4]School of Computing Science and Engineering Galgotias University, Greater Noida, Delhi-NCR, India

Abstract

Blockchain technology facilitates a way to organize business activities, commercial transactions, minimizes costs and time incurred because of intermediaries, and increases trust of the complete ecosystem. Blockchain is a decentralized transaction technology that was first developed for the cryptocurrency known as bitcoin. Since the concept was first proposed in 2008, there has been a growing interest in blockchain technology. The primary traits of blockchain are as follows: provide security, data integrity and anonymity without the involvement of any third-party organization for tracking the transactions, which drives interest in this technology and opens up new research areas, particularly in solving several technical challenges. A systematic review is conducted to present all relevant fundamental concepts on blockchain technology in this study. Our goal is to gain a technical understanding of current research issues, challenges, and future directions in blockchain technology. The focus of this research work is in providing a high-level overview of blockchain from the context of its categories and various use cases. Researchers interested in this area would gain a better understanding of this technology with this article.

Keywords: Blockchain, bitcoin, cryptographic, private, public, consortium

Corresponding author: aradhnasaini13@gmail.com

T. Poongodi, D. Sumathi, B. Balamurugan and K. S. Savita (eds.) Digitization of Healthcare Data Using Blockchain, (1–24) © 2022 Scrivener Publishing LLC

1.1   An Overview of Blockchain Technology

Blockchain in the early stage is known by cryptocurrency, which is known as bitcoin. It is peer-to-peer network and everyone can use without their authentication details. The public can be a part of blockchain and also carryout transactions. According to Gartner report, the estimation of blockchain till 2030 is $3.1 trillion investment. Blockchain plays a very vital and important role in digital cryptocurrency bitcoin [1]. Blockchain can be defined as a scatter database include information or a set of sheets that spot each and every event and agreement, implement and split into examine parties. The transaction data between sender and receiver can never be removed, and each and every transaction had checkable documentation. Blockchain emulates an assigned database by including information by assimilate information identical across the web in real time. At present has become a slang in both industry and academic community [3]. As one of the most victorious cryptocurrencies, bitcoin has appreciated with its capital retail reaching 1 tn dollars in February 2021. In the beginning, scalability is a colossal have to do cover. The size of bitcoin block is restricted to 1MB, at the moment spam a block is mined regarding about every 10 minutes.

There are some properties of blockchain:

i.   It has authenticated data, if data change or improve, it has to be confirmed by users using a cryptographic approach.
ii. It has a database that is secured by cryptographic symmetric and asymmetric public/private key.
iii. The transaction of bitcoin between two devices/parties is very trustworthiness.

Blockchain is conceivable consider as a general ledger, and all carry-out transactions are stocked in a record of blocks. These bonds expend as latest blocks are attached to it continuously. Asymmetric cryptography and allocated consensus algorithms have been executed for customer safety along with register stability. The blockchain technology normally has pointer attribute of decentralized, persistency, anonymity, and audibility. Using these properties, blockchain save cost, improve ability, and increase security.

1.1.1   Evolution of Blockchain Technology

Blockchain has progressed into an additional established technology, and the merchandise for the technology is stretching very fast. The blockchain contributes fetters market awaiting to enlarge at a CAGR of 81.7% atop predict interval 2021 to 2026. Blockchain technology is most intelligible independent, and consortiums from incompatible pasture are applied on different applications of blockchain that expand far away from the origin of cryptocurrency and other different intelligent models. In the uncondensed shareholder, banking plays the earliest major industry investor in the blockchain. Simultaneously, blockchain flatters as undetectable in the online pursuit, and it is very significant to resolve the cybersecurity problem or prevent from methods of attack.

1.1.2   Significant Characteristics of Blockchain Technology

A blockchain is registered effectively in all production in which benefits are supervised and undertaking takes place. It is very powerful in the main aspect of security, it is imparts immovable fetters of tutelage for both, first is digital and second is physical benefits through its protection characteristics that provide between transaction between two different compatible devices. In Figure 1.1 it is very clear to understand the characteristics of blockchain. There are important characteristics described below as coincidental, security, consensus, and other as decentralized. These details of blockchain are very helpful in the research of following transaction. Transaction is the interchange of recommendation that helps to control under the whole amenities rules. These rules help to up and run, with the help of scripting language as bitcoin and also used for state-of-the-art performance. The behavior of blockchain is very credulous, and it is also delineated to get rid of the requirement for all or one setup to gate transactions. Blockchain can be confidential like public, private, or hybrid modification, turn on their appeal public. In the public blockchain, there are no possessors, and anyone can easily access without any authorization, and they are overflowing broadcast. An example of public blockchain is bitcoin. In private blockchain, there are uses of concession to authorize to read and write to the blockchain. Consensus algorithm and mining are not required as sole operation has possession and power block formation. In hybrid blockchain, it works as public but only for a privileged category, and it is controlled by consensus, privileged dependent using a group of rules concurred by all functions. The different characteristics of blockchain is shown in Figure 1.1.

- **Faster settlement:** The head ascendancy of blockchain technology is that it can pace up settlement, twain by acquiring purge of a shattered gestation framework and

Figure 1.1 Different characteristics of blockchain.

by instrumenting a more settlement rotation. It decides to clasp time transaction between parties (sender/receiver). It helps to settle the payment broadcast to Peer-2-Peer (P2P) network consisting of devices that are known by nodes. The payment between these parties, cryptocurrency involved, consists of all records of transactions or also other information.

- **Distributed ledgers:** It is represents the database that is a two-way split and harmonized covering different sites and foundations. This technology is the one important key of technologies, and it is responsible for conducting the cryptographic. Block represents the records, each block keeps the encipher hash of the last block and checksum onward the transaction data.

- **Consensus:** As it is known, the blockchain works on block, and using blocks create a blockchain, the consensus use for surety that every block is added in blockchain [9]. It is the only version that decides which block is added or rejected.

- **Enhanced Security:** Blockchain automation has superior security, it is almost impossible to shut down the system. In history, bitcoin is the second decentralized and had never been hacked, and the single reason is that blockchain trellis is highly secured by a number of computers, which is known by nodes, and nodes are used to affirm the transaction of bitcoin on this network.
- **Decentralized:** This technology plays a vital role in the administration of resources, for both hardware and also for software [7]. Blockchain is worn in a decentralized procedure where a single person nor groups has control, preferably everyone in concert keep jurisdiction.
- **Immutability:** Generating immutably is the foremost values of the blockchain. Blockchain like bitcoin keeps its register in a never-finished state of redirecting momentum. The database is not hacked because of a third party, a third party keeps the data more secure. To command the bitcoin, first, it needs to command over 51% of the whole market.

1.2   Blockchain Architecture and Its Components

A structure of blockchain is an order of blocks, blocks work as a store in an out-and-out list of transaction information like conventional public ledger [5]. Figure 1.2 refers the architecture of blockchain (a) that represents the connection between parties, whole system, and BitCoin connected with each other and create a blockchain. Multiple devices and academics are

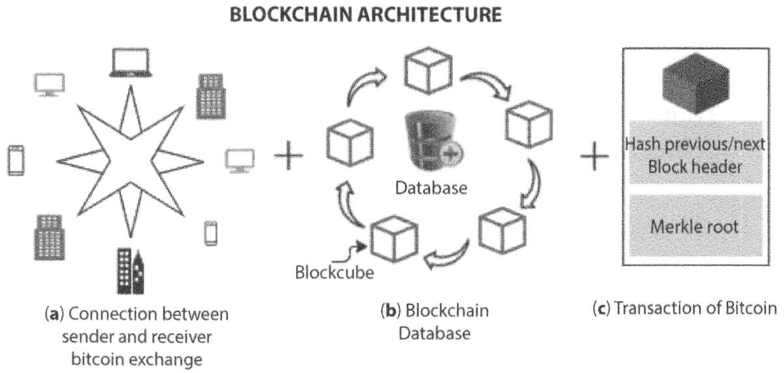

BLOCKCHAIN ARCHITECTURE

(a) Connection between sender and receiver bitcoin exchange

(b) Blockchain Database

(c) Transaction of Bitcoin

Figure 1.2 Blockchain architecture in different ways. Panel (a) represents the connection between parties. Panel (b) represents the blockchain database. Panel (c) represents the transaction using hash.

connected with each and create a network to exchange their bitcoin. The transaction of bitcoin is highly secure, no one can hack the transaction of bitcoin and it is easy to transfer bitcoin from one place to another place [6]. In a standard consolidate bargain arrangement, a one and all arrangement requires to be certified through the halfway believe in organization, inescapably takes place to the fetch and the staging constriction at the median hostess.

> **Cryptographic Hash Functions:** Cryptographic, this word is mostly used for encryption, and decryptions have been worn for centennial to safeguard military and political confidential. The dialectics was if elucidation of an encipher narrative decision in a consequential communication it should have been formulated by dignitary who realize the confidential leading. In the course of all this terms, the field of paleography was domain of favored few i.e., it was deliberate and accomplished by hardly any [4]. The tendency alteration was Diffie and Hellman, which are ascribe for arrival of public key cryptography in mid 1970s.

> **Asymmetric-Key Cryptography:** It is also known as public key encryption, a structure of information encipher where the encryption key and another correlate with decryption key are dissimilar. A note inscribed with the general (public) key can be deciphered narrowly in agreement with a particular (private) key [2]. The general key and the particular key are connected numerically, even so, it is estimating absurdly to obtain the particular key from the general key. Figure 1.3 shows a key exchange between plain text to decryption document. There are two keys, one is a general key and another is a particular key, a general key is used for

> **Transactions:** A transaction indicates an interchange between parties (receiver to sender and vice-versa). With

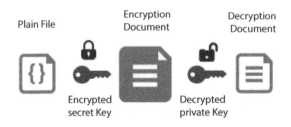

Figure 1.3 Security key exchange.

the help of cryptocurrency, for instance, an arrangement represents a relocation of the cryptocurrency betwixt blockchain user networks. For business-to-business framework, a transaction could be a way of recording a venture happening on the digital or physical forte. It is the most elementary backbone of blockchain system. In the advancement of transmitting the transaction, the customer dispatches the funds, indicating its use in their private key and a particular terminus address. In Figure 1.4, the process of bitcoin transaction is depicted.

> **Ledgers:** It is use for store documentation structure. It helps to keep going the engage recognition incognito, their separate micropayment equilibrium, and an information of fully the veritable compact achieved betwixt crisscross joiner [8]. It somehow differed from blockchain; in blockchain, it creates a sequence of blocks, but in ledger, there are not any chain. A ledger is one kind of database that lays out between collective sites.

> **Blocks:** In simple terms, block helps to store new records of bitcoin transactions that have not yet go in for precedent blocks. Blockchain webwork enjoyer consent applicant deals with the blockchain web via operating system (electronic publishing applications, cellphone applications, electronic handbag, netting services, etc.). The operating dispatch these

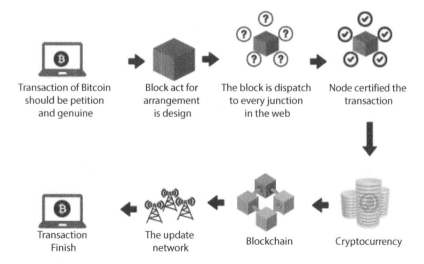

Transaction of Bitcoin should be petition and genuine

Block act for arrangement is design

The block is dispatch to every junction in the web

Node certified the transaction

Transaction Finish

The update network

Blockchain

Cryptocurrency

Figure 1.4   Transaction of bitcoin between parties.

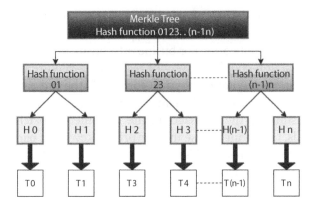

Figure 1.5 Hash tree.

transactions to a junction or a junction inside the block-chain webwork. The selected junction may be nonproducing complete junction, as well as producing junction. The conformed transactions are then breed to the further junction in the web, but they are not taken place itself.

➤ **Consensus algorithms:** Blockchain automation materialize to overcome the threat and inefficiencies in the vocation agreement. It has transfigured the structure of production and vocation [9]. Blockchain can be expound as a distributed ledger, a portion among the nodes of a vocation network.

➤ **Merkle tree (inclusion):** Merkle tree is the structure, these data are hashed and integrate until there is an extraordinary radicle hash that act for the whole structure. It is used for verifying data on Merkle tree using mathematical. These are used of cryptocurrency for sure data blocks, which is passed in the middle of peer-to-peer network. Figure 1.5 represents the Merkle tree structure, hash function indicates the set of inputs in a tree structure with their size.

1.3   Comparative Analysis of Blockchain Categories

As blockchain is in its embryonic and the massive rate of acceptance in all level of business activities extending from small-, medium- to large-scale industries in all domains has brought into it a various number of subspecies in its deployment based on the type of network and the access control, i.e., who is allowed into the P2P network and what type of access control

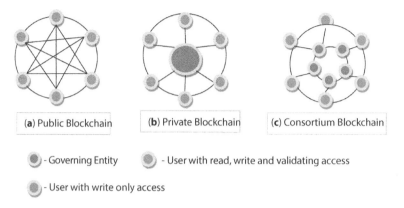

(a) Public Blockchain   (b) Private Blockchain   (c) Consortium Blockchain

- Governing Entity   - User with read, write and validating access

- User with write only access

Figure 1.6 Types of blockchain.

they have. The type of blockchain to use is based on the business need and unique to the problem to be solved. Most often, the selection of the paradigm has been deluding to a larger group and thus makes the selection of blockchain paradigm as a mood one. Before associating to one type of blockchain, it is important to fathom about the various categories in blockchain like permissionless or public blockchain and permissioned or private blockchain, hybrid healthcare and consortium blockchain variants in detail, and it is shown in Figure 1.6.

1.3.1 Permissionless or Public Blockchain

Permissionless or public blockchain is a complete decentralized open network as shown in Figure 1.6a. In this type of blockchain network, anyone who wants to be a part of the blockchain network can join the network at any time and can take participate in the transactions, can add, read and write data to the chain and also participate in the consensus using the mining mechanisms. The data in the chain will be maintained by everyone participating in the network, and so it is accessible by all participants in the network. Also, there is no central controlling point, which makes it an authority free network. In this network, once the data are validated by all the participating nodes, then the data become immutable from there as it is maintained by all the nodes participating in the network. The data validation is done based on the Proof of Work (PoW) or Proof of Stake (PoS) consensus algorithms, and each user in the network will be provided with an incentive if they involve themselves in the data validation to make the network more alive and supple.

In the PoW, the users, called miners, are asked to solve a mathematical puzzle, which needs a lot of computational power both in terms of electricity and resources used. In PoS consensus algorithm, the amount of data validation the user can do is directly proportional to the stake value he holds. The data validation will be allocated to the users randomly and the user will be rewarded if the block is added to the blockchain else the user will be fined with the same level of reward he receives. The other types of consensus algorithm are as follows: Tindermint, Proof of Luck (PoL), Proof of Personhood (PoP), Ripple [10, 11] and etc. The user incentives are provided in the name of tokens of two types, namely monetary value tokens and utility tokens where the monetary tokens have exchanged values and the utility token do not have exchanging values but have intrinsic values. The users involved in the blockchain process are anonymous, and only their blockchain address is needed. In public blockchain network, no third-party intervention is needed as it is an open network with no single controlling authority. The public blockchain has its application in digital currencies, public sector like education and healthcare, consumer to consumer, and business to consumer model. Bitcoin, Ethereum, Tezos, and Litecoin are the most popular platforms, which uses the public blockchain networks. The average size of the blocks in Bitcoin is 1.3MB with an average transaction of 285111 per day [12].

Characteristics of Public Blockchain:
There are some unique characteristics for the public blockchain that makes it differ from other types, which are as follows:

- fully decentralized,
- no restrictions to join the network,
- offers anonymity for the users,
- all users can involve in all activities of blockchain,
- no single controlling points,
- complete transparency,
- incentives for the users.

Advantages of Public or Permissionless Blockchain:
Public or permissionless blockchain type comes with a number of advantages in its deployment style. The strong security in this type of blockchain can prevent the skullduggery or the impact made by this activity can be reduced because of the large volume of the users in the network. The public blockchain network will be propelled by providing the incentives to its users.

Disadvantages of Public or Permissionless Blockchain:
The main disadvantage of public or permissionless blockchain type is its complete transparency, which leads to the lack of privacy. This type of blockchain is slow in operation, and thus, the number of transactions for the given time is very limited. Bitcoin can take 10 minutes to create a block in the chain. Energy consumption will be more because of the maintenance of distributed ledger. The energy consumed by the bitcoin in 2019 July is equal to that of the power consumption of Switzerland. The network can be more vulnerable if a small part of the user behaves maliciously, and this type of blockchain has a risk of around 51% of the total attack in the blockchain. The user when using the PoW needs high computational infrastructure resources, like application specific integrated circuit (ASIC) or graphics processing units (GPU), which are expensive. The size of the block is limited because of the need of large computational resources.

1.3.2 Permissioned or Private Blockchain

The hefty attacks and the openness of the information in the public blockchain have made a path to the more private and secured category of blockchain named private or permissioned blockchain [13, 14] as shown in Figure 1.6b. A private or permissioned blockchain is a network with preselected participants based on the digital signatures as a validating element and controlled by a single authority or governing body within an organization. Not all the users are provided with the access to read, write, or validate the data which prevent data leakage. Different levels of access control will be maintained for the user group by the authority body to maintain the transaction speed and privacy. Private blockchain cannot offer the same level of decentralization provided by the public blockchain, thus it is more centralized as they are controlled by a single authority. Anonymity of the users is not allowed, and every user needs to authenticate him using a valid identity. The immutable of the blocks can be broken by the governing body, thus the data in the blockchain can be modified [15]. It is easy to get the consent from the small group of participants when compared with that of a public blockchain. This type of blockchain is more scalable and saves a lot resource and avoids useless resource usage. It is more robust in nature and has very efficient architecture.

The data can be encrypted based on the commercial needs. The number of computational resources needed will be less, and less time is required to get a consensus among the users because of the limited users in the network. The different consensus algorithms used in the private blockchain are Proof of Authority (PoA), Raft, Proof of Elapsed Time (PoET), Practical Byzantine Fault Tolerance (PBFT), Delegated PoS (DPoS), and so many other algorithms. The users are not provided with any incentives for validating the data block [16, 17]. Private blockchain finds its application in financial services, retails, healthcare, and supply chain management and in business-to-business model. IBM's Hyperledger [18] Fabric and Ripple are the best examples of private blockchain. Other private blockchain are EOS, R3 Corda, Monax, and Multichain.

Characteristics of Private Blockchain:
The private blockchain has its unique characteristics, which makes it differ from other types of blockchain, are as follows:

- highly secured,
- faster transactions,
- renowned users with restricted access,
- centralized control,
- economical,
- efficient,
- scalable,
- robust architecture.

Advantages of Private or Permissioned Blockchain:
The private blockchain comes with a spare of advantages, which makes it utilitarian type among the distinctive organizations. In a private blockchain network, only authenticated users can participate, and thus, the security and privacy of the data in the block are increased. Each private blockchain network will function based on certain regulations guided by the governing authority. The amount needs to complete a transaction, which will be lesser when compared with the public blockchain. Limited resource usage and the speed of transaction processing with scalability features make the private blockchain best suited for many environments [19].

Disadvantages of Private or Permissioned Blockchain:
On the side, the private blockchain has handful of disadvantages to it. Because of the limited number of users in the private blockchain network, it is easy that the malicious attacker can take control of the network. Thus, the security of the private blockchain is in mood. Private blockchains have trust issues in the network among the users. The information in the block can be modified by the authority person. As it is more centralized, unavailability of the system is possible. The private blockchain will not grow as it is more toward private network with limited users.

Both the public and private blockchains can be either open or closed network based on how the users of these networks access the data in the blockchain. Four different characteristics can be formed by using their combination as follows:

1. public and open,
2. public and closed,
3. private and open,
4. private and closed.

Public and Open:
This characteristic is related to the normal public blockchain type where all the users with the computational resources can join the blockchain network, and all have the access to read, write, and validate the block in the blockchain. No one will be the controlling authority for this type of network. It is mainly suitable in crypto currencies, like Bitcoin, Ethereum, and Litecoin, in games.

Public and Closed:
In this type, any user can join the blockchain network, but only few users will be providing the access to read the data from the blockchain. A company named "FollowMyVote" is currently designing a blockchain technology, which can be implemented in the election, where everyone can participate in the voting process, but only certain users have the rights to read the voting [20] count. It can also be used in medical and financial organizations where the need of securing the data is very important.

Private and Open:
In private and opened model, only the invited user can participate in the blockchain network where certain user can write the data into the block and the others can read and consume the data from the block. A use case for this type of blockchain is the supply chain management in which only the manufacturer will add the information to the blockchain, and all other parties involved can access the data in the blockchain.

Private and Closed:
Private and closed type of blockchain is also known as private blockchain or permissioned blockchain. In which, only trusted users are allowed in the network to participate in blockchain activities with different level of access control. Private and closed blockchain is used in insurance industries, DHL is using it for its logistics management, and Walmart is using this technology for its supply chain management.

1.3.3   Consortium Blockchain

The openness of the public blockchain and the centralization of the private blockchain led to a new category of blockchain known as consortium blockchain or federated blockchain, where multiple organizations will participate in the network and have the authority over the blockchain whereas in private blockchain only one organization will have the authority. As per Figure 1.6c, the users of the network are culled identified users who can read, write, and audit the data in the blockchain network. All the users have the equal access control on the data in the blockchain. It is a decentralized network where the consensus process involves all the organizations involved in the blockchain. In this blockchain, the immutable of the data is preserved as no single organization controls the blockchain. Every organization will maintain individual copy of the record of data and any modification can be easily identified and proved in the blockchain network. No incentives are provided for the users in the network for the data audit or validation. The consensus algorithm used in consortium blockchain is Proof of Trust (PoT) and Proof of Vote (PoV) and these algorithms need very limited resources and the transactions are speedy. In PoT, the validators are selected based on their trust value and in PoV the validators will consensus based on the voting mechanisms. Consortium blockchain is mainly used in financial sectors followed by logistics, healthcare and cross sectors. Quorum, Hyperledger, and Corda are the well-known examples of consortium blockchain. The performance of this blockchain is around 1000 to 2000 transactions per second.

Characteristics of Consortium Blockchain:
Consortium blockchain has bulged itself from other blockchain in various industries where the organization needs to collaborate among them based on its unique characteristics. The characteristics of consortium blockchain are as follows:

- decentralized nature,
- renowned users with equal access rights,
- faster transactions,
- limited resource need,
- scalability,
- high security,
- immutable nature of data.

Advantages of Consortium Blockchain:
The consortium blockchain head start with splashy advantages in the field of blockchain. Consortium blockchain is a private blockchain but with decentralized control on the network. Because of the limited authenticated users in the network, it is free from malicious activities and uses constricted

resources which results in the speedy transaction with privacy of the data. It includes the regulation to follow in the network as it is a corporate-controlled private network. Consortium blockchain is unsusceptible to 51% attack as we will not have 51% of the user from a single organization. The energy consumption and fee for each transaction to be made is less compared to that of public blockchain.

Disadvantages of Consortium Blockchain:
The disadvantage of consortium blockchain is because of its decentralization. The minimum number of users in the network will lead to malicious activities. The transactions are not completely transparent and the anonymity of the user is not preserved as in original blockchain.

Table 1.1 describes the comparative analysis between the various categories of blockchain.

1.3.4   Hybrid Blockchain

It is formed with the benefits of both the public and private blockchain. The hybrid blockchain has the features of public blockchain like transparency, immutable, decentralized, and also have the features of private blockchain, like access restriction in write or change data, validation to particular user only [21]. Here, the ledger is placed in the public blockchain and the access to the ledger, such as modification or validating or auditing activities, can be done by selected users or nodes in the network. The various advantages of hybrid blockchain are that it still preserves the privacy of the data in the blockchain even though it is public in access.

1.4   Blockchain Uses Cases in Healthcare

Patient-Digital Identity
Exchange of health information requires patient identification matching for identifying a patient uniquely. This is implemented using system like the master patient index and enterprise master index [22]. Mismatching of patient identity may lead to duplication of patient records, resulting in inconsistent and incomplete medical data. This may result in wrong or repeated tests or treatments, delays in the treatment and reimbursement of medical claims. Also, there can be typing errors, which is common when a huge amount of data are entered. This incurs huge cost in maintaining and correcting the errors. Thus, a common standard for collecting patient identification information is needed as different healthcare providers follow different formats for storage of data which may lead to inconsistencies.

Table 1.1 Comparison between the various categories of blockchain.

Features	Public blockchain	Private blockchain	Consortium blockchain
Authority	Decentralized	Centralized—one organization	Decentralized—group of organization
Access	Everyone	Preselected	Preselected
Transaction speed	Low	High	High
Cost per transaction	High	Low	Low
Energy consumption	High	Low	Low
Consensus algorithm	PoW, PoS, DPoS, etc	PoA, PoET, Raft, PoM, etc	PoV, PoT, etc
Immutability	Yes	Partial	Partial
transaction per second	Around 4 transaction/sec	Several 1000 transaction/sec	Several 1000 transaction/sec
Infrastructure need	High	Low	Low

(Continued)

Table 1.1 Comparison between the various categories of blockchain. (*Continued*)

Features	Public blockchain	Private blockchain	Consortium blockchain
Consensus type	All nodes Without Permission	Selected nodes with permission	All nodes With Permission
Data handling	Any node	List of predefined nodes	Any node
Incentive	Yes	No	No
User anonymity	Yes	No	No
Through	Low	High	High
Example	Bitcoin, Ethereum	Multichain, Monax	HyperLedger, Coda, Quorum,
Application	Crypto currency, public projects	Organization Blockchain (Walmart, DHL)	Supply Chain Management, Healthcare industries

A common identity management system is required across all health-care providers and this can be implemented using blockchains in which each patient can be identified using a cryptographically secured address linked to a unique key. Universal Patient Index Registry, which can be shared across all healthcare providers, can be enforced for standardized identification of patients.

Accessing Medical Records
Medical records can be accessed by patients in an IOT-based blockchain system where organizations, patients, and blockchain are integrated in a complex manner through the use of wearables, sensors, actuators, and cloud services based on prespecified business agreements. A user can fetch EHR data from the local health organization with the help of APIs. Interfacing among the healthcare organizations is provided which helps in proper communication among the healthcare entities. Smart contracts are used to provide authorization from the user for sharing of medical data by an organization.

Assessment of EHR Claims and Billing
Fraudulent EHR claims and billing are regular activities that take place in e-healthcare system which impose major loss for the industry. Fraudulent activities include billing for health services which are unperformed, e-health services being overcharged, unwanted health services being leveraged for a patient, and representing non-covered e-healthcare services in a wrong way [23]. In existing system, though the transactions can be validated, there is no effective communication among the participants involved in the billing. Thus, IOT-based blockchain e-health system with its transparent and decentralized nature can be used to solve majority of the problems by automating the needed workflows and sharing a copy of the transaction by the participants.

Drug Supply-Chain Management
Many patients are affected because of counterfeited drugs entering the supply chain which are done intentionally or by mistake. In the traditional method, the activities are not transparent and hence mistakes are common and unidentified. By implementing IOT-based blockchain, the blockchain itself stores the supply chain data, making it transparent and thereby minimizing fraudulent actions.

Clinical Research
Clinical research involves clinical trials in which anonymity of the patients should be maintained, incurring high cost in terms of time, effort and money. Also, the consent of the e-health consumers, in sharing their

medical data is also mandatory. Hence, blockchains can be used in which anonymity of the patients can be achieved and also the patients can privately store their own EHR data, and publicly modify them using an integrated hybrid blockchain facility [23]. Also, patients can either grant or revoke back their rights in sharing data to a healthcare provider community with the use of hybrid key cryptography.

Opioid Prescription Tracking

Opioids are commonly used in the treatment of pain which contain compounds having the property of interacting with the opioid receptors in the brain. Apart from their benefits, there is increase in the improper usage of opioids leading to public health crisis. According to WHO, more than 70% of the total 0.5 million deaths related to drugs are due to improper usage of opioids [24]. At present, there is lack of effective technology for prescription tracking and blockchain technology with its decentralization, and auditable nature can be effectively used in handling opioid epidemic. By establishing a network of associated shareholders in a blockchain based system can ensure storing and sharing of opioid-associated transactions, which can improve the quality of patient care by monitoring and tracing opioid prescriptions.

Data Sharing in Telemedicine

Telemedicine uses more advanced technology to offer medical care for patients located at a distant place. With telemedicine patients can save time waiting at doctor's place, but can get treatments immediately with the help of many user-friendly apps. Telemedicine is wide ranging, wherein providers treat patients from different networks or regions. This results in reduced care to the patients. Also, data collected during the period of treatment may not be accessible to the patient's primary care providers resulting in incomplete medical history of the patients thereby reducing the quality of service. By incorporating blockchain technology into existing telemedicine can improve the direct communication between the participants thereby eliminating third party intervention.

Cancer Data Sharing

In the existing health systems, data sharing, which is controlled by the patients, would allow cancer patients in easy sharing of their EHR data with the intended care providers and avoids in treatment delays.

Cancer registries play a vital role in population wide control of cancer. However, these registries are isolated and fragmented providing minimal benefits. With the use of blockchain technology for data exchange, several patients serve as a source of data creating an enriched cancer data set. Predictive models can be built by using artificial intelligence on these richer data sets, which aids the health providers in decision making [25].

1.5   Research Opportunities and Challenges of Blockchain Technology in Healthcare

Despite various advantages of blockchain technology, there are inherent challenges associated with it, which needs further research. Some of the major challenges are depicted below.

- Storage
  Health industry generates massive amount of sensor and EHR data coming from various sources. However, blockchain technology, because of its decentralized nature, has a very limited online storage of data [26]. Also, the cost of storing and maintaining this big data in the blockchain architecture is very high. Hence, further research is needed in designing blockchain applications considering the storage factor.
- Scalability
  Health industry is multidimensional encompassing various stakeholders. It is a big challenge that an increase in the number of users in the system requires an increase in the computational requirement of the blockchain system. Also, in the healthcare system, the usage of IoT-based sensors or smart devices is high, which are computationally slow. Thus, these devices are constrained to be benefitted by the blockchain capabilities, resulting in the overall slowdown of the system. Hence, much research is needed in handling the scalability issue.
- Interoperability
  As health industry is vast spreading across many countries, there are differences in formats of data storage, infrastructure, applications, and policies in each region. Thus, there are interoperability challenges in communication among various service providers, which hinders effective data sharing. Hence, further research is needed in this area by increasing more security and transparency.
- Privacy and regulations
  Healthcare contains more sensitive data, and hence it is a huge challenge in making strong privacy policies for sharing medical data among various care providers.

Also, blockchain, being a growing technology, faces challenges related to taxation, and acceptance of legal regulations and policies. Hence, much focus is needed on these factors.

- Modification
  The immutable nature of blockchains provide no rooms for data modification and deletion. However, as deletions and changes are inevitable, blockchain applications should be designed such that changes are minimal.
- Standardization
  As blockchain is a new technology and is in the developing stage, a high level of standardization is required to make function different infrastructure and applications across various countries.

1.6   Conclusion

Blockchain technology operates in a decentralized environment for transactions, with all transactions documented on a public ledger that is accessible to all. The objective of blockchain is to provide all of its users with anonymity, privacy, transparency and security. However, these characteristics create several technical issues that must be addressed. The purpose of this systematic approach is to understand the present state of blockchain technology and its primitive characteristics. With the rise in popularity of cryptocurrencies and blockchain technology in general, there has been renewed interest in its practical applications. Because of some serious limitations, it is highly complex to meet the needs of large-scale deployment in real time. Hence, the primary focus in the quest to develop more suitable realistic blockchain systems by choosing the appropriate blockchain category. The primary motivation of this article is to synthesize some basic ideas under a systematic study in order to advance knowledge in this domain.

References

1. Yaga, D., Mell, P., Roby, N., Scarfone, K., *Blockchain technology overview*, p. 1906.11078, US, arXiv preprint arXiv, 2019.
2. Asaithambi, N., A study on asymmetric key cryptography algorithms. *J. Comput. Sci. Mobil. Appl.*, 3, 4, 8–13, 2015.

3. Komalavalli, C., Saxena, D., Laroiya, C., Overview of blockchain technology concepts, in: *Handbook of Research on Blockchain Technology*, pp. 349–371, Academic Press, Stockholm, Sweden, 2020.

4. Sobti, R. and Geetha, G., Cryptographic hash functions: a review. *Int. J. Comput. Sci. Issues (IJCSI)*, 9, 2, 461, 2012.

5. Syed, T.A., Alzahrani, A., Jan, S., Siddiqui, M.S., Nadeem, A., Alghamdi, T., A comparative analysis of blockchain architecture and its applications: Problems and recommendations. *IEEE Access*, 7, 176838–176869, 2019.

6. Zheng, Z., Xie, S., Dai, H., Chen, X., Wang, H., An overview of blockchain technology: Architecture, consensus, and future trends, in: *2017 IEEE international congress on big data (BigData congress)*, IEEE, pp. 557–564, 2017, June.

7. Diallo, N., Shi, W., Xu, L., Gao, Z., Chen, L., Lu, Y., Turner, G., eGov-DAO: A better government using blockchain based decentralized autonomous organization, in: *2018 International Conference on eDemocracy & eGovernment (ICEDEG)*, IEEE, pp. 166–171, 2018, April.

8. Kadam, S., Review of distributed ledgers: The technological advances behind cryptocurrency. *International Conference Advances in Computer Technology and Management (ICACTM)*, 2018, March.

9. Chaudhry, N. and Yousaf, M.M., Consensus algorithms in blockchain: Comparative analysis, challenges and opportunities, in: *2018 12th International Conference on Open Source Systems and Technologies (ICOSST)*, IEEE, pp. 54–63, 2018, December.

10. Jalal, I., Shukur, Z., Bakar, K.A.A., *A Study on Public Blockchain Consensus Algorithms: A Systematic Literature Review*, vol. 2020110355, Switzerland, Preprints, 2020.

11. www.blockchain.com//en/stats.

12. Casino, F., Dasaklis, T.K., Patsakis, C., A systematic literature review of blockchain-based applications: Current status, classification and open issues. *Telemat. Inform.*, 36, 0736-5853, 55–81, 2019, https://doi.org/10.1016/j.tele.2018.11.006.

13. Feng, Q., He, D., Zeadally, S., Khan, M.K., Kumar, N., A survey on privacy protection in blockchain system. *J. Netw. Comput. Appl.*, 126, 45–58, 2018, https:// doi.org/10.1016/j.jnca.2018.10.020.

14. Joshi, A.P., Han, M., Wang, Y., A survey on security and privacy issues of blockchain technology, in: *Mathematical Foundations of Computing*, vol. 1, 2, 121, 147, 2018-5-3.

15. Li, X., Jiang, P., Chen, T., Luo, X., Wen, Q., A survey on the security of blockchain systems. *Future Gener. Comput. Syst.*, 107, 0167-739X, 841–853, 2020, doi: https://doi.org/10.1016/j.future.2017.08.020.

16. Elisa, N., Yang, L., Chao, F. *et al.*, A framework of blockchain-based secure and privacy-preserving E-government system. *Wirel. Netw.*, 1–11, 2018, doi: https://doi.org/10.1007/s11276-018-1883-0.

17. Chen, G., Xu, B., Lu, M. *et al.*, Exploring blockchain technology and its potential applications for education. *Smart Learn. Environ.*, 5, 1, 13, 2018, https://doi.org/10.1186/s40561-017-0050-x.

18. Zhong, B., Wu, H., Ding, L. *et al.*, Hyperledger fabric-based consortium blockchain for construction quality information management. *Front. Eng. Manage.*, 7, 512–527, 2020, doi: https://doi.org/10.1007/s42524-020-0128-y.

19. Yang, R., Wakefield, R., Lyu, S., Jayasuriya, S., Han, F., Yi, X., Yang, X., Amarasinghe, G., Chen, S., Public and private blockchain in construction business process and information integration. *Automat. Constr.*, 118, 0926-5805, 103276, 2020, doi: https://doi.org/10.1016/j.autcon.2020.103276.

20. Pawlak, M., Guziur, J., Poniszewska-Marańda, A., Voting Process with Blockchain Technology: Auditable Blockchain Voting System, in: *Advances in Intelligent Networking and Collaborative Systems. Lecture Notes on Data Engineering and Communications Technologies, INCoS*, vol. 23, F. Xhafa, L. Barolli, M. Greguš (Eds.), Springer, Cham, 2019, 2018, doi: https://doi.org/10.1007/978-3-319-98557-2_21.

21. Cao, Y., Sun, Y., Min, J., Hybrid blockchain–based privacy-preserving electronic medical records sharing scheme across medical information control system. *Meas. Control*, 53, 7-8, 1286–1299, 2020.

22. C. Feied and F. Iskandar, Master patient index. Patent Application No 11/683,799, 2007.

23. Ray, P.P., Dash, D., Salah, K., Kumar, N., Blockchain for IoT-based healthcare: background, consensus, platforms, and use cases. *IEEE Syst. J.*, 15, 1, 85–94, 2020.

24. https://www.who.int/news-room/fact-sheets/detail/opioid-overdose.

25. Zhang, P., Schmidt, D.C., White, J., Lenz, G., Blockchain technology use cases in healthcare, in: *Advances in computers*, vol. 111, pp. 1–41, Elsevier, US, 2018.

26. Onik, M.M.H., Aich, S., Yang, J., Kim, C.S., Kim, H.C., Blockchain in healthcare: Challenges and solutions, in: *Big data analytics for intelligent healthcare management*, pp. 197–226, Academic Press, US, 2019.

2

Geospatial Blockchain: Promises, Challenges, and Scenarios in Healthcare

Janarthanan S.[1]*, S. Vijayalakshmi[2], Savita[1] and T. Ganesh Kumar[1]

[1]School of Computing Science and Engineering, Galgotias University, Greater Noida, Delhi-NCR, India
[2]Department of Data Science, Christ (Deemed to be University), Lavasa, India

Abstract

Geospatial blockchain technology already do exist in similar geospatial applications, making the multiple number of transactions of digital tokens more suitable for spatial applications. It includes more sensitive data communication in public with more autonomous devices and sharing the information from one point to another point in a fully secure way. The data need to be verified with more number of shared networks. The misleading or stealing of information would be almost much more difficult, by using the system with so many dispersed and most connected copies of the shared content with digital timeframes. It is more difficult to change the original, because any data information changes to a particular document information will invalidate all of the other content pieces of the copies. Even though these possibilities were completely open to the public, once created, it becomes very difficult to change it in block. All blocks hold current information with hash and earlier hash consisting of an alphanumeric value for uniqueness to find the content. Geospatial blockchains are more suitable for storing the information or data with confirmation about the location for the proof. The challenges are related to security and privacy model implementation, which are required to overcome these intermediate processes and commercial.

Keywords: Geospatial, blockchain, remote monitoring, security, privacy model, healthcare records, shared network, digital transaction with time frame

Corresponding author: jana.mkce@gmail.com
Janarthanan. S: ORCID: https://orcid.org/0000-0003-3003-6621
S. Vijayalakshmi: ORCID: https://orcid.org/0000-0002-0310-5495
Savita: ORCID: https://orcid.org/0000-0002-4826-4721
T. Ganesh Kumar: ORCID: https://orcid.org/0000-0002-2712-712x

T. Poongodi, D. Sumathi, B. Balamurugan and K. S. Savita (eds.) Digitization of Healthcare Data Using Blockchain, (25–48) © 2022 Scrivener Publishing LLC

2.1 Introduction

Blockchain technology is getting more attention nowadays due to its development in the field of cryptocurrencies such as bitcoin. More innovative and secured developments are required in terms of applications, where frequent changes of information sharing may update a block with cryptographic security environment. It is an open and more common design which allows real time and without disconnection transactions. To observe the earth using spatial technologies and development in this area, more wide and new ideas for the application of blockchain for earth observation has come [1]. China developed a protocol, based on Consultative Committee for Space Data Systems (CCSDS), Trusted Compute Framework (TCF) format for sending the data, which can overcome the repetition of other satellites functionality. This will increase frequent work using common data sharing and communication each other [2]. Involvement in terms of medical data exchange has made blockchains much more useful and will make creating such a model more difficult.

To track remote patient monitoring in healthcare, use the most appropriate wearable devices with secure symmetric key encryption to ensure data exchange. To secure healthcare, blockchain technology for IoT medical devices will be significantly more useful for tracking inpatient and outpatient care and will be particularly well suited for use with smart wearable devices. In terms of earth observation, blockchain technology plays a more critical role and is used more frequently. Exploring for sharing and providing patient medical credentials that must be secured without putting the patient's safety at risk is a difficult task in the field of medicine, which has experienced tremendous growth. In these cases, using the crypto spatial coordinate systems. Time series and spatial indexing are stored as part of the record. The integration of artificial intelligence (AI) and blockchain to predict and forecast patients and the healthcare industry was more advanced. It will provide frequent monitoring day to day [3]. More other fields are also involved in blockchain development, such as land cover and its management where many applications parallel have frequent access to have real-time knowledge about the land, such as vegetation, soil, tenure, and more importantly, climatological changes [4].

2.1.1 Basics of Blockchain

A shared and immutable ledger allows for the storage of additional transaction records, as well as the tracking, conforming, and providing confidence

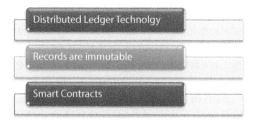

Figure 2.1 Key elements in blockchain.

Figure 2.2 Types of blockchain networks.

in them. In IBM, older methods of record keeping were converted into new technology development for records-keeping for trust and transparency in nature using blockchain [5]. Some key elements in blockchain are in Figure 2.1.

- **Distributed Ledger Technology:** Everyone in the network community has an access with this common shared ledger with a single transaction record due to elimination of the duplicates in it.
- **Records are immutable:** Once shared records have been altered, they cannot be changed again until the error has been corrected or a new transaction is required to replace the error in it, and both may be accessed.
- **Smart Contracts:** Set rules for automatic execution in blockchain to increase corporate compatibility and travel insurance required to pay a lot to speed up the transaction.

Blockchain network can be private, public, permissioned, and consortium as shown in Figure 2.2.

2.1.2 Promises and Challenges in Blockchain

Promises may be met by user's needs, but there have been many challenges since the initial investment of around 800 million in blockchain-related projects in 2014 and 2015 [6]. With four distinct characteristics, the decentralized validation is critical for validating the particular's authority. And second, redundancy ensures that each node is connected to the group ensuring that no failure occurs. Because of the immutable nature of blockchain storage, hackers can manipulate not only a single data block but also the entire chain of subsequent blocks. As a result, in addition to its data being registered with a digital fingerprint that includes time and date frames to prevent tampering, the data may not match with the previous one. Encryption is digital signatures using public and private cryptographic key pairs to ensure network participants ownership of copyrighted data and transactions.

In other words, businesses are required to be more transparent about their customer needs. In some cases, opportunities for insurers with additional assistance required to implement blockchain technology were a significant challenge because of the ageing factor in digital transformation. Reduced costs and a more efficient way of operating will increase customer access at this stage, and blockchain may be used. Another way to meet customer needs is to make all products tailored, simple, and transparent while making the policy more difficult to understand in the traditional manner. This will frustrate buyers, and for multifactor verification, will frustrate customers by making providing data more difficult to provide repeatedly. In that case, sharing with third parties or another client permission is required. This was one of the difficulties inherent in blockchain. The concerned authority will provide customer authentication to conduct know your customer (KYC) for multifactor authentication, which will eliminate unnecessary time taken for access to the customer or client data.

2.1.3   Comparative Study

All of these issues and challenges will be resolved through the use of smart contracts, thereby reducing the handling costs as said in a comparative study and analysis discussing how to identify insurance fraud claims. To overcome the distributed environment, blockchain may be used to detect fraud. To unlock the access for blockchain, all types of more valuable transactions must be tracked in this study.

In this case, efficiency may increase to reduce costs. Automation of the process will expedite the consumer's claim to accelerate market growth and, in conjunction with smart contracts, will encourage farmers to insure at the micro and nano level. It will also facilitate payment and access, as well as ensure a more reliable metrological availability. This will eliminate the issue of fraudulent companies and allow for

Table 2.1 Difference between blockchain and geospatial.

Blockchain	Geospatial
Data and records stored same way	Data and records along with time series data stored, keeping and managing the records
Tampering the data and records will be overcome if we use blockchain	This will overcome by hashing or encryption
Reasonable cost for implementation	Both had same operational cost
More transparent	Most improved transparency
More efficient	Most efficient one as blockchain
Risk identification will easy in terms of fraudulent services	Identify the risk and within a particular community only

more targeted user access. Table 2.1 presents difference between blockchain and geospatial.

2.2   Geospatial Blockchain Analysis Based on Healthcare Industry

Geospatial objects are phenomena that have a specific location on the earth's surface. This could be anything from a specific road to a natural disaster, such as an earthquake or the poverty of living peoples. As a result, geospatial will collect all available information along with earth coordinates. In general, almost all geospatial data available were free with the content, such as roads, localities, and public amenities. Some of the more useful factors when using geospatial data are listed in Figure 2.3.

The primary goal of this analysis was to reduce costs and improve management by utilizing available data or information. As a result, insurance pricing, GIS technology development, and modern electronic usage in humans will be far more beneficial for high performance in database management in encoding engines. It will be more precise and specific with the user's latitude and longitude format, so that we can easily identify the customer or user address or regions, for example, more accurate technology development in the field of smart communication like smartphones and smartwatches will support this more [7].

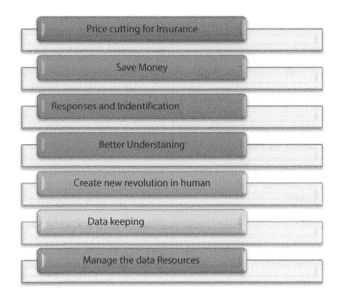

Price cutting for Insurance

Save Money

Responses and Indentification

Better Understaning

Create new revolution in human

Data keeping

Manage the data Resources

Figure 2.3 Geospatial analysis.

Another end usage is not only by user saving, and cost cutting is the primary concern about geospatial, so application will give a lot of improvements and efficiency for fast delivery in terms of truck delivery or other way of transportation process may reduce the time is taken or another way to find the best route for transfer. This will make customer service more useful than usual. Traditional or older modes of transportation for amenities, such as large oil, gas farms, and other logistics organizations to make their physical assets available on the field. As a result, GIS will assist and respond in identifying the location of assets to exact identification with less time delay and more accurate response in the event of an emergency.

2.2.1 Remote Monitoring and Geospatial Healthcare System

Remote monitoring mainly uses digital technology to gather information about medical claim forms for further assistance required for one point of manual form transfer securely to the healthcare providers for additional support and recommendations [8]. GIS has to be used in all health analyses for tracking the origins and location of a specific disease to respond with a more effective disease identification [9]. More health departments and policies, as well as various medical and research organizations, such as medical centers and insurance, will be provided to find more suitable and flexible cost-cutting solutions. Secure, patient information accessibility, and confidentiality were more accurate terms. The healthcare industry spans both the public and private sectors. To monitor the patient's health, GIS primarily employs private sector technologies and various applications, such as business and marketing management.

Wealth tool management uses a GIS-based system, which identifies specific care and location monitoring systems for patient beds, as well as demographic and specific treatment center details. GIS analytical and more accurate solutions are used by many millions of healthcare clients around the world. In all of these, GIS plays a critical role, which provides quality services to all healthcare providers with accurate solutions in less time stream for the client. This will reduce the time it takes to process a claim for the patient and health industry. This will be overcome by GIS and remote monitoring for larger industries and medical alliances that are using in the field of sales, marketing, and various materials today and tomorrow greater importance in system data and image to understand in a very short amount of time. Satellite geospatial in data positioning systems require monitoring services and the most advanced system-level application to track.

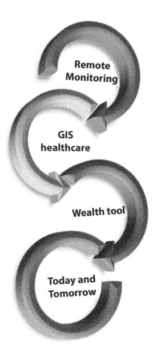

Figure 2.4 Remote monitoring and geospatial steps.

Large level of transactions and movement supply chain and larger industries management tracking the larger products for this purpose, but at the medical level, small network management either usual internet management via mobile network or regular internet connectivity availability will maintain all those data in the own storage of the medical management software or cloud management system for multiproduct management. All subsequent growth will be much easier to track and maintain than with traditional file management systems. Figure 2.4 shows all steps involved in remote monitoring and Geospatial.

2.3   Smart Internet of Things Devices and Systems

The Internet of Things (IoT) is a network of interconnected computing devices, digital and mechanical machines, used to identify objects, animals, or people that are uniquely identified and capable of being transferred without human intervention as presented in Figure 2.5. For example, the

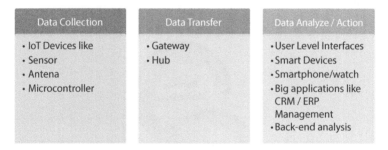

Figure 2.5 IoT in different connections.

Figure 2.6. IoT devices and systems.

patient's heart monitor implant can be monitored. Another method assists the driver with smart sensors to notify the driver through an alert-based system. So how is it possible that it will work?

The IoT system and devices are much more useful than other regular procedures. In terms of medical diagnosis, more accurate results can be obtained in a shorter period. Typically, user data is collected, compiled, and transferred to nearby hubs or gateways for analysis and action via various applications [10] as shown in Figure 2.6.

2.3.1   Main Challenges and Importance in Smart Convention

The IoT devices and smart conventions will make daily life more enriching and improve in a technology-driven approach to complete access control. When we implement IoT devices for operation-level processes, the logistics and supply chain management systems will become more precise and accurate. Employee affordability will be reduced, the nature of customer delivery and support will be more transparent, and customer delivery and support will be very understandable. All of the difficulties will be overcome [10]. How come more benefits for the organization? Overall, we are monitoring the process to improve the experience to save time and money, which will increase productivity, and we are integrating many business models to create a better business environment for the customer and industry. This will result in increased revenue generation for the system as a whole.

In many ways, we can implement this transportation and manufacturing with the help of sensors and other supporting devices, and also helps the farmers by reducing human intervention for monitoring and predicting the solution of seed plantation to the final stage of crop management, like rainfall, temperature, and soil content too.

- **Advantage:** Access it anywhere at any time, regular connection interval, transfer data will save money and time. Improve the quality and reduce human interaction.
- **Disadvantage:** Much complex in nature shared multiple devices. Information security is a primary concern. Data collection and management became more complex.

2.3.2   Recent Innovations in Healthcare

The IoT is changing everyone's lives, such as monitoring patients in real-time records, communicating with healthcare industries, and more accurately calculating related data in report preparation and claim processing [11]. Electronic health records (EHR) will have access to the patient's entire medical history, as well as all diagnosis information. One of the major benefits of remote care is that it allows doctors and clinics to track patients in both inpatient and outpatient settings using smart wearable devices with alerts based on their location. This allows doctors and clinics to track the patient's basic information in case of an emergency and reduces the time spent repeating tests. For major corporations, 3D printing will lower costs in prototyping, skin, and tissue, and even pharmaceuticals. The conversion from 2D to 3D will improve the accuracy of identifying burn victims, resulting in a longer service life.

LASIK: More advancements in laser technology for easy and convenient in nature for doctors, in terms of vision issues will permanently correct the vision correction, instead of regular surgery will be overcome by this laser treatment. More suitable in nature may be more expensive. Other include augmented reality, precision medicine, and blockchain technology.

2.4   Implementation Strategies and Methodologies

In many cases, implementation will be more understandable to both customers and businesses, such as a step-by-step approach in blockchain and geospatial. In a distributed ledger, only the concerned authorized personnel will be able to authorize a transaction based on a customer's request for a secure transaction hash algorithm for random number generation [12]. The complete transaction system process flow is presented in Figure 2.7.

Because the transactions are more virtual and decentralized with interconnected systems, a transaction validation function is not required here,

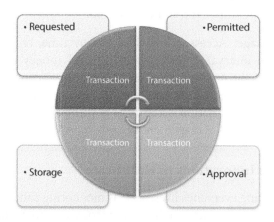

Figure 2.7 Transaction system in blockchain.

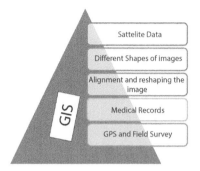

Figure 2.8. Geospatial system.

which will create a blind system level that is immutable and cannot be tampered with; instead, a time series coordinated with many systems levels is required. With proper authorization, it is more suitable for a wide range of transactions. This will increase the security of the process and build trust in these transactions. In addition, geospatial medical geographic information is used in both public and private healthcare for disease and the environment in all areas. In particular, rural areas in the case of childcare, as well as surveillance systems with proper database access. As in intensive care in hospitals, management systems must meet all of the requirements of the customer and companies that are much more interconnected [13]. All transactions requiring proper request for access and update, and once permitted by the concerned authority or management for accessing in the blockchain transaction management system, will make it possible for more interconnected virtual management systems with proper validation function for centralized system services. All medical illnesses and treatments that require proper surveillance for the patient and others for the purpose of proper diagnosis will be provided on-time delivery and supply chain in rural areas. Figure 2.8 presents different fields of the geospatial system.

2.4.1   Promises and Challenges in Implementation

Both promises and challenges at the blockchain, and geospatial levels will improve system-level access and user-level challenges [3] required to identify the original claim in terms of the healthcare system and management more suitable to the client and industrial system. More accurate results and less time spent processing forms for various purposes, such as patient-to-doctor treatment and medical claim process will also necessitate more transparency in cost management, and treatment should be mandatory in

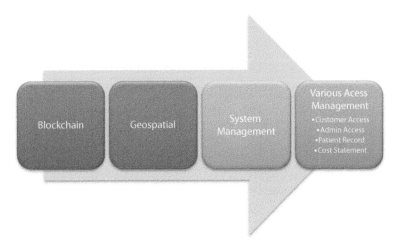

Figure 2.9 Geospatial and blockchain system management.

nature. If additional assistance is required for processing after the claim and during medical treatment, which is the primary concern and challenge in implementation, see the largest analysis in healthcare data breach in Table 2.2.

Figure 2.9 representation will overcome delays in processing and detail analysis with proper proof available in a distributed connection, but this will overcome the traditional method of report management and generation and also manual intervention will be completed, but sometimes technical issues or other causes must be considered in this process both the document and records requirement.

Table 2.2 Report for largest healthcare data breaches.

Rank	Year	Covered sector type	Breach impact on individual	Breach method
One	2015	Health plan	78,800,000	Hacking/IT Issues
Two	2019	Business associate	26,059,725	Hacking/IT Issues
Three	2015	Health plan	11,000,000	Hacking/IT Issues

2.5   Information Security and Privacy Protection in Geospatial Blockchain Healthcare Systems

Information about the patient is a primary concern in sharing the data or information record in the public domain with possible issues, such as security and privacy protection in blockchain and geospatial healthcare systems [6]. For a security reasons, using hashing functions prevents tampering with the data and information, making hacking the data much more difficult.

2.5.1   Security and Privacy Protection Framework

In the age of IoT, all traditional methods of storing and retrieving records have given way to online cloud storage for quick retrieval and storage. System management is highly recommended for this concern because security is much more important in every credential [14]. More security and privacy protection are required in the geospatial system framework. And the primary concern in the data sharing framework was data storage and retrieval. Either in an online storage system or in a cloud-based system, the credential, which was the primary concern in this process for the system, must be secured.

2.5.2   Data Access Control System

The data access control system is a system that provides assured user-level access from the company in which provide security-based or authenticate with properly authorized personnel, with a selective level of restriction for accessing [15] for more secure sharing content, and any information related to that should be addressed with company policy, which was the most important challenge for the security. Let me explain what access control is, access control for user access requires proper permission with two primary concerns, which should be followed by authorization and authentication, which was the primary concern for data level security. As a result, authentication is required, and the appropriate level of user level roles will determine the data level access and full permission provided by the authorization for the user who wants to access the specific data that is required for accessing it.

However, in both cases, there is a risk of a security breach in terms of public servers, which can be disastrous. And cybercriminals, such as IP addresses of personal and specific domains, as well as user data, such as usernames and passwords, maybe stolen and leaked to the web if proper data access control system is not provided [16]. Different access control systems are mandatory, discretionary, and user-level roles are also given in Figure 2.10. More data on confidentiality and classification can be found in the representation below. The necessary security policy and guidelines enable the proper channels for accessing the more sensitive credentials.

And the discretionary will make the decision for access to a specific area to be done only by approved personnel and only to specified areas. Most situations may result in malware attacks due to end user level access, so malware will be executed without the user's knowledge. Finally, user level roles may lead to overcoming the aforementioned issues and increasing the security of the credentials within it. In terms of administrator rights with proper roles and usage level access, the proper level of usage may only be available to approved personnel. We can learn more about the advantages of access control systems by looking at Figures 2.11 and 2.12. The primary business objective was to maintain an access control management system with and in and out registration process in the traditional manner. However, digital transformation may result in the appropriate level of code for an easy employee management system in a high level of employees.

Figure 2.10 Types of access control system.

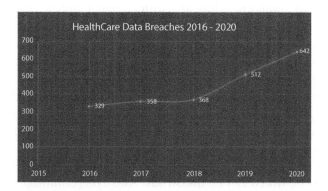

Figure 2.11 Healthcare data breaches.

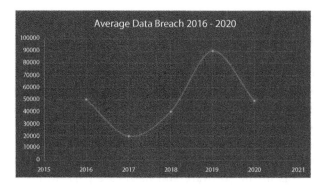

Figure 2.12. Average data breach.

(Graph source: hippa journal—reported to the department of health and human services office of civil rights, 2020. Average data breach size from 2016 to 2020 individual affected below.)

The manual may take a long time to calculate in and out, but other levels of the procedure provided by the system may make it easier to resolve manual efforts. To secure sensitive documents and data, limiting access control mechanisms may result in proper user-level access. It will reduce the loss or theft of data, and accidental theft may be overcome by this access control issue in which specific areas are concerned. Levels in the access control system are presented in Figure 2.13.

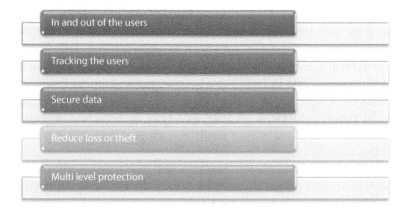

Figure 2.13 Levels of access control system and benefits.

2.6   Challenges in Present and Past and Future Directions

Most of the challenges in blockchain may lead to the present, past, and future directions. In the current challenges in healthcare, providers may be faced with a plethora of scenarios, which I will go over one by one. Advanced healthcare technology was the primary and most difficult challenge in medical development and all the ways new diseases spread all over the world, such as coronavirus. In this case, more challenging was in the software and hardware part, where continuous changes into this may not be able to predict the proper diagnosis [17]. The AI and machine learning will make automated suggestions based on proper software management applications maintained by the hospital management system with comparing and learn. For technology-driven approaches to medical development, growth will increase in this process as it is applied.

2.6.1   Present Challenges in Healthcare

More advanced sharing may shorten the lifespan of medicine development in terms of doing research from the ground up being completely removed if technology driven was sharing the global information will lead to new technology growth in medical history and healthcare industries growth as well. Some current challenges are given in Figure 2.14.

In the present scenario, health development with connected healthcare may lead to many solutions and a faster guidance system. And other end health service providers may lead to a solution, while customer need on time may cause a delay. Healthcare industries will provide AI-supported applications with larger data sets in an easy-to-use manner in the health services. Relational databases may lead to unstructured data from various sources, but this is not always the case for databases of structured and unstructured data in healthcare organizations. Another end security requirement in most cases is that connected medical devices should be secure in nature, otherwise security data may be breached or stolen by malware attacks or hackers. As a result, it is more secure than type checking in this case.

Even obtaining the credential was one goal, but rising healthcare costs will have an impact on healthcare providers in the following ways. Despite the fact that the insurance will not be able to cover the entire policy from the concern.

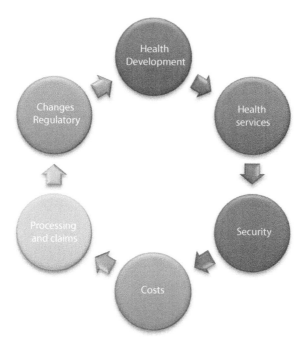

Figure 2.14 Present challenges in healthcare.

2.6.2   Past Challenges in Healthcare

The main challenge in geospatial data sources is that discovery and new things, as well as up-to-date information from time to time and region to region changes, must be updated in a timely manner with primary concern for geospatial data. This chapter goes into detail about the challenges and issues to obtain a possible solution to the associated problem statement. Furthermore, the operation will lead to increased tool usage in geospatial data sources. The most important feature was the search grid. They aid in locating a specific location's latitude on a map, as well as providing ground-level detail information. For geospatial data analysis, more details are required for visual clarity with 2D and 3D visual representation.

In healthcare identification, patient details with accurate location of region-based requirements was the primary concern at this level. To overcome previous health issues, monitoring and tracking their live location will help to find nearby hospital availability along with doctor details, which may lead to first aid support in case of illness and other treatment-related issues [18]. Geospatial data collection and

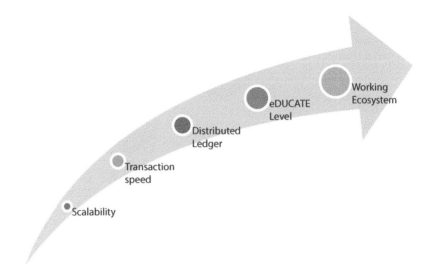

Figure 2.15 Blockchain challenges in healthcare.

processing, as well as representation, are much more difficult to use [19]. Let us look at another blockchain based on the IoT that is needed for authentication, security, and data privacy, as well as how to validate image identification and validation using blockchain and data transactions. Every aspect of this is only required in the case of image processing and analysis in healthcare for patient MRI and CT scan images to be shared via a secure in nature. This paper processing may lead to a secure communication channel that will overcome the previous challenges in the sharing of information in the common access which will be denied in nature due to the secure connection. Some challenges are given in Figure 2.15.

2.6.3   Future Challenges in Healthcare

In the future, all aspects of blockchain and geospatial development will improve the healthcare industries, and service providers and service personnel may lead to easy accessing and claiming the processing in medical treatment and medical practitioners may lead to easy access in secure cloud storage and worldwide data sharing may lead to new innovation and the development for researchers for economic growth rate for new medicine development may be introduced due to credential sharing in the security level with the same or different organization in pharma, and pharmaceutical level growth will boom by this research of patient analysis report with proper approval for sharing the personal concern as the primary reason for research growth and development [19].

In another way, the global sharing community prioritized data sharing with high data transaction speeds. For example, in 2019, blockchain will perform seven transactions per second. Thousands and millions per second may be achieved over the course of development. Furthermore, because of the enterprise level, they may have limited access to their environment with user-level privilege.

Figure 2.16 representation depicts the future challenges in healthcare in this processing and tasking, monitoring, and surveillance on another object detection, and primarily moving from one point to another point and location to another location object detection. All information sharing with larger and multinational corporations must be more secure in nature, and all people who have access to information must be secure in nature, so security and support were one of the important concerns for sharing the information for patients and others, and trust and trustworthiness are more important for the company concern or service provider. During and after the claim process, the insurer and those who obtain health insurance have much simpler and time-saving experience, and other document processing is much easier for all users.

In all aspects, the future generation for healthcare was more advanced in nature with all the people's needs much more fulfilled in nature with all requirements must satisfy the customer or users and service provider of the health insurer much easier for accessing with secure in nature was the primary concern in healthcare. However, many technological

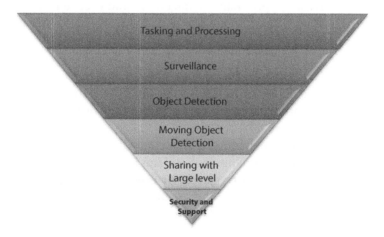

Figure 2.16 Future challenges in healthcare.

advancements and innovation growth will answer this question and solve many issues and problems nowadays by virtual chatbot with new AI and machine learning and very useful in now a day with instead of voice over call to overcome and because the customer waiting time will be removed, and this will be much easier than dialing. The primary advantage for all-over support with natural language of the user level understanding and time saving for the users and customer support assistant for understanding the issue may balance because of the advanced natural language processing concept almost supported by many regional languages supports.

Chatbots and voice assistants are both much more helpful to future generations in healthcare and medicine level usage, but I am not sure how secure their data is for this processing and tasking. More security measures are required to complete this process. The technical scalability of the networking process was a major challenge in the blockchain. Specifically, with public level transactions, the ability to perform thousands of transactions per second or million and a greater number of transactions per second was one of the most important factors, as was the amount of energy consumed [20] for processing. According to the survey, the error rate will be reduced by around 95%. However, network traffic may cause processing and transaction delays.

In the future, blockchain distributed ledger technology will have a greater impact on financial growth rates, be more transparent, have a faster transfer rate, and be more beneficial to blockchain technology users rather than regular usage pattern followers. So, with rapidly advancing technology development and innovation, more advancement will increase supply chain management and cycle enormously in the future market. Also, on the other end, the main challenge was geospatial in nature, which needed to be more accurate and challenging in all locations, specifically being able to identify the object detection either in one location or in the moving object location that needs to be tracked in a specific identification of the object, which was one of the challenges, and more improvements are required in the latitude and longitudes of a person.

These two are the main future challenges in healthcare industries 4.0, with revolutionary development and implementation both required in this domain at all industry levels or elsewhere where it has been required for implementation in the specific only in terms of healthcare level and more advancement will be introduced for economic growth, which will also increase if being followed above any of the metrics.

2.7   Conclusion

We have discussed various mechanisms and services available to users and service providers in this chapter. And previous promises and challenges in blockchain and geospatial, with a comparative study of both, as well as remote monitoring in geospatial healthcare systems and smart IoT devices and systems with additional challenges. Few implement strategies and methodologies then go through information security and privacy protection in the geospatial blockchain data framework for next-generation healthcare systems and how data are traditionally managed and the modern way of distributed ledger technologies with immutable records with smart contracts. In addition, data and analysis are available in the form of public, private, permission, and consortium blockchain networks. Price reductions to save money with identification and responses for the most understanding in nature create a revolution in it for storing data and managing various data resources.

Tracking and monitoring were the primary concerns for healthcare with IoT devices and systems for health monitoring with specific sensors, as well as smart devices network communication channels, with remote monitoring and GIS healthcare and wealth tools. For example, data collection from IoT devices, sensors, antennas, and microcontrollers for data transfer via a proper network gateway and hub, followed by data analysis and action with user-level interfaces and access via smartphone/watch to CRM and ERP level application management systems, as well as larger back-end analysis, customer access, user access, administrator access, and so on. Industrial development with geospatial or blockchain management for more common development and innovation will be followed by the most recent technology or digital transformation will improve healthcare promises and challenges in both in the future. This allows us to see what the challenges and opportunities are in the geospatial blockchain in healthcare.

References

1. For More on blockchain and how europe is seeking further application of blockchain for earth observation, European Space Agency, vol. 1, pp. 1–28, 2019 see: https://eo4society.esa.int/2019/04/09/blockchain-and-earth-observation-a-white-paper/.
2. Ma, N., Wang, X., Li, Z., Zhan, P., He, X., Zhang, X., Liu, Z., Design of Routing Incentive Protocol for Space Network Based on Blockchain Technology, in:

Probability-2, vol. 95, pp. 123–131, 2019. https://doi.org/10.1007/978-981-13-6553-9_14, 2019.

3. Kamel Boulos, M.N., Wilson, J.T., Clauson, K.A., Geospatial blockchain: Promises, challenges, and scenarios in health and healthcare. *Int. J. Health Geogr.*, *17*, 125, s12942-018-0144–x, 2018. https://doi.org/10.1186/s12942-018-0144-x.

4. Bennett, R.M., Pickering, M., Sargent, J., Transformations, transitions, or tall tales? A global review of the uptake and impact of NoSQL, blockchain, and big data analytics on the land administration sector. *Land Use Policy*, 83, 435–448, 2019. https://doi.org/10.1016/j.landusepol.2019.02.016, 2019.

5. For more on the blockchain in basics, See: IBM Blockchain Technology https://www.ibm.com/blockchain, 2017.

6. For more on the promises and challenges, See: https://www.mckinsey.com/, 2018.

7. For more geospatial data analysis, See: https://www.geospatialworld.net/blogs/top-7-benefits-of-geospatial-data-in-driving-analytics/, 2019.

8. For more remote monitoring in healthcare system, See: https://www.cchpca.org/about/about-telehealth/remote-patient-monitoring-rpm, 2019.

9. For more geospatial healthcare system, See: https://www.geospatialworld.net/article/geospatial-technologies-iot-healthcare/, 2016.

10. For more IoT devices and systems, See: https://internetofthingsagenda.techtarget.com/definition/Internet-of-Things-IoT, 2020.

11. For more recent innovations in healthcare, See: https://getreferralmd.com/2018/09/9-recent-medical-innovations-disrupting-healthcare/, 2018.

12. For more strategy, See: https://www.strategy-business.com/article/A-Strategists-Guide-to-Blockchain?gko=9d4ef, 2016.

13. Ali, M., Emch, M., Ashley, C., Streatfield, P., Implementation of a medical geographic information system: Concepts and uses. *J. Health Popul. Nutr.*, Jun. 19, 2001.

14. Yu, Y., Li, Y., Tian, J., Liu, J., Blockchain-based solutions to security and privacy issues in the internet of things. *IEEE Wirel. Commun.*, 25, 6, 12–18, December 2018.

15. Martin, J.A., 21, 1, 1–10, 2019. For more information, see https://www.csoonline.com/article/3251714/what-is-access-control-a-key-component-of-data-security.html.

16. For more reference, See: https://www.tedsystems.com/3-types-access-control-which-right-building/, 2020.

17. For more information, See: https://www.finoit.com/blog/top-10-healthcare-challenges/, 2019.

18. de Miguel González, R., Koutsopoulos, K., Donert, K., Key challenges in geography research with geospatial technologies, in: *Geospatial Challenges in the 21st Century. Key Challenges in Geography (EUROGEO Book Series)*, K. Koutsopoulos, R. de Miguel González, K. Donert (Eds.), Springer, Cham, https://doi.org/10.1007/978-3-030-04750-4_1, 2019.

19. Vivek Anand, M. and Vijayalakshmi, S., Image validation with virtualization in blockchain based internet of things. *J. Comput. Theor. Nanosci.*, 17.5, 2388–2395, 20202020.
20. For more information, See: https://medium.com/dataseries/7-blockchain-challenges-to-be-solved-before-large-scale-deployment-3e 45b47eee6, 2019.

3

Architectural Framework of Blockchain Technology in Healthcare

Kiran Singh[1]*, Nilanjana Pradhan[2] and Shrddha Sagar[1]

[1]School of Computing Science and Engineering, Galgotias University, Greater Noida, Delhi-NCR, India
[2]Pune Institute of Business Management, Pune, Maharashtra, India

Abstract

Blockchain is one of the most vital technology for discoveries and creative developments. It moves in constant pace for the changes and revolution. It is a blockchain that covers data and maintains trust between people, no matter how far they go. In the last few years, the growth of blockchain technology has forced academics and experts to examine new ways. The application of blockchain technology has a wide range of domains, as there is drastic increase in the implementation of blockchain technology in various applications like bitcoin, banking, payment and transfer, healthcare, law enforcement, voting, Internet of Things (IoT), online music, real estate, supply chain management, digital IDs. The researcher has done a lot of studies in the healthcare system on the application of blockchain technology. By using blockchain technology, it is possible to reform conventional healthcare procedures by delivering accurate diagnosis and proper treatment through safe and secure data sharing. In this chapter, we have done a thorough study of existing and latest improvement in the domain of healthcare, and it is discussed in this chapter. We also explored the use of blockchain in healthcare along with obstacles and future prospects.

Keywords: Smart healthcare, blockchain, distributed system, security, privacy, Internet of Things, sensor

*Corresponding author: kiran13.singh@gmail.com
Kiran Singh: ORCID: https://orcid.org/0000-0003-1711-7371
Nilanjana Pradhan: ORCID: https://orcid.org/0000-0002-8082-5867
Shrddha Sagar: ORCID: https://orcid.org/0000-0003-3647-1384

T. Poongodi, D. Sumathi, B. Balamurugan and K. S. Savita (eds.) Digitization of Healthcare Data Using Blockchain, (49–72) © 2022 Scrivener Publishing LLC

3.1 Introduction

Blockchain is analogous to the repository distributed among the network's partners, and the network architecture it creates is peer to peer, so a centralized entity is not required. Blockchain is a decentralized distributed ledger (Novo, 2018). Blockchains are essential as they provide users with a trusted environment to make any sort of transaction without having to trust anybody. It is possible to think of blocks in a blockchain as a piece of paper. Blocks can carry any form of data on them, just like paper [1]. In the blockchain, the first block is considered the block of genesis. When the blockchain network first begins, the genesis block is enabled. The second block has the first block's transactions and cryptographic hash value. The next block is going to be the same.

A sequence of transactions is blocked for every payment transfer values between businesses. Pool miners are solitary miners mine blocks. Mining process incorporates transaction collection into blocks. Miners are chosen by consensus method (proof of work [PoW] in the case of bitcoin). When mining is finished, transaction fees are awarded, typically some bitcoin in the bitcoin network. The difficulty level in the PoW method is increased after mining a number of blocks. Both pairs in the blockchain network will review transactions [1] to avoid a double problem. Each pair receives a network update and checks the block Testing transaction validity and previous block hash. The guy attaches the block to his local blockchain afterward. Each pair will have a set of transaction validation rules. The peer nodes will verify the transactions using these guidelines.

Initially established as a system to power Bitcoin, blockchain has now become recognized as a key technology for different decentralized applications. Blockchain is a valuable technology for the management of sensitive data, especially in the healthcare, medical research, and insurance sectors. It is possible to consider healthcare as a system comprising three key components: (i) healthcare as a framework comprising three main components can be considered; (ii) health services–related basic schemes, such as medical tests and health insurance; and (iii) health and health-oriented service recipients, such as patients or public service recipients. We agree that the health system needs contact-based and technology-based remote monitoring programs extended by constituent service providers to support, protect, and restore the well-being of the beneficiaries. Healthcare breaches of privacy and security reportedly rise every year, with over 300 breaches reported in 2017 and 37 million patient records affected between 2010 and 2017. In addition, digitization of healthcare has contributed to the identification of concerns relating to safe storage, ownership, exchange of personal health information for patients, and related medical data. Blockchain has been proposed as a means of addressing key health problems, such as the safe exchange of medical records and compliance with data privacy laws [2].

3.2   Healthcare

Healthcare is a clinical area that is data-intensive and produces a large amount of data, which are accessed and regularly disseminated. The storage and distribution of this large amount of information is because of the confidentiality of data and restricting factors, protection and privacy, for example, are important as well as significantly difficult [3]. Data sharing is highly safe, secure, and scalable (SSS) in the healthcare sector and clinical settings. It is appropriate for diagnosis and medical judgement in combination. The process of data exchange is crucial in enabling health professionals to move clinical data from their patients to the patients. Involving power for rapid follow-up, it should be possible for these caregivers and general practitioners to transferring their patients' clinical data, which are highly to ensure that all parties have complete and up-to-date details on patient's health issues in a privacy-sensitive and timely manner.

Telemedicine and e-health, on the other hand, are two widely used areas where clinical data are used. From an expert opinion, it is transmitted remotely to a professional (at a distant location) [4]. The patient data are transmitted either via a "store-and-forward technology" or via online real-time clinical monitoring in these two online clinical configurations (e.g., telemonitoring, telemetry, and the like) [5]. Patients are remotely diagnosed and treated by healthcare professionals using these online clinical environments through the sharing of clinical data. Security, sensitivity, and privacy in all such clinical arrangements, which are of case-sensitive nature for the patient's clinical records, are some of the major challenges that will arise. The capability for the secure conversation of information is, therefore, extremely significant for helping remote patient cases to have a healthy and meaningful clinical communication. Because this is a secure and effective exchange of information, which helps clinical communication through the collection of references or authorizations from clinical experts, it will help make a more accurate diagnosis and a more efficient treatment [6, 7].

3.2.1 Electronic Healthcare

The need for a sheer increase in the digitization of patient health records over the past decade has led to the digitization of this information to help medical professionals, healthcare centers, and devices of healthcare that will help to digitize the records. It has simple access and sharing, as well as being the basis for a better and quicker decision making. Currently, in the field of electronic medical records, the most popular healthcare implementation of blockchain technology is electronic health records (EHRs), which are never produced to manage lifetime records. As life circumstances split them from the data of one provider into another, several institutions and patients share their knowledge dispersed between different organizations; therefore, losing the access of information more easily [8]. Faced with a pressing need to monitor EHRs in a way that enables patients to engage in their current and historical health data, we came up with a novel solution, a number of scholars have developed technology for blockchain to preserve EHRs.

The Norwegian Electronic Patient Record format, Elektronisk pasient-journal (EPJ), documents user health information and has been mainly used to record user health information, which that is used in Norway by health professionals. An EPJ framework stores EPJ records in databases and provides an interface to register, scan, and view EPJ file data, and so on. Users and other providers with different defined permissions are (partly) available to such databases. Actually, like many other countries' electronic health record (EHR) systems, this EPJ system is fragmented across health providers and the whole healthcare system. The device must also be integrated.

Because of its inherent characteristics, it is assumed that the e-healthcare system is one of the areas in which blockchain has great potential, particularly for the administration of EHRs. In the last few years, in this direction, major research efforts have been made. A decentralized record management system called MedRec was proposed, which was built on Ethereum blockchain and created an intelligent representation of existing medical records stored on the network within individual nodes using Ethereum smart contracts [9]. Patients have control over their medical records by manufacturers and care centers in this scheme although stakeholders in healthcare are encouraged to engage in the mining of the blockchain, such as academics, public health officials, and so on.

Patients, professionals, and regulators will all keep track of their medical experiences on the blockchain ledger. This solution raises concerns about how much control patients can have over their medical records and how much data should be exchanged. Similar regulations have been debated in different situations and, in most cases, health authorities have agreed on them. As a result, the available variation of the system under which patients do not have full control over their medical records and data shared at various levels by all medical stakeholders should be considered.

3.2.2   Smart Healthcare

Any country's most precious commodity is its people's well-being. Because all patient-related data are centralized in traditional healthcare, it is not advisable to give data access to any untrustworthy third party. In addition, because it is vulnerable to a number of threats, the privacy and protection of patient data must be protected [10]. These specifications cannot be met fully by a centralized architecture. As a result, smart healthcare was built to resolve the abovementioned concerns in traditional healthcare systems. Smart healthcare focuses on remotely tracking and diagnosing the well-being of patients through a wireless means of communication.

It gathers valuable information from a variety of patients using a variety of wearable devices and sensors. For a large number of patients, vast quantities of data are obtained. Analyzing and storing this information in a safe way is a major challenge. Such information should also be securely shared among trusted parties, such as hospitals, patients, physicians, and medical stores. Safe communication of these data is vital since important decisions are affected, such as the preparation of future medical facilities, the advice of physicians, the review of symptoms of various illnesses or health conditions, and the development of the overall system to make it intelligent.

Patients' data must be exchanged on a daily basis for different medical research programs, care decisions, and disease symptom analysis. Traditional access control policies are insufficiently secure to allow highly confidential patient information to be exchanged from one party to another. In addition, patients should not discuss their medical history with physicians in the majority of cases. Medical records of the patient are needed in the event of a medical emergency, but they are not accessible because of poor record maintenance. Smart healthcare will resolve any of the abovementioned concerns by using EHR.

While smart healthcare has the potential to solve many of the industry's major problems, there are some hurdles to overcome. In smart healthcare, access control policies for EHR, privacy, protection, and availability are open issues. These problems can be solved with the aid of blockchain technology. Indeed, the distributed ledger of the blockchain has the potential to help smart healthcare among various users, such as patients, physicians, medical stores, and insurance companies.

3.3   Blockchain Technology

System architecture

In the system architecture of healthcare, there are four participants, the patient, the clinician, and the lab and machine supervisors. Blockchain has been suggested to solve key health concerns, such as the protected sharing of medical records and compliance with data privacy laws. Figure 3.1 shows the workflow of the scheme is simple to use.

Participants register via the client application or SDK and apply through the Member Service Provider (MSP) to the certification authority for certificates of registration [11]. Then, the certification authority issues the certificate and personal key with a new ID. All transactions are distributed through the Hyperledger fabric blockchain network. Contributors have

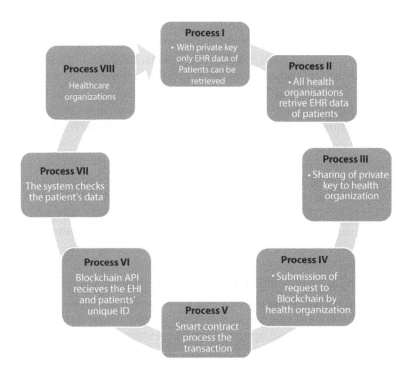

Figure 3.1 Processing steps in blockchain-based smart healthcare.

many computer functions and can only display documents with access [11]. By using client software that invokes the chain code to commit a network transaction, patients can add records. Modified transactions are distributed across the network after the transaction is committed via the blockchain network, ensuring that each network transaction is distributed to any part of the system and that unauthorized users are unable to change or erase each transaction [11]. Transactions are only applied with a time stamp from the previous to any user. Providers can query the necessary data over the network, such as clinicians and hash, making the network fully secure on the blockchain network, records are modified and available to laboratory personnel. The clinician or laboratory participant will be able to view and update patient consent documents when required if the patient needs access to view and update their records on the EHR ledger network [12].

There are four groups of participants in the EHR sharing scheme, including administration, patients, physicians, and laboratory workers. The exact execution of administrators is exposed on a blockchain network in Algorithm I. An administrator's registration certificate is requested by the certification authority. Administrator's absolute framework regulation, including posting, viewing, upgrading, and withdrawing users. If doctors, patients, or laboratory personnel are legitimate, a relevant ID can be given to each participant to allow admin access to the blockchain network. The administrator can remove the participant with a message on the hyperledger blockchain network if the participant's activity is considered satisfactory.

Algorithm II reveals the patient module's structured execution. In this, the patient node requires a private key to log into network administration. After access to the blockchain network has been given, the patient has various privileges, such as reading, writing, and revoking EHR records [13].

3.4   Architecture of Smart Healthcare

Sensor-based devices that also operate with emergency medical service (EMS) patients: AI allows EMSS to make decisions and provide emergency care for vital patients, such as stroke patients. To monitor patient status and provide immediate assistance for a short time, computers that are friendly with AI algorithms need some inputs, such as illness, BP, and so on. In the patient's blood drawing, the AI plays a part, also giving nurses instructions. With the help of AI, nurses update the status of patients. It also helps guide patients to a particular diagnosis at the designated hospital. Figure 3.2 shows the AI

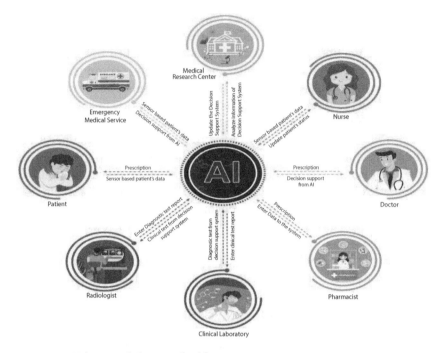

Figure 3.2 AI framework for smart health system.

framework for smart health system. With the support of intelligent AI-based systems, nurses can handle large volumes of patient information easily without having to manually enter the details. The AI-based system is also updated by nurses, which gathers patient data from their smart devices and allows nurses to evaluate the status of diseases and helps them predict future therapies.

Physicians: By tracking and screening the patient and conveniently providing assistance for decision-making, AI makes it easier and quicker. Artificial intelligence can quickly convert unstructured knowledge into a standardized form, generating reliable results and offering the ideal diagnosis. The proposed approach allows researchers to gather data more efficiently and to evaluate new drugs or new diseases more predictively. Artificial intelligence can automatically write the stories given by doctors and nurses, and researchers can use structured data for testing purposes to achieve a perfect and reliable study. This study allows researchers to understand the key cause of the disease and to obtain the best proof of its associations with various biomedical institutions and to strengthen the development process. AI also allows researchers to determine the biomarker blend and recruit the patient, providing the potential for diagnosis. Artificial intelligence enables researchers to repurpose different drugs with current targets and to extract biological knowledge to develop new ones. In assessing different substances, AI also plays an important role.

3.5 Blockchain in Electronic Healthcare

Initially formed as a way to power Bitcoin, blockchain has now grown to be referred to as a basic technology for various decentralized applications [14, 15]. Blockchain, especially in the healthcare, medical research, and insurance industries, is considered a key tool for critical data management. For healthcare as a system, the three main components are as follows:

- providers of healthcare facilities, such as physicians, nurses, hospital administrators and technicians;
- required medical facilities such as medical tests and services for healthcare;
- participants in the health and health business, such as patients, or pub facilities.

In addition, healthcare computerization of issues linked to security storage, possession, patient disclosure of particular health data, and appropriate medicinal data [16]. To address major health problems, such as the safe exchange of medical records and compliance with data privacy laws, blockchain has been proposed. Blockchain is a distributed network of public ledgers run by a certified user or node network that stores immutable information blocks that can be exchanged securely without interference from third parties. The use of consensus algorithms and cryptographic signatures is preserved and is documented as key enabler of their implementation. Usage of consensus algorithms and cryptographic signatures are maintained, and registered data are used as key enablers of their implementation.

This data security capability is an important explanation of blockchain in healthcare form implementation, where a large amount of data is subject to comprehensive sharing and dissemination [17]. For addressing crucial issues, blockchain has the ability, like automatic claim authentication, leading to the discovery public health management, where the healthcare sector is a prime candidate for blockchain technology. It will make it possible for patients to own and pick data from which it is exchanged, resolve existing data ownership, and share concerns with patients [17, 18]. Figure 3.3 shows the architecture for healthcare systems. In several healthcare applications, blockchain technology redefines data modelling and governance.

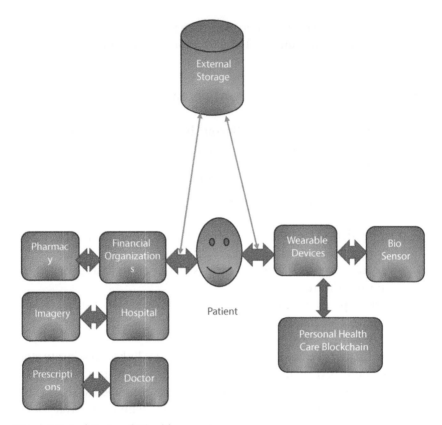

Figure 3.3 Architecture for healthcare system.

This is primarily because of its flexibility and ability to segment, protect, and share medical data.

For data and services in an unprecedented manner, blockchain technology is at the forefront of many current developments in the healthcare field. The concept is organized through four layers of evolving blockchain-based healthcare technologies, namely data sources, blockchain technology, healthcare implementations, and stakeholders. With developments in electronic health–related data, cloud health data storage, and patient data privacy security regulations, new opportunities for health data management, as well as health data management, are opening up, for the patients' convenience, accessing and exchanging their health data [19].

Data security, storage, transaction, and management of their seamless integration are extremely critical for any data-driven organization. Particularly in healthcare, where blockchain technology has the potential to robustly and efficiently deal with these critical issues.

3.6   Architecture for Blockchain

Cryptocurrency has become a buzzword in business and academics nowadays. As one of the most popular cryptocurrencies in 2016, Bitcoin achieved considerable popularity, with its stock market reaching $10 billion [20]. Without any third party with a specially built data storage system, Bitcoin network transactions will take place and a blockchain that was first suggested in 2008 and introduced in 2009 is the central framework of Bitcoin construction technology [21]. Blockchain is a block series with a complete set of records of transactions, such as traditional public ledgers [22].

Figure 3.4 shows the basic block structure is defined by the block header and the transaction counter (Block version, Merkle Tree Root Hash, nBits, Nonce, Parent Block Hash). Below is an overview of the functionality of each are discussed:

- The block version determines the list of rules to be followed for block validation.
- Block of hash value, transactions is determined by the root hash of the Merkle Tree.
- Since January 1970, time stamp is set as second.
- The threshold value of an authenticated block hash is set by nBits.

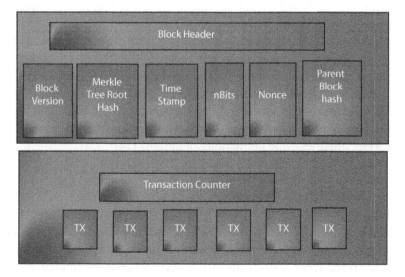

Figure 3.4 Basic framework of block.

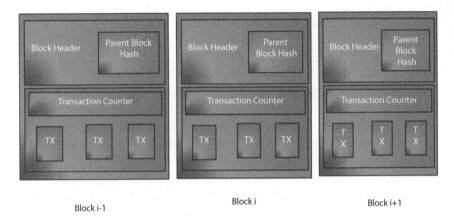

Block i-1   Block i   Block i+1

Figure 3.5 Basic structure of block.

- A 4-byte area that typically begins with 0 and increases for each measurement of the hash.
- Parent block the hash value referring to the previous block is 256 bit.

Create the body of the block with a transaction counter and transactions as the transactions are huge in number, which can be monitored in a block and will be contingent on the size of the block and transaction of each size. To check transaction authentication, an asymmetric cryptography mechanism is used by blockchain [23]. For uncontrolled environment, asymmetric cryptography-based digital signatures are used. Figure 3.5 shows the example of blockchain.

Blockchain, called blocks, is a constantly growing list of documents that use cryptography to be connected and secured. The P2P protocol that can withstand a single fault point is used by blockchain. The consensus mechanism ensures that transactions and blocks are generally arranged unambiguously and ensures the consistency and accuracy of the blockchain across geographically distributed nodes. Blockchain has features, such as decentralization, openness, and auditability of designs [24].

3.7 Distributed System

Knowledge of distributed systems is basic to comprehend blockchain on the grounds that fundamentally, blockchain at its center is a distributed system. All the more specifically, it is a decentralized distributed system.

Distributed systems are an enumerating criterion, whereby at least two hubs work with one another in a planned design to accomplish a common outcome and it is demonstrated so that end clients consider it to be an individual logical platform. One of the biggest challenges for design of distributed system is the organization among the nodes and adaptation to internal failure. Irrespective of few nodes are imprecise or the breakage of the network links, the distributed system ought to endure this and should keep on working impeccably to accomplish the ideal outcome. This has been the latest domain for research for a long period, and few algorithms and components have been proposed to resolve these issues.

Blockchain technology, as a cryptographic-based technology, allows trusted transactions between untrusted network participants. Since the launch of the first Bitcoin blockchain in 2008, many blockchain networks, such as Ethereum and Hyperledger Fabric, have appeared beyond traditional fiat currencies and electronic voucher schemes of public and private connectivity. Recently, blockchain technology has also been the subject of an increasing number of academic investigations. The creation of illegal dark web markets was encouraged by commercially accepted, affected by the markets for world currencies. The emergence of financially motivated cyberattacks, such as ransomware and denial of service, against retailers and other online organizations has also been a significant factor affecting. There is an emerging trend in particular that will open up a new generation of applications that are decentralized and function as the basis for main components of the security of Internet infrastructure beyond intermediary-free payments for cryptocurrency payments. It is, therefore, important to understand that current studies, specifically, relevant blockchain, apply blockchain to a cyber security issue to solve how to treat digital technology which can provide counter emerging threats as solutions. It is important to systematically map out relevant articles and academic work to determine what research has already been done regarding blockchain and cyber security.

3.8   Security and Privacy

Using private and public keys is a main feature of concealment in blockchains. To safeguard transactions between users, blockchain systems use asymmetric cryptography. Each user has a public and private key in these systems. These keys are random numbers, each of which is cryptographically related. Blockchain technology in an open networked environment with no centralized authority is a new breakthrough for trusted computing. A blockchain is a type of database that, from the perspective of data management, logs an emerging collection of a hierarchical blockchain of transactions records. The blockchain, an overlay network which uses peer-to-peer networking, which also utilizes intelligent and decentralized use of crowd computing cryptography, is utilized, created, and maintained from a security perspective. A blockchain serves the functional role of a distributed and stable transaction log archive. To switch bitcoin from A to B on a Bitcoin network, via A, it will build a bitcoin transaction. Before the Bitcoin network is dedicated, the transaction has to be accepted by miners. Any node on the network receives the transaction to start the mining process. For this bitcoin to move from A to B, which has been permanently registered with the blockchain, will become official and legal. The implementation of blockchain in Bitcoin's main feature (transaction handling) offers three basic and important capabilities for the project:

- stored as a storage chain with hash-connection,
- signature on digital signature,
- the overall consensus of engagement.

To provide the means for a new globally chained storage block to be built, if a block has been successfully added to the blockchain with a series of common blockchain-based security techniques, such as Hash chains, Merkle trees [25], digital signatures, and consensus mechanisms, Bitcoin's blockchain can protect both double spending and hold transaction data unaltered.

Storage Using Hash-Chaining

The hash pointer and Merkle tree are the two primary parts of the blockchain structure, which can be implemented using hash chain storage in Bitcoin. Hash's pointer. The hash pointer refers to where the information is stored in the data. Because a hash pointer may be used to evaluate whether or not the information has been tampered with, therefore, a hash pointer can be used in verification. To build a sequence of data blocks, a hash pointer chain is used. The address of each block is exposed, and the hash pointer shows where the data were copied from the previous block. The hash pointer points to the block that goes before it. In addition, by publicly verifying the hashing of that data, users can be assured that the stored information has not been tampered with and can reveal it. If there has been tampering, the adversary must make all previous blocks contain a different hash pointer, as chain changes must spread to every block in the chain.

In the end, the opponent must cease attempts to interfere because there is no way to refute the data on the chain head that was generated before the system is mounted. We call this the block of genesis, as it is the first link of the chain to be opened. It is only by looking back at the genesis block's root hash pointer (i.e., back at the block on which the chain was created) that evidence of tampering can be found, so it can be demonstrated that the entire chain has tamper-resilient properties by simply finding the genesis block's root hash pointer. New users are expected to start and then return to any previous block from the beginning of the chain to check its validity.

Signature on Digital

The use of a cryptographic algorithm acts as a digital signature to verify the validity of a piece of data. A form of data verification also helps to ensure that no changes to the data have been made. There are three main elements, which must be present to have a system of digital signatures. The algorithm used to produce two keys: one is kept secret and a private key is given a name, whereas the other is made public, and a public key is used. This second key is used to verify that the key generation algorithm has signed a message using the generated secret key needed. The signing algorithm's own implementation is the second critical component of the entire algorithm. The cryptographic hash function produces a digital signature on the input message, which is affixed with the user's private key. The algorithm's verification is the third major component. The data must contain an input signature, message, and public key, after which the value returned [26] may be either true or false. Two properties of a well-defined and secure signature algorithm are being well-defined and protected. They must be able to authenticate the first property's signatures. The second property is unforgeable signatures. If an adversary has your public key, they cannot convincingly fabricate your digital signatures on any messages.

A Consensus on Dedication

Each node may choose whether or not to include the new block in their copy of the global ledger when a new block is broadcast to the network. To keep the ledger extension (the blockchain) secure and to prevent deceptive attempts or malicious attacks, contracts are used to settle on one unified state shift for the majority of the network. For specific purposes, because the blockchain is a huge, decentralized global ledger, if a node attempts to tamper with the ledger's state, or if several nodes act in concert to tamper with it, an adversarial offense occurs, and it can be changed by anyone.

One easy way to do this would be to make sure that no one on the network can alter the transaction's contents and turn 10 bitcoins into 100 bitcoins. A decentralized public ledger necessitates an effective and accurate consensus algorithm to ensure the blockchain operates globally and has transparency and protection. This can only be done with fault tolerance and (ii) does not rely on a central authority to keep malicious adversaries from violating the coordination. The network as a whole should also be resistant to malicious community of nodes, messages in transit being intercepted, and individual nodes acting against the whole network. To enforce the blockchain, we need a high degree of consensus. The consensus procedure secures two important features: long-term durability and responsiveness. The persistence of the mechanism ensures a crystal-clear response. In general, liveness implies that all nodes or processes come to agreement on a decision or value [28]. Finally, the use of persistence and liveliness in the incorporation of transaction ledgers ensures the system is secure, in such a way that only true transactions are accepted and irreversibly occur.

3.9   Applications of Healthcare Management in Blockchain

The use of healthcare blockchain technology for various tasks include maintaining a traditional healthcare information system, performing services that include, but are not limited to, backing up stored data, following up on recovery mechanisms, and keeping up-to-date areas. There is no single point of failure because data are distributed through the network through a blockchain (Table 3.1).

3.9.1   The Use of the Blockchain for EMR Data Storage

Many pilot projects around the world have explored blockchain's potential use in hospitals. The Food and Drug Administration's Office of Translational Sciences has developed a blockchain-based pilot platform to explore how to use the technology for healthcare data management. The pilot project is currently being integrated into four large hospitals, using Ethereum for data sharing via virtual private networks. To allow user sharing, project participants use encryption and off-chain cloud components with cryptographic algorithms [29].

Table 3.1 Blockchain healthcare data processing firms [27].

	Blockchain company		
	Name	Country	Website
EMR data management	PokitDoc Gem YouBae	USA	http://pokitdoc.com http://enterprise.gem.co/ health http://www. youbase.io
EHR data management	Medicalchain	USA	http://www.medicalchain. com
	HealthWizz	USA	http://www.healthwizz. com
	Curisium	USA	http://www.curisium.com
	Hearthy	Spain	http://hearthy.co
	Iryo	Slovenia	http://iryo.io
	Robomed	Russia	http://www.robomed.io
PHR data management	*Medcredits*	USA	https://medcredits.io
	MyClinic	UK	https://myclinic.com
Point-of-care genomics	Nebula Genomics	USA	www.nebula.org
	In Genomes.io	USA	/www.genomes.io
	TimiCoin	USA	http://www.timicoin.io
	Shivom	Switzerland	http://shivom.io
Oncology patients network	OncoPower	USA	http://oncopower.org
Pharma &drug development	Embleema	France	http://www.embleema.com
	BlockPharma	France	http://www.blockpharma. com
	Chronicled MediLedger	USA	http://www.mediledger. com

3.9.2 Blockchains and Data Security are Related

General Data Protection Regulation (GDPR) is a widely disputed regulation in Europe, and GDPR is an idea of healthcare data protection alignment (as an example or in regard to data portability, with respect to consent management, data traceability, and the traceability of consent data). However, various problems can be found with regard to the right to be forgotten, (although with smart contracts in place, this may undermine actual control over data by allowing the data to be executed automatically), the technical implementation takes precedence. In line with the GDPR consent provision [28], dynamic consent management is one potential approach to addressing this problem. Finally, it is also assumed that "private blockchains," such as Enterprise blockchain, are able to comply with GDPR directives because digital records of the stored information can be updated and removed by unique consensus algorithms, which are run by private entities or organizations that own and manage this network. A single entity, which is usually an organization, operates private blockchains that give access to their users that meet certain preestablished qualifications or requirements. When thinking of how a corporation deals with its private web applications, their systems are handled in the same manner. They could involve government agencies' record keeping, owners of public health records, and healthcare providers in the payment process. The future of healthcare policy and management may rely on these private blockchains. The future applications of blockchains are discussed by the EU-backed Innovative Medicine Initiative (IMI) pilot project, Blockchain Powered Healthcare, which is led by Novartis, which aims to use standards, such as Ethereum, to introduce new services to the healthcare sector.

3.9.3 Blockchain for Personal Health Information

A broad range of wearable sensors and Internet of Things (IoT) medical devices gather information about our personal lives, and these data have recently begun to be stored in personal health information. Healthcare analytics powered by real-time artificial intelligence (AI) can be reported to concerned parties, such as patients, doctors, and customers representatives of pharmaceuticals. These real-time, AI-powered healthcare analytics would then help blockchain service providers. Based on the blockchain, open source, distributed and decentralized applications (Dapps) allow physicians and patients to function more securely and safely with reduced intermediary costs. This, in essence, encourages more autonomy for patients over healthcare and increases their autonomy.

3.9.4   Blockchain is a Strong Technology at the Point of Treatment Genomic Analytics

Timi Inc., a blockchain technology organization, predicts that any patient's data are worth between $7,000 and $7. This is true regardless of how long the patient uses the service. Although several mHealth companies emphasize patient capacity to use and monetize their personal health data stored in EHRs and wellness routine profiles measured by wearable sensors, as well as the patient (at-home) genome, this generalization is not always right. For one thing, several consumer-based DNA sequencing companies have been in the market for quite some time now. In 2006, "23andMe" was established, and today, it is the most prolific of the direct-to-consumer genetic testing firms. However, patient safety is very critical in the healthcare industry, of course. GlaxoSmithKline charged $300 million for 23andMe, which provides consumers with data in return.

3.10   Applications of IoT in Blockchain

The decentralized and scalable ecosystem that is created by blockchain enables IoT devices, networks, and applications to exist. To validate the blockchain technology, banks and financial institutions, like ING, Deutsche Bank, and HSBC, are conducting proof of concept (PoC) projects. Besides financial companies, various other businesses are preparing to make use of the blockchain's ability [29]. On the other hand, the IoT would open up limitless possibilities for businesses to operate productive operations. All our devices now have sensors mounted, which pass data to the cloud. It can be inferred that using these two technologies would result in productive systems.

Examples of how IoT and Blockchain can have a huge effect across various industries:

- logistics and supply chain,
- industry automotive,
- intelligent homes,
- economy sharing,
- industry in pharmacy,
- for agriculture,
- the management of water.

3.11   Challenges

There are many benefits to the blockchain concept, but it also has disadvantages:

Scalability issues and the size of the blockchain ledger have evolved over time. This will lead to centralization, as the technology casts a shadow on the future of blockchain [30].

The computing power and amount of time needed to perform encryption algorithms for those involved in the blockchain-based IoT ecosystem; IoT ecosystems are very diverse and are made up of diverse device types, and not all of them can perform the same encryption algorithms at the required rate.

The ledger will get larger over time as nodes store transactions and device IDs. The limits of a wide range of smart devices, such as sensors, and with only small storage space, stop such a device from being used.

3.12   Conclusion

Emerging smart contracts have become a common topic for research in both academic and industrial communities as blockchain technology gains widespread acceptance and complexity increases. Decentralization, enforceability, and verification of smart contracts make it possible for contracts to be agreed upon. Participation in an untrusted party of a reputable entity or a central server must be avoided if possible. Today, various studies are focused on the use of blockchain in healthcare. The quantity and quality of publications in the academic sector are on the rise. This also happens in global healthcare. The demand for blockchain technology is anticipated to reach 500 million dollars by 2022 in the industrial sector. Hospitality companies have a strong demand for innovative and improved trust-preserving solutions because of the significant demand for data sharing in the healthcare ecosystem. Because of the lack of publications on knowledge infrastructures, image archiving and communications networks, and pharmaceutical supply chains, the health information system domains that have not been adequately addressed include automated patient diagnostic facilities, administrative systems, community health management systems, and pharmaceutical supply chains. This chapter is an in-depth analysis of blockchain and the healthcare system as well as the architectural nature of e-healthcare systems. Additionally, we have written about the difficulties and the recent developments in the area of healthcare and the introduction of blockchain. It is imperative that the study agenda be broadened to address these issues. Additionally, you must focus on tackling the mission of seeking blockchain-based solutions that preserve trust by minimizing risk from inside as well as from the outside as an outsider to the healthcare sector.

References

1. Ravi, C. and Manimaran, P., Introduction of blockchain and usage of blockchain in internet of things, in: *Transforming Businesses With Bitcoin Mining and Blockchain Applications*, pp. 1–15, IGI Global, USA, 2020.

2. Tandon, A. *et al.*, Blockchain in healthcare: A systematic literature review, synthesizing framework and future research agenda. *Comput. Ind.*, 122, 103290, 2020.

3. Griebel, L., Prokosch, H.U., Köpcke, F., Toddenroth, D., Christoph, J., Leb, I., Engel, I., Sedlmayr, M., A scoping review of cloud computing in healthcare. *BMC Med. Inform. Decis. Mak*, 15, 17, 2015.

4. Houston, M.S., Myers, J.D., Levens, S.P., McEvoy, M.T., Smith, S.A., Khandheria, B.K., Shen, W.K., Torchia, M.E., Berry, D.J., Clinical consultations using store-and-forward telemedicine technology, in: *Mayo Clinic Proceedings*, vol. 74, Elsevier, Rochester, MN, USA, 1999.

5. Bhatti, A., Siyal, A.A., Mehdi, A., Shah, H., Kumar, H., Bohyo, M.A., Development of cost-effective tele-monitoring system for remote area patients, in: *Proceedings of the 2018 IEEE International Conference on Engineering and Emerging Technologies (ICEET)*, Lahore, Pakistan, 22–23 February 2018.

6. Castaneda, C., Nalley, K., Mannion, C., Bhattacharyya, P., Blake, P., Pecora, A., Goy, A., Suh, K.S., Clinical decision support systems for improving diagnostic accuracy and achieving precision medicine. *J. Clin. Bioinform.*, 5, 4, 2015.

7. Berman, M. and Fenaughty, A., Technology and managed care: Patient benefits of telemedicine in a rural healthcare network. *Health Econ.*, 14, 559–573, 2005.

8. Mandl, K.D., Markwell, D., MacDonald, R., Szolovits, P., Kohane, I.S., Public Standards and Patients' Control: how to keep electronic medical records accessible but private. *BMJ*, 322, 283–287, 2001.

9. Azaria, A., Ekblaw, A., Vieira, T., Lippman, A., MedRec: using blockchain for medical data access and permission management. Paper presented at: *IEEE International Conference on Open and Big Data (OBD)*, Washington, DC, 2016.

10. Tanwar, S., Parekh, K., Evans, R., Blockchain-based electronic healthcare record system for healthcare 4.0 applications. *J. Inf. Secur. Appl.*, 50, 102407, 2020.

11. Kumar, A. *et al.*, A Novel Smart Healthcare Design, Simulation, and Implementation Using Healthcare 4.0 Processes. *IEEE Access*, 8, 118433–118471, 2020.

12. Kamruzzaman, M.M., Architecture of Smart Healthcare System Using Artificial Intelligence. *2020 IEEE International Conference on Multimedia & Expo Workshops (ICMEW)*, IEEE, 2020.

13. Nakamoto, S., A peer-to-peer electronic cash system. Available online: https://bitcoin.org/bitcoin.pdf, 2008.

14. Iansiti, M. and Lakhani, K.R., The truth about blockchain. *Harv. Bus. Rev.*, 95, 1, 118–127, 2017.

15. Meinert, E., Alturkistani, A., Foley, K.A., Osama, T., Car, J., Majeed, A., Van Velthoven, M., Wells, G., Brindley, D., Blockchain implementation in healthcare: protocol for a systematic review. *JMIR Res. Protoc.*, 8, 2, e10994, 2019.

16. Zhang, A. and Lin, X., Towards secure and privacy-preserving data sharing in ehealth systems via consortium blockchain. *J. Med. Syst.*, 42, 8, 140, 2018.

17. Dimitrov, D.V., Blockchain Applications for Healthcare Data Management. *Healthc. Inform. Res.*, 25, 51–56, 2019.

18. State of blockchain q1 2016: Blockchain funding overtakes bitcoin, 2016. [Online]. Available:http://www.coindesk.com/state-of-blockchain-q1-2016/.

19. Nakamoto, S., Bitcoin: A peer-to-peer electronic cash system, 2008. [Online]. Available: https://bitcoin.org/bitcoin.pdf.

20. Lee Kuo Chuen, D., Ed., *Handbook of Digital Currency*, 1st ed., Elsevier, 2015. [Online]. Available: http://EconPapers.repec.org/RePEc: eee:monogr:9780128021170.

21. NRI, *Survey on blockchain technologies and related services*. Tech. Rep., 2015. [Online]. Available: http://www.meti.go.jp/english/press/2016/pdf/0531 01f. pdf.

22. Yuan, Y. and Wang, F.-Y., Blockchain and cryptocurrencies: Model, techniques, and applications. *IEEE Trans. Syst. Man Cybern. Syst.*, 48, 9, 1421–1428, Sep. 2018.

23. Zhang, R., Xue, R., Liu, L., Security and privacy on blockchain. *ACM Comput. Surv. (CSUR)*, 52, 3, 1–34, 2019.

24. Peng, L., Feng, W., Yan, Z., Li, Y., Zhou, X., Shimizu, S., Privacy preservation in permission less blockchain: A survey. *Digit. Commun. Netw.*, 7, 3, 295–307, 2020.

25. Li, X., Jiang, P., Chen, T., Luo, X., Wen, Q., A survey on the security of blockchain systems. *Future Gener. Comput. Syst.*, 107, 841–853, 2020.

26. Dimitrov, D.V., Blockchain applications for healthcare data management. *Healthc. Inform. Res.*, 25, 1, 51, 2019.

27. Cyran, M.A., *Blockchain as a foundation for sharing healthcare data*, vol. 1, pp. 1–6, Blockchain in Healthcare Today, 2018.

28. Kaye, J., Whitley, E.A., Lund, D., Morrison, M., Teare, H., Melham, K., Dynamic consent: a patient interface for twenty-first century research networks. *Eur. J. Hum. Genet.*, 23, 2, 141–146, 2015.
29. Ali, M.S., Vecchio, M., Pincheira, M., Dolui, K., Antonelli, F., Rehmani, M.H., Applications of blockchains in the Internet of Things: A comprehensive survey. *IEEE Commun. Surv. Tutorials*, 21, 2, 1676–1717, 2018.
30. Zheng, Z., Xie, S., Dai, H.N., Chen, X., Wang, H., Blockchain challenges and opportunities: A survey. *Int. J. Web Grid Serv.*, 14, 4, 352–375, 2018.

4

Smart Contract and Distributed Ledger for Healthcare Informatics

Yogesh Sharma[1]* and B. Balamurugan[2]

[1]*Maharaja Agrasen Institute of Technology, G.G.S.I.P. University, Delhi, India*
[2]*Galgotias University, Greater Noida, U.P., India*

Abstract

From the past decade, information technologies have gained various new technologies in the industries. One industry, unfortunately, was left behind or lagged, the healthcare sector. The reason could be a number of factors, like a couple of activities in healthcare or healthcare services and the utilization of charting paper-based information. If given a thought, every time a person goes to a doctor, there are questions about the last treatment, which are written down on charts, or in the hospital, nurses generally input things on charts and paper records, as well as the doctors. The problem with this is the collection of hundreds of records for every hundreds of patients over a 2-week period, and the result is a stack of charts. In analyzing a stack of written information, what you have is the possibility of illegible information, lost information, or just the inability to say what is in there. Now what is happening in the healthcare sector is the incorporation of new technologies that are digitizing this paper-based resource or information resource into computerized type of information. Now instead of writing this in the paper-based form, information is being input into the computer for creating electronic health records (EHR). This is where technologies, like distributed ledger and blockchain, comes into play. These technologies have gained a lot of appreciations in the past decade for safely handling a user's data and provide a strong privacy and security to the data of the users. The idea of distributed ledger helps the user's data to be shared with all the users of the data, be it a patient, doctor, and/or the administrator of the data.

Keywords: Healthcare, blockchain, distributed ledger, EHR, patients, records, privacy, security

Corresponding author: yogeshsharma027@gmail.com

T. Poongodi, D. Sumathi, B. Balamurugan and K. S. Savita (eds.) Digitization of Healthcare Data Using Blockchain, (73–92) © 2022 Scrivener Publishing LLC

4.1   Introduction

Health informatics is not simply upcoming area of the healthcare industry but more essentially the health of all of us. Health Informatics is combination of both health and technology. Health informatics deals with health data and the way data can be used in helping to improve health. The patient's data are warehoused in a record, and these records are kept for healthcare workers and for the patients themselves. These stored data can then be used to help make well-versed decisions and track progressive analytics.

The process of storing data can be done in 4 steps. Initially, the data are formed. The patient's health symptoms, medical diagnoses, treatments received, and other individual data are logged by healthcare professionals, or sometimes by devices like smart sensors. These collected data are then fed into an electronic health record system or an EHR. In the next step, data are taken out from EHR databases, which can be examined. This is the time when superior analytics techniques, machine learning, and artificial intelligence techniques are applied to find different patterns and make predictions. Finally, at the end, the collected data and the result found from the process of analytics are then provided to healthcare professionals, so the patient may get treatment accordingly. By applying a more superior analytics technique in health informatics, a patient's risk for certain diseases, like anemia and diabetes, can be evaluated and foreseen according to their medical history. Similarly, these advance analytics have the capability to detect even much smaller symptoms that may have been undiagnosed or not exposed to the healthcare provider. If in case the patient is admitted to the hospital within 30 days of discharge, this type of information could also be calculated or if a patient may develop some reactions to certain medications. There are many instances where informatics and artificial intelligence can improve care for a patient. Thus, Health Informatics is transforming the lives of everyone. Healthcare informatics not only expand the results in hospitals and medical facilities but also could be very useful in an administrative type of work and, more importantly, in everybody's home. The idea of using the health-based applications is also changing the lives of many, even on a smaller scale. With thousands of applications that help in storing the healthcare or fitness data, people start to understand their health and habits. The health record collected in these applications not only help the patients to keep track of their health but also the clinicians or healthcare workers keep track of their patients timely and in a better way [22].

4.1.1   History of Healthcare Informatics

The healthcare informatics has rapidly come from the last decade or so. There are multiple organizations and consumer-related technologies that have transformed multiple folds in the last decade and is in the growing phase at a much quicker pace. In earlier times, the disease diagnosis, action, and medication totally depends on the discoveries of in what manner patients respond to the external spurs [1]. In the 1920s, the healthcare informatics depends on the type of treatment given to the patient, every time the patient comes up with some health-related problem to healthcare worker and treatment is given based on the medical diagnosis. After every treatment to one person for some medical problem, the doctor can then be able to give same treatment to any other patient for same medical problem. Thus, a record can be maintained by the doctor for a given medical problem and the treatment given.

Earlier the data and analysis used to be written on papers to record the healthcare data for the healthcare experts but in 1960s/1970s when the era of computer system arrived, this changed the tuning and allocation of patients' health record [2]. Dr. Lawrence Weed, professor of medicine and pharmacology at Yale University, formed the initial Problem Oriented Medical Record (POMR). POMR has helped various medical practitioner and medical organizations to check the whole medical history of the person. In 1965, the authorized electronic medical record (EMR) was built and was taken into use by around 73 hospitals (www.vertitechit.com). During this era, healthcare services were very costly and very few of the person could be able to use it.

In 1980, the individual desktop system came that have changed the healthcare sector and during this time, not only hospitals, individual doctors were capable of investing in buying the computer machine which has transformed the structure of healthcare industry. In late 1980s, window-based computer systems became top priority in the offices of medical staff but the use of systems were limited to only billing and scheduling doctors relatively than maintaining the electronic health records of an individual patient.

In the mid of 1980s, the Institute of Medicine (IOM) has initiated work on the electronic health records, and lots of research were made to find the advantages of electronic medical records [3]. The research, however, could not come into existence as there were lot of issues related like the criteria, safety, and price connected with the adoption of EMRs. This was the time, during which the health-based records were not higher and collection of these data was not a big problem, nor the handling and analysis of the data.

However, after some time, the health-based data increase quickly, and suddenly, there are no systems that can handle these huge data coming and storage of data becoming problem for the healthcare industry. Clinics and medical staff do need EMRs. The EMR provides the solution for medical industry in analysis of disease diagnosis, its treatment, and proper medication. The EMR could play a useful role for any patient because the patient need not to carry all the records with him while traveling from different doctors or from one clinician to other. The electronic medical records can be used by the patient anywhere and anytime [4].

4.2   Introduction of Blockchain Technology

The blockchain technology came into existence in the financial sector with the arrival of cryptocurrency Bitcoin in 2008 by Satoshi Nakamoto [6]. Since then, the technology has emerged multiple folds and the technology along with other concepts is getting into various different sectors. A blockchain can be considered as a structured database like a linked list, all the data nodes connected with each other with a pointer.

A blockchain technology will be very useful where all the nodes in a network want to share their work and information on a common platform. Bringing the multiple authoritative domains on this single platform will make them work in a trusted environment, so that they can cooperate, coordinate, and collaborate [23] with each other in a decision-making process in the network.

In the traditional way of sharing the documents, one person writes a document, which might contain some data or information and send it to the receiver. The receiver again writes some data on that and share it with the sender again. With this kind of sharing, there is a lot of time consumed and the sender and receiver not able to write the document simultaneously also if in case the number of users will be more in this kind of network it might take huge amount of time. Now if we use some google doc. Application for sharing the information the time will cut down to very less but then come the problem with the single authority. First, network is still not decentralized and suffer from single point of failure, it could be a problem if the central authority may go down or server crashes. Second, every user needs sufficient bandwidth for the simultaneous update of the document. So, these are some of the disadvantages of centralized system and necessity of moving the system on a decentralized system.

A blockchain technology is a distributed and decentralized technology, distributed means everyone in the network collectively executes the job. Blockchain is based on the concept of Distributed Ledger Technology

(DLT) and is known as one of the types of DLT. Whereas in the blockchain technology there is no centralized/ single authority or a node which have the complete control over the chain thus called as a decentralized technology in which there are multiple points of coordination. A network created using a blockchain technology is a tamper evident and tamper proof network. A blockchain is a digitally implemented network as all the records in a blockchain network are secured cryptographically.

In the blockchain network, every node in the network maintains a local copy of the complete information. A decentralized system must ensure the consistency in the local copies with the node so that the copies at every node is identical with all other copies on other nodes and that all the local copies are getting updated based on the global information in the network.

4.2.1   A Blockchain Process

A typical blockchain process is shown in Figure 4.1. The process shows a transaction that has been made by a user. The transaction could be of any type, it could be financial transaction or it could be just sharing an information to the other nodes of the network. It is to note that all the nodes connected in the network has a ledger with them, which is a decentralized ledger and is used to store every transaction happening in the network, which means whatever be the transaction happening in the network will be

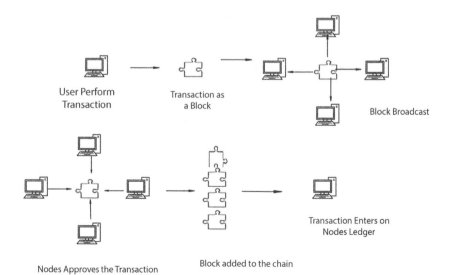

Figure 4.1 Blockchain process.

updated to all the nodes present. Any node that wants to create a transaction has to write the transaction in a block. A block is a kind of container that can take up around 500 transactions on an average, although the size of a block is just up to 1 MB [20]. Once a node finishes a transaction, this information is added in the block. This newly created block will get a new block number and a unique ID attached to the block. This unique ID is known as a *Hash Value*. A hash value is a value created by the hash function which is to make a transaction secure. This newly created block is now going into the blockchain network where all other nodes are present, whose duty is to verify and validate the newly created block. Now if the transaction made in the block is correct and authenticate and is no false information the transaction got accepted by the nodes of the network based on a consensus algorithm applied on the blockchain by the creator of the network. Once a transaction is validated by the nodes, the valid block gets added into the block. All the blocks that got validated are added one after another and forms a chain called blockchain. All the blocks that are added in the chain have their own hash value, and the hash value of the preceding block makes all the blocks connected with each other. The first block in the blockchain has its own hash value and does not have the hash value of previous block [24]. This first block in the chain of blocks is called a Genesis Block.

A blockchain works like a Public Ledger that means anyone can join this type of blockchain. However, there are some different aspects that need to be confirm.

When a transaction is created by some node during a time that it is needed to ensure that this particular transaction is valid, it should be dedicated to the current public ledger or blockchain, otherwise that item will not be in the blockchain. Once the transaction is verified and validated by the other nodes of the network, all the information should be consistent and updated on all local copies. The blockchain has to be secure enough that once the information is updated on all the nodes, no else could modify the data present the nodes or if some node does some modification in the data and broadcast the information in the network, the other nodes should be capable of detecting that there is some change in the data and that information should not be included. Privacy and authenticity are important factors in a blockchain that need to be ensured because the data belong to different clients.

4.3 Types of Blockchains

There are three major types of blockchain chain, Public, Private, and a Consortium Blockchain. Depending up on the architecture and the work, these types of blockchains are used in various organization and industries. There are advantages and limitations in these types of blockchain; however, whichever type of blockchain benefits and improves the quality of an organization, it will be used despite the limitation.

4.3.1   Public Blockchain

The public blockchains are very well known due to the invention of cryptocurrencies, like bitcoin and Ethereum. Now, as the name says, Public, means anybody can join this type of blockchain network and is open to everyone and essentially read the data, and also, the identity of the participant is almost impossible to gather. Being open to all does not mean here that the public blockchain is insecure and not as secure as other types of blockchain. Every blockchain is essentially secure by the power of cryptography. A public blockchain is also known as a permissionless blockchain because no permission is required in this type of blockchain to join the network.

In a public blockchain, any number of anonymous users can join the network and keeps on announcing the transactions created. All of these transactions are recorded on to the block until the block gets full. Once the block is filled with the transactions, all the transactions are compared, and the consensus is taken by the other node for validation of the transaction. If the transaction is verified and validated to be true, the transaction is accepted. Proof of Work and Proof of Stake consensus algorithm are widely used algorithms for a public blockchain. Bitcoin and Ethereum are the example of Public blockchain.

4.3.2   Private Blockchain

A private blockchain is also known as permissioned blockchain because any participant who wants to join the network needs to take permission from the owner of the blockchain, and all the permissions of the private blockchain are kept centralized. However, some people say that blockchain is decentralized technology then how come a private blockchain be a centralized one. Well, the organizations and many other sectors like banking and finance supports the private blockchain for being centralized. So, in a private blockchain, the control is with the owner of the blockchain, and all the rules and regulations are made by the owner. It is the owner who decides who can join and who cannot. Since all the participants in a private blockchain are authorized participants once the transactions are added in the ledger, there is no requirement of further audit. The details of all the transactions are visible only to participants of the network. When in a private blockchain, the entire history of the assets can be tracked down and managed accordingly. All the participants are in hold of a ledger that gets updated every time there is any new information or transactions added in the block. The private blockchain are highly secure, and the cryptographically linked ledgers are almost impossible to tamper.

4.3.3   Consortium Blockchain

This type of blockchain is not a fully public blockchain, which means it is not possible to join the blockchain like anybody. A consortium blockchain is actually controlled by pre-selected nodes in the network. A consortium blockchain are not considered as fully decentralized as everybody cannot just involved in the network. However, they can be called partial decentralized type of network. In a consortium blockchain, the consensus mechanism is controlled by few selected participants, and it is the decision of these node whether to allow other nodes to read the records or not. Although with this decision, there might be a possibility that some wicked participant could tamper the records. The efficiency of consortium blockchain is high as compared with a public blockchain, and the consensus process in this type of blockchain is a permissioned one.

4.4   Blockchain in Healthcare

A blockchain is a sequence of blocks connected in a form of chain. This method was initially defined in 1991 by a set of researchers for the innovative purpose for timestamping digital documents to avoid their back dating and tampering. In 2009, Satoshi Nakamoto [6] adapted this technique to make a digital cryptocurrency bitcoin. A blockchain is a type of distributed ledger that is not closed to anyone with an exciting property that when data are logged inside a blockchain, it converts into permanent data and cannot be altered. This immutableness characteristic of blockchain comes very strongly where there is any need for storing healthcare data, which is the requirement to provide the security and validity of patient's health records. One of the biggest properties of blockchain that prove advantageous to the health records of patient is that it is not a centralized one, this makes it possible and allows scattered healthcare applications, which does not believe on a single central authority. Moreover, considering the statistic that the record in the blockchain is virtual among each node in a network and creates an environment of precision and sincerity that enables the healthcare users and patients, in order to realize who is handling their data, when and how. Notably in the blockchain network, adjusting any single user does not impact the position of the record as the data in the record is duplicated among several user in a network. Hence, according to the nature of block-chain, it can protect healthcare data from possible loss, scam, or safety of the data from different types of attacks, like the ransomware attack. For better health records exchange, many systems are not proficient of contrib-uting their health information, which could be a huge task for health IT and EHR. Blockchain technology in true sense is potential in addressing the multiple platform tasks by being used as a mutual technical standard to safely distribute the electronic medical data. The security and information privacy issues hamper the meaningful coordination and collaboration in healthcare. There is always some risk of cyber attacks and uncertain mul-tiplatform standards keep the information at risk and bound the way it might be dispersed and retrieved. Although, sometimes, even the collected information is not reliable, even though it is swapped partly because the files might be corrupted or contain faults that are to be corrected manually. Blockchain technology guarantees open control through collective public and private types of chains while public data is accessible to all users of the network. Private data are encoded, and only authorized users can access these private data. Thus, blockchain-permitted structures protect EHR and also enhance the privacy essential by HIPPA trust and medical research. Blockchain technology can tackle the problems of result instability and data prying [21]. The system allows shifting the time marked stable ledger of medical trials and investigation results. Hence, reducing the incidence of cheat and error in medical test, validate billing, correctness. Blockchain's self-regulating structure provides a highly integrity for tracking the option and allows uplifting of the data instantly. Any attempt of data alteration should be confirmed by every block in the system. After authorization, current information becomes a steady part of the record and could not be altered or modified. Blockchain can diminish financial crashes, as well as considerably break the scam and unlawful shifting of data, empowering the clinical supply chain. According to some estimates, 10% of health materials streaming in multiple nations are either low in quality or fabricated. It is assumed that a small percent of all drugs currently in the market are fake. However, a system based on blockchain technology can assure a chain of safekeeping. Tracing of record at all the level of the drug supply chain could also enhance the functionalities, like secret key and smart contracts, brace the trustworthiness of the medicinal supplier at any distribution step, and preserve the agreements among multiple parties well. Blockchain technol-ogy has the ability to convert medical care by putting the patient in the middle of the medical care ecology and growing the security, privacy, and ability to work on multiple operating systems handling the health data. Last, but not the least, as nowadays, COVID-19 is spreading all over the world, it is very important that medical reports of a person should be kept private and secured from others. The blockchain technology does help in providing the right kind of security and privacy to patients suffering from corona virus.

4.5 Distributed Ledger Technology

A distributed ledger technology also known as DLT is a technology that is based on peer-to-peer network, which is very secure. A Distributed Ledger can also be termed as a ledger that is shared among other nodes. A distributed ledger is a type of database in which the shared data are replicated, meaning the data are geographically expanded across multiple nodes, placed in different countries or multiple institution. A decentralized authority exists in a distributed ledger system. Each node present in the DLT updates their own records on time-to-time basis on their own. A distributed ledger system is a node-to-node network and uses some type of consensus algorithm, the algorithm ensures that the duplication method among multiple nodes. A distributed ledger system can be characterized into a permissioned or permissionless ledger. The type of ledger depends on the fact that if the users of the distributed ledgers is open to all or only some pre authorized participants can use the record. The technology came into existence with the concept of cryptocurrencies like bit coin but the technology has moved three folds and now the technology is being used in many use cases and many organizations are investing lot of amounts in DLT as the technology helps in saving money and, in same manner, or other the risk involved in the operation also gets reduced [19].

4.6 Evolution of Distributed Ledger Technology

Earlier in the banking system all the records used to be maintained manually in registers and on papers. With the invention of computer in around 1980's and 1990's the records were shifted into some database which was controlled by a single server or a centralized server also called as Centralized Ledger System [4]. However, the problem with this centralized ledger system was that this system was controlled by a single authority, and also, a single point failure may disrupt the complete network.

Lamport *et al.* [5], the concept of distributed ledger arrived in late 1982 with the Byzantine Generals Problem theorized by whereas the concept of blockchain came into existence in 1991 by Damgård [7], but the real existence of blockchain technology came with the concept of cryptocurrencies like bit coin in 2008 by Satoshi Nakamoto [6]. A distributed ledger technology is based on the trust between the peers connected in the network. A distributed ledger technology adds the trust, transparency, security and traceability to a network [8]. The distributed ledger technology is a decentralized technology, i.e., without any central authority. The DLT has evolved since then and many blockchain use cases are following the distributed ledger technology.

4.7   Smart Contract

In 1997 "Smart Contract" was initially used by Nick Szabo [9], way back Bitcoin was formed. Smart contracts are similar to simple contracts in the real world. However, the smart contracts are entirely digital. In fact, a smart contract is truly a small computer program that is placed inside a blockchain. A smart contract first of all should not be called a smart contract but, should just be called a contract. Actually, a smart contract is nothing more than certain computer code built within to the blockchain cryptocurrency network that computers or the nodes execute. Once the computers or the nodes execute this contract, they update the ledger. smart contracts, first relate it to something called automation where certain tasks are executed. Once something is reached or once something is triggered, for example in email marketing when somebody goes to your funnel certain laws exist where if a person enters the email, email one can be seen, if email one opened up, second email will be received so what this refers to is IFTT (If This Then That) logic. So, that's what smart contract is in a nutshell If This Then That Logic When a code for smart contract is created online on the blockchain and the law states that if a person puts in money into this contract, then that will execute a next action that next action will then send a digital contract to somebody's email and that person will get this contract to sign off and then that trigger will go back to the smart contract code on the blockchain which will again execute something else. Vending machine could be the best real-life example to better understand the smart contract idea, where, by putting a dollar in the vending machine is the first trigger, which executes a bag of chips falling from the vending machine Thus, smart contract is a domino series where there is a pre-existing event to trigger the next event. The smart contracts are both immutable and distributed. By immutable means, smart contracts cannot be altered once they have created. That means no one will be allowed to modify the contract even accidentally. When it is said that smart contract is distributed, it means once the smart contract is executed, its output will be validated by all the users present in a network. Thus, no one user can influence the contract to issue the assets since other users on the network will find this execution and mark it as unacceptable. Thus, modification with smart contracts is not possible in true sense. The smart contract is programmed onto the blockchain and run by all the computers. The system will automatically then update the transparent ledger that everybody can see. Thus, in a simplest term, a Smart contract is a tiny section of written code inside a blockchain that can execute a bunch of different actions such as keeping money in it or executing a contract to buy something. Currently, there are very few blockchains that support smart contracts, but the most popular one is Ethereum. Ethereum was explicitly created and designed in order to support smart contracts. Solidity programming language is a special programming language that is useful in creation of smart contracts and was specifically created for Ethereum. The Solidity Programming language resembles the syntax of JavaScript. It's worth noting that smart contracts also support Bitcoin although the scope is more limited compared to Ethereum.

Let us see few examples to better understand the smart contract and its advantages, when buying a car, two options are either online to find a car or go to the dealership, either way, the process takes a while, maybe takes a couple of days to execute. Now imagine if there is a smart contract than buying the car, the ownership, the information, everything about it is executed on that smart contract. Now, the information or the ownership of that car, a digital identity, is on the blockchain ledger. Every single node, every single computer part of that blockchain ecosystem automatically updates the ledger. So, everybody now knows on a network that a car was just sold. This means everything is updated in the ledger of the blockchain.

Imagine a situation where 10 people want to buy piece of property which can be like multi equity buys with in a house on a smart contract that executes everything and this might have exponential effect as, smart contract is multi-purpose buying a multi signature bind where even if a person wants to sell something or one third of something. However, in this situation, all the 10 persons are legal owners and have to sign off of it automatically on its smart contract.

Smart contract especially on the blockchain, a digital identity can also be created with the social credibility so the more that that individual is trustworthy paying on time, their social credit Rises and if their social credit is good that individual can get better credit or get better loans or might even get a reduced cost, when it comes to paying rent by a tenant. So finally, a smart contract is just an agreement between couple of multi parties (may be all at one time) online that can be automatically executed on a transparent blockchain using weather tokens or cryptocurrencies.

4.7.1 Limitations of Smart Contract

Smart contracts can be called as the automation of the legal contracts. Smart contracts have recently gained popularity with the popularity of blockchain in various other fields other than just cryptocurrency. Smart contracts are a low-level code that runs on the blockchain. A recent study has shown some challenges associated with the smart contact in their development. Since the smart contract are still in their initial phase according to the survey, there are still no perfect path to secure the smart contracts [10]. The toolchain that exists for the development of the smart contract are less powerful. The programming languages and virtual machines that are used in development and the runtime platforms does have lots of limitations. Talking about the support from the blockchain community and the resources available online for learning purpose are also very less or are limited.

4.7.2 Smart Contract in Healthcare Informatics

Electronic health record can be hard to approach in part as the ability to assess and alter them needs to abide by an array of rules and privacy as the private health information increases by time and the number of medical facilities, an individual receive grows, it sometimes become difficult to keep track of the database that have been created in the past. Smart contracts can restructure the possession and gets to the important healthcare data for both patients and the doctors or healthcare providers. These healthcare providers store the healthcare records on the blockchain, which permits only those have the authority to view, and secure access records any time. The functionality of smart contract means that only the verified users can simply accept and make variations to the data received. With this process only the authorized party can add new documents or update the existing document abide by the new regulations. The changes made will be backed up by blockchain network and authenticated cryptographically [11]. So, they are more secure and traditional electronic health records.

Let us take an individual who purchases health insurance and what happens then is, the particulars of their strategy get connected to their profile.

Inside the blockchain when that person undergoes a healthcare process which is covered by their strategy then the smart contract will inevitably be activated and the correct payment from the insurance company to the hospital will instantly be made, and this will show optimistic result on the reasonable implementation of the person's insurance policy and it will decrease the non-efficient result and stresses that arrives with in the process of completion in the insurance forms.

The biggest problem in the basic supply chain of pharmaceutical was of counterfeit medicine being supplied to the retailers. Now, with the blockchain technology, this problem can also be removed by using another element that is Internet of Things (IoT). The IoT devices can help track the medicines from the manufacturer or from the production to the consumers. With IoT devices in place, manufacturer and the consumer will be able to get the complete information when the medicine left the production unit and when it reaches to the consumer through which path. Consumer can also track if the medicine is coming from the trusted pharmaceutical company and not the fake one. At the end of the process the smart contracts can be used for the transfer of the funds from the consumer to the pharmacist. The smart contract helps in direct fund transfer from without any intervention of the medical practitioner.

4.8   Distributed Ledger in Healthcare Informatics as Blockchain

Blockchain can simply also be known as Distributed Ledger Technology, or DLT in short. This is because of the publicity of the cryptocurrency Bitcoin, based on Blockchain technology. DLTs can be described as a digital database where in each user can add the data kept there — not specifically on the cloud, but on every local computer on the network, working as a decentralized node-to-node network [12]. One feature is that, decentralized consensus algorithms that are executed over on the active computers. This supposed mining confirms the data in the non-central network — makes DLTs transparent, secure and non-central, and these features makes the backbone for the transactions in the future and confirmation processes [13]. While if thought of Blockchain, it is block with a distinct signature comprises of the hash value of the previous block which is created for each new set of data [14].

The users of the blockchain looks for the new data by means of a consensus protocol before it is merged as a block inside the chain and converts into an unchallengeable from then on. "Proof-of-work," is one of the best consensus mechanisms developed. This mechanism incorporates the computing power of the user for the purpose of validation of a given transaction executed by the user. The proof of mechanism is a resource-based mechanism because of difficult computing due to the complex mathematical calculations, although this type of work is one part of the protocol design of secure consensus and in order to secure the network from any kind of modifications and thus reduces the attacks. There is other easier manner that can secure the consensus, like "proof of stake," in which not much of the safety requirements needed. Proof of stake is based on the number of tokens a user added. The more the number of tokens are, the more power is there in finding the consensus [15]. This occurs with a hypothesis that the user is not interested in destroying the values of the token nor does the user going to harm the system. If in case a user has much higher speed requirements then the user can opt for DLT framework and complete the information interchange by second layer mechanism. On these second layer, the transactions are managed at a much-advanced rates. Distributed ledger technologies quite applicable in future, as they permit an Economy of Things. Secure transactions among the humans and machines, unchallengeable, undeniable information, and as a consequence, the competence for smart contracts, implanted in a program code to be able to promise non-central automatic prescribed transactions [16]. Distributed Ledger Technologies provide and authorize the foundation for faith, justice, and involvement in the decision-making process. Thus, DLT permits the intersectoral value forming the networks. Distributed Ledger can also be advantageous in the Healthcare Informatics [17].

Blockchain and healthcare is today, the first of which is that, there are new business networks being formed, companies joining together using shared infrastructure to create value in healthcare and life sciences. There is a huge level of investment, and it is an all-time high doubling the pace of previous years, in a new way of forming capital is emerging using security tokens to fund drug development for early-stage biotech companies. Another trend to highlight is that out of all parts of healthcare right now, there is the most activity within pharma and all outline sort of what ways that is happening.

There are small business networks like healthcare and life sciences enterprises. They are joining together to solve all the problems in new ways using blockchain technology. The way that blockchain enables this is because companies' enterprises non-profits that would normally be competitors are able to come together in a business network to trust the shared infrastructure that are building on and solve some complex issues that they can't solve alone. Now this is happening in a number of different consortiums.

Machine learning ledger arrangement for drug discovery or melody project. There are ten of the world's largest pharmaceutical companies that have proprietary data around molecules that they are using. A blockchain and federated learning to allow these businesses to train a single machine learning model without giving up the privacy of their data. They are using a blockchain to arrange the learning process to position when and how data is accessed, shared and trained. Using this distributed infrastructure where no single party has control over, so they can have trust that they are extremely proprietary the data that is not breaching and neither getting shared with their competitors. Distributed ledger creates one single source of truth and shares the data between the parties which reduces the redundant workflows in order to improve the accuracy of their directories which in turn lowers the costs associated with administrative overhead. So, the value that blockchain provides in this case, is a single source of truth for data sharing between companies that traditionally would not be sharing the data.

4.9   Distributed Ledger Technology in Healthcare Payments

In last decade or so because of complicated agreements between the parties the healthcare or medical sector has suffered a lot. Thus, the result of it was delayed payments and also resulted in complicated errors in the claim process and multiple disputes occurred during the settlements. Consider a situation where different users in a business network may get the same kind of information or an update, that means all the user in the business network are in coordination with the one kind of fact only. Many different companies working on the idea of distributed ledger technology. A Distributed Ledger or can simply be called as blockchain, is a shared distributed ledger that enables the logging of transactions and asset tracking for anything of value. The shared ledger allows all parties to monitor and analyse the status of an asset near real time enabling end-to-end tracking. There are four key dimensions of blockchain, one is the shared ledger which is a simply records on a distributed system which is shared across a business network, second is the smart contract which is a term for business purpose and can be used for both embedded and executed in a transaction database. Third is the consensus in which all parties agree to the validity of a transaction and committed to the blockchain and the fourth one is, privacy, so that transactions are secure authenticated and verifiable [18]. One major point today is free authorization process, this is an extra step required by some insurance companies before they decide, if they want to pay for certain services determining if a given expense for event is medically necessary and covered by a members insurance policy. This process can be a slow process for many reasons such as, one the involvement of multiple stakeholders, second the variance and amount covered based on the payer provider relationship, three, the processes that are typically complex and involves several manual steps and finally there could be errors that occurs with deprived communication and technology.

Blockchain technology will speed up in streamline pre-authorization. With blockchain a single ledger shared among the healthcare stakeholders that contains the patient's entitlement and smart contracts which code the prior authorization conditions. This mechanizes the information gathering and sharing, permitting for real-time determination of benefits. Some advantages of using blockchain for pre-authorization include, improvement in cash flow which is due to the faster transaction settlement, timely treatment of the patient, accurate payment to the provider and reducing administrative costs and less double record-keeping.

4.10   Conclusion

Healthcare informatics is a vast area in terms of data as well as accessibility. The healthcare informatics allows the users of the system to access the data in a secure manner in order to check the health-related information of a patient. The healthcare informatics carries very sensitive for both the patient and the healthcare workers. To secure the information and data one way could be storing the information on cloud but that is not secure enough. So this chapter discussed about distributed ledger which helps in sharing the information only to the users connected in a distributed ledger environment. Blockchain technology, also based on the distributed ledger concept, makes the data and information secure and provide high level of privacy. The smart contract is another technology that came with the blockchain technology which is small piece of code the executes automatically when a particular condition is met. The smart contract also helps not only in sharing the healthcare information like reports, and other sensitive documents to the users of distributed ledger but smart contract can also be useful in making payments to the healthcare worker joined in network by the patients in the same network.

References

1. Dada, M. and Chambers, C., Healthcare Analytics, in: *International Series in Operations Research and Management Science*, pp. 765–791, Springer, New York LLC, 2019.
2. VeritechIT, *The History of Healthcare Technology and the Evolution of EHR*, *https://www.vertitechit.com*, Holyoke, Massachusetts, 2018, Available at: https://www.vertitechit.com/history-healthcare-technology/ (Accessed: 8 April 2021).
3. Evans, R.S., Electronic Health Records: Then, Now, and in the Future, in: *Yearbook of medical informatics*, pp. S48–S61, Thieme Medical Publishers, (Suppl 1), 2016.
4. Sharma, Y. and Balamurugan, B., A Survey On Privacy Preserving Methods Of Electronic Medical Record Using Blockchain. *J. Mech. Contua. Math. Sci.*, 15, 32–47, 2020.
5. Lamport, L., Shostak, R., Pease, M., The Byzantine Generals Problem, in: *ACM Transactions on Programming Languages and Systems (TOPLAS)*, vol. 4(3), pp. 382–401, ACM PUB27 New York, NY, USA, 1982.
6. Nakamoto, S., Bitcoin: A Peer-to-Peer Electronic Cash System, 2008, Available at: www.bitcoin.org (Accessed: 31 July 2020).
7. Damgård, I., Towards practical public key systems secure against chosen ciphertext attacks, in: *Lecture Notes in Computer Science (including subseries Lecture Notes in Artificial Intelligence and Lecture Notes in Bioinformatics)*, pp. 445–456, Springer Verlag, 1992.
8. El Ioini, N. and Pahl, C., A review of distributed ledger technologies, in: *Lecture Notes in Computer Science (including subseries Lecture Notes in Artificial Intelligence and Lecture Notes in Bioinformatics)*, pp. 277–288, Springer Verlag, 2018.
9. Szabo, N., The Idea of Smart Contracts, pp. 2–3, Satoshi Nakamoto Institute', (c), 1997.
10. Zou, W. *et al.*, Smart Contract Development: Challenges and Opportunities. *IEEE Trans. Software Eng. Institute Electrical and Electronics Engineers (IEEE)*, 10, 1–1, 2019.
11. Omar, I.A. *et al.*, Ensuring protocol compliance and data transparency in clinical trials using Blockchain smart contracts. *BMC Med. Res. Methodol. BioMed Central Ltd*, 20, 1, 1–17, 2020.
12. Marks, J., Distributed Ledger Technologies and Corruption the Killer App. *Colum. Sci. Tech. L. Rev.*, 20, 1, 42–49, 2018, Available at: https://heinonline.org/HOL/Page?handle=hein.journals/cstlr20&id=42&div=&collection= (Accessed: 12 April 2021).
13. Zhang, R., Xue, R., Liu, L., Security and privacy on blockchain. *ACM Comput. Surv. Association for Computing Machinery*, 52, 3, 1–34, 2019.

14. Aste, T., Tasca, P., Di Matteo, T., *Blockchain Technologies: foreseeable impact on industry and society*, Discovery.Ucl.Ac.Uk, University College of London, 2017, https://discovery.ucl.ac.uk/id/eprint/10043048/.
15. Sunyaev, A. and Sunyaev, A., Distributed Ledger Technology, in: *Internet Computing*, pp. 265–299, Springer International Publishing, 2020.
16. Antal, C. *et al.*, Distributed ledger technology review and decentralized applications development guidelines. *Future Internet. MDPI AG*, 13, 1–32, 2021.
17. Kaya, F., Gordijn, J., Wieringa, R., A minimalistic decision tree for blockchain business cases in healthcare, in: *CEUR Workshop Proceedings*, pp. 16–25, 2020.
18. Sultan, K., Ruhi, U., Lakhani, R., Conceptualizing blockchains: characteristics & applications. 11th IADIS International Conference Information Systems, arXiv preprint arXiv:1806.03693, 2018.
19. Bashir, I., *Mastering Blockchain: Distributed ledger technology, decentralization, and ... - Imran Bashir - Google Books*, Packt publications, 2018.
20. Madeira, A., *What is the Block Size Limit | CryptoCompare.com*, CryptoCompare, Available at: https://www.cryptocompare.com/coins/guides/what-is-the-block-size-limit/ (Accessed: 8 April 2021), 2018.
21. Shi, S. *et al.*, Applications of blockchain in ensuring the security and privacy of electronic health record systems: A survey, in: *Computers and Security*, p. 101966, Elsevier Ltd, 2020.
22. Yogesh Sharma, B. and Balamurugan, F.K., *Blockchain, Big Data and Machine Learning, Blockchain, Big Data and Machine Learning*, 2020.
23. Vedpal, Jain, V., Bhatnagar, N., Four C's in supply chain management: Research issues and challenges, in: *Proceedings - 2012 3rd International Conference on Emerging Applications of Information Technology, EAIT 2012*, pp. 264–267, 2012.
24. Di Pierro, M., What is the blockchain?. Computing in Science & Engineering, 19, 5, 92–95, 2017.

5

Consensus Algorithm for Healthcare Using Blockchain

Faizan Salim[1], John A.[1*], Rajesh E.[1] and A. Suresh Kumar[2]

[1]*School of Computing Science and Engineering Galgotias University, Greater Noida, India*
[2]*Department of Computer Science and Engineering, Graphic Era University, Dehradun, Uttarakhand, India*

Abstract

Blockchain was first invented in 1991 by Stuart Haber and W. Scott Stornetta. They wanted to create a system where tampering of time-stamps in documents could be stopped, which ultimately led to the blockchain's creation. There is a myth that blockchain can store only financial transactions, which is false because we can store any type of data in the blockchain. The network of computers connected mining the blocks for rewards, this connected group of networks is called a peer-to-peer network and is also referred to as p2p network. The main types of types of blockchain are Public Blockchain, Private Blockchain, Consortium Blockchain, and Hybrid Blockchain. Usage of consensus in the blockchain is very important because blockchain is based on a distributed network, where we always need to decide fairly which node should be the next primary node that will be able to add the next block to the chain. Consensus algorithms work as the basic building block of the blockchain, without which, the whole technology is a failure. There are various consensus algorithms available, which need to be chosen wisely, depending on the type of application and sector in which we are implementing blockchain as a technology. The main problem with proof of work is that it is very expensive and requires a lot of computing power to solve complex mathematical problems, which are of no use to humanity. The healthcare system can get revolutionized with the implementation of blockchain-based mechanisms. Personal healthcare and external record management are the two main blockchain networks that could help implement blockchain in the healthcare system. The main problem with the current healthcare system, that is, data are not available to all, research fields are very

---

Corresponding author: johnmtech@gmail.com

T. Poongodi, D. Sumathi, B. Balamurugan and K. S. Savita (eds.) Digitization of Healthcare Data Using Blockchain, (93–116) © 2022 Scrivener Publishing LLC

slow due to lack of data, and the available data are also inefficient and adequate. The practical Byzantine Fault Tolerance algorithm enables us to communicate with other peers without having a third party in between, hence decreasing the risk of fraud and removing the high costs charged by the middlemen, thus making blockchain cost-effective. The primary concern in the management of healthcare data is the security of the healthcare data and maintaining the data's ownership. With the present proposed implementation, almost all the concerns have been addressed and those remaining will be soon worked upon.

Keywords: Blockchain, blockchain database, consensus algorithm, healthcare systems, and algorithms

5.1   Introduction

Blockchain was first invented in 1991 by two researchers named Stuart Haber and W. Scott Stornetta. Their main objective was to design and implement a system where tampering of timestamps in a document could be stopped. Hence, an attempt to make something immutable and they succeeded too. In 2009, with the incoming of Bitcoin in the market which Satoshi Nakamoto invented, Blockchain technology got its first real-world usage, and since then, there was no looking back [1].

Blockchain is an immutable database in which data are stored in blocks, then chained together using cryptographic techniques. These interconnected blocks are dependent on each other for completing a valid transaction. A block in the blockchain mainly consists of a body and a header.

    a.   A version of the blockchain: Currently, we have three versions of the blockchain. Version depicts which version of the blockchain we are using. Its size is 4 bytes.
        1.0 Currency
        2.0 Smart contract
        3.0 Distributed applications
    b.   Hash of the previous block: the previous block's hash is also attached to the new block to form a chain of blocks called a blockchain. Its size is 32 bytes.
    c.   Timestamp: it is a piece of information depicting the time utilized in the creation of the block. It is 4 bytes.
    d.   Merkle tree root hash: This contains the hash of data present in the block to protect the data's immutability. This is done through cryptographic techniques, and the size is 32 bytes.

e. Difficulty target: It is of 4 bytes and helps in the validation of the new blocks.
f. Nonce: It is of 4 bytes and contains any random number starting from zero. Miners solve for the nonce, this is simply a random number that helps in reaching consensus. Moreover, Nonce is an abbreviation used for numbers used only once.
g. Data counter: Its size can vary between 1 and 9 bytes approximately and consists of the number of transactions for the particular block in the blockchain.

5.2 Types of Blockchain

There are primarily two types of blockchain—public and private blockchain; however, over time, we have found few more variants like hybrid blockchain and consortium blockchain. The diagrammatic representation of more variant of blockchain shown in Figure 5.1.

The common thing between all the types of blockchain is as follows:

- All the blockchain consist of a peer-to-peer network consisting of nodes connected.
- All the nodes share a common ledger, which is constantly updated.
- Any node present on the network can create blocks, verify a transaction, or send or receive transactions on the network.

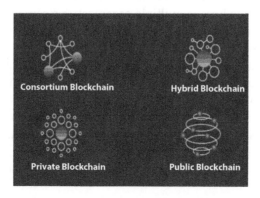

Figure 5.1 Diagrammatic representation of types of blockchain.

A. **Public blockchain:** Public blockchain is a distributed, noncentralized blockchain that anyone on the Internet has access to. Anyone with an Internet connection can easily become a part of this blockchain network as a node and start participating in the transactions. The node can access the complete ledger of past and ongoing transactions and is also authorized to verify the transactions. Bitcoin is a famous public blockchain-based decentralized system. Public blockchains need to implement some serious security algorithms to make sure everything is secure. Because the number of participants cannot be controlled, we need to make sure everything is safe and free from malicious nodes, for example, Ethereum, Dogecoin, Bitcoin, Litecoin, and so on.

B. **Private blockchain:** The main difference between the public and the private blockchain is that in a private blockchain, any random nodes on the Internet cannot join the peer-to-peer network and start doing transactions. This type of blockchain implementation is used inside a particular organization, where the organization owner manages all the permissions and access rights of the allowed nodes in the system. The primary use of such implementation can be voting, digital identity, private data management inside an organization, and so on, for example, Corda, Multichain, and so on.

C. **Consortium blockchain:** In this type of blockchain implementation, we have a semidecentralized type of structure where multiple organizations are involved in managing the blockchain, unlike private blockchain. The significant difference here is multiple organizations can act as nodes and do transactions like exchanging information or mining new blocks into the blockchain, this type of implementation is used mainly by government organizations and banking systems, for example, R3, E.W Foundation, and so on.

D. **Hybrid blockchain:** Hybrid blockchain is an excellent combination of the public and private blockchain. A limited section of data is allowed to go public rest is kept private. In a hybrid blockchain, users can enjoy the freedom of both public and private blockchain by easily keeping the data private and are also able to verify it on a public network when required, for example, Dragonchain.

Public Blockchain vs. Private Blockchain

1. **Public blockchain:**
   The main advantages of the private blockchain over the public blockchain are:

   - *Speed*: Because of a smaller and constrained peer-to-peer network, the transaction speed is very fast compared with that of a public blockchain where the number of nodes can be large.
   - *Scalability*: Another advantage of using private blockchains is that it is way more scalable when compared with the public blockchain because it is to be used within an organization to easily define the size required by the blockchain. This property makes private blockchain very flexible and scalable [2].

2. **Private Blockchain:**
   - *Secure*: Public blockchains are comparatively secure because the number of participants or nodes is large. The security also improves automatically by decreasing the chances of a 51% attack.
   - *Transparency*: Public blockchains are transparent, and all the transactions stored in the ledger are shared with all the networks in the node without any central authority controlling it, which makes things to be fairer, and this property makes it usable in lots of different sectors.
   - *Trustworthy*: The nodes in the network need not worry about others' authenticity in the network. With the implementation of a proof of work algorithm, hacking a blockchain becomes extremely difficult. Even if someone tries to do so, the investment done by him would be more than what he will earn from the attack, thus making the system secure, robust, and trustworthy.

So, in a nutshell, both the public and the private blockchain have their pros and cons making it very difficult to give a clear verdict on which blockchain is better than the other. Hence it depends on the industry's demand which type of blockchain should be used, without considering the demand factor it would not be fair to declare anyone better than the other [3].

5.3   Blockchain Database

The data in the blockchain can be essentially of any type. There are no restrictions on the type of data that can be stored in a blockchain.

Peer-to-Peer Network: This property of blockchain helps ensure that it is completely safe and the transaction cannot be tampered with. By P2P network, we mean that data are stored in a publicly available ledger stored on multiple computers connected to the network. Thus, even if someone tries to change the data, he has to update the data in all connected peers, which is an impossible task [4]. Whenever new data are received, a new block is formed. Once the data enter the new block, it is chained together by adding the hash of the previous block to the newly formed block.

Other than these, another essential property of blockchain is its *immutability*. It means data, once written into a block. can never be erased or edited. Even if someone tries to change the data, the hash would also change, leading to disconnection of the connection between blocks. However, because the ledger is available with everyone in the network and networks keep on growing more prominent, the security and immutability of data are ensured.

Because blockchain is distributed and a decentralized database or a distributed ledger where no central authority is present to validate the transactions, this blockchain is considered entirely safe and secure [5]. It is because of the consensus algorithms, which are an integral part of any blockchain network.

5.4   Consensus Algorithm

A consensus algorithm is used to solve a significant problem in blockchain, that is, which node among the connected peers on the network will add the new block to the network and subsequently update the data in the publicly available ledger in the blockchain network. In other words, a consensus algorithm helps in agreeing and finalizing a particular state of the block-chain network [6].

Depending on the type of blockchain, we have a variety of consensus algorithms available. Some of them are as follows:

1. **Proof of Work (PoW):** PoW is famously used by bitcoin as its consensus algorithm. The main working principle of the PoW algorithm is the validation of new blocks to be added into the blockchain, i.e., to decide which node from P2P will add the new block. This is done by multiple computers trying and competing to find a predefined puzzle by constantly updating their Nonce number. The first computer on the P2P network to find the solution can add the block and get rewarded. For example, in bitcoin, the miner gets some bitcoins as a reward for solving the puzzle. This process of validation and mutual agreement of adding the blocks to the blockchain requires heavy computing power. This is generally done using GPUs and powerful CPUs. Standard daily usage computers or personal computers cannot be used to mine bitcoins [7].

2. **Proof of Stack (PoS):** PoS is considered the most preferred and the best alternative for PoW because of the high-energy consumption property of PoW. For using proof of stake algorithm, the validators instead of solving complex mathematical problems and investing in high-cost equipment, invest in some coins of the system. Depending on their investment, the chance of forging the next block is determined. Unlike in PoW, where the person adding the block is called a **miner**, in PoS, the person adding the block is called the **Validator** and thus the process is known as **Minting or Forging**.

   Now, the question arises how the P2P network can trust the validator or the node that it is not malicious. This is where the investment or the deposit comes into play. If the node is malicious, then the validator will lose part of his investment, which will be more than what the validator has earned as a reward for adding the new block into the blockchain. When the node stops being a validator, all the invested stake and transaction fees earned will be released after a certain period. The reason behind this is if the P2P network finds out some of the blocks that we added were fraudulent, they should be able to deduct the punishment amount [8].

3. **Proof of Capacity (PoC):** PoC is another consensus algorithm that entirely depends on the hard disk space present in a computer. It discourages the practice of using costly equipment and a lot of electricity for mining. Instead, the higher the capacity available, the higher will be the chances to add the new block to the network and get rewarded.

4. **Proof of Authority (PoA):** The PoA is a bit different consensus algorithm as compared with the other algorithms. The main difference here is that the nodes present in the network carrying out the transaction are verified and are known to the organization for which they are working. Depending on the reputation of the nodes, the primary node is chosen arbitrarily. The main application of this algorithm could be utilized in trading.

Similarly, there are various consensus algorithms available like Proof of Activity, Proof of Elapsed Time, Proof of Importance, and so on. It is crucial to choose a consensus algorithm wisely to facilitate a fraud-proof and safe blockchain network.

5.5   Healthcare System

A healthcare system or health system is a group or different organizations combining and working together to facilitate better health for the country's population. A country's healthcare system depends on multiple factors, and almost every country needs a different type of healthcare system for its population.

A generalized picture of the healthcare system consists of hospitals, patients, governments, pharmaceutical companies, NGOs, doctors and nurses, clinics, insurance companies, and so on. All these work together to enhance the healthcare system of any country [9].

1. Prevention and care: This is the main element of the healthcare system and consists of clinics, doctors, nurses, NGOs, pharmaceutical companies, hospitals, and so on. They are responsible for maintaining enough supply of medicines and other healthcare techniques to maintain the public health of the country's population. In return for the services offered to the public, they get paid.

2. Patient: The population or the patients with complaints related to health reach out to the hospitals or clinics so that the doctor and nurses could take care of their health issues and help them regain everyday healthy living. Without patients, no healthcare system is possible.

3. Payment: The third and last pillar of a generalized healthcare system are payments. The patients pay to the hospitals, clinics, and other organizations included in the prevention and care system, whose services were used by the patient. Now the payment does not need always to be direct.

   With time, the healthcare services have become very expensive. As a solution insurance companies have come up, where the patient has already paid the premium for some time and when needed, the insurance company pays for the patient's hospital bills.

   Other than this, depending on the government's policies and the employer, sometimes these are too involved in clearing bills of their citizens or employees, respectively. This varies from country to country.

5.5.1   Healthcare and Blockchain

The current healthcare system continues with many flaws, bad practices, health data breaches, or essential health data being lost altogether. Blockchain can be used to fix all this by chaining all the essential information that is correct, transparent, and immutable. With blockchain in healthcare, we can maintain an electronic medical record of data that does not change [10]. Blockchain and healthcare systems together have a great future ahead. Blockchain has the power to revolutionize the complete healthcare system and even stop the high costs of the current healthcare system.

5.5.2   Benefits of Blockchain in Healthcare

Using blockchain in the healthcare system is a massive step toward a revolution in the healthcare system [11].

The areas in healthcare where blockchain will be used are:

1. Protection of the health records, which sometimes are misplaced.
2. Management of personal health records.

3. Management of EMR data.
4. Management of point of care genetics.

Other exclusive, essential benefits and use that implementation of blockchain in the healthcare system will provide are as follows:

- **Healthcare will be cheaper and faster:** With blockchain, we can create a single database where all the information regarding patient's health will be recorded and quickly retrieved by healthcare professionals for a better and much more personalized treatment patient. This will reduce the miscommunication between the doctors and other healthcare professionals, which may lead to severe patient problems [12].
- **Data security:** In the recent past, there have been millions of data breaches where personal data have been widely compromised. Blockchain, with its compelling safety features, can help protect the records in a much better way.
- **Patients can switch among healthcare organizations:** Sometimes, if there is a need to change the doctor, we need to share the exact information and health records of the previous diagnosis, which possibly may not be available all the time, leading to a lengthy process of redoing all the tests and compromising on health. Using blockchain, a decentralized database, will be formed to easily share all the records in a single click and receive the best possible care from the prevention and care department.
- **Research:** Creating a decentralized database accessible to the researchers and all the concerned people who require the data can be used to research better healthcare alternatives and develop effective medicines or better insurance plans. The availability of such a considerable amount of data would primarily give a great boom to the research industry.
- **Insurance claims:** Blockchain can be adapted to settle the insurance claims legally and prevent fraud because the insurance companies can always check for the previous data that are immutable and cannot be changed.
- **Tracing and preventing outbreaks of pandemics:** With real-time reporting and updating of data in the blockchain, concerned healthcare departments can easily trace the root

of any disease and prevent it from affecting humans at a very early stage.

- **Preventing theft of genomic data:** In the present scenario, genomic data theft has become a significant issue. This can easily be fixed and prevented by blockchain. Moreover, other than safeguarding the genomic data, we can also sell the data to the researchers and also cut middlemen costs, making it safe and economic both at the same time.

5.6 Algorithms

In the healthcare system, a large amount of data are processed and recorded daily. These data are crucial because it contains essential and confidential information about an individual's health. All these data need to be secure and easily accessible for future references, hence, storing it in any regular database will lead to various problems like data loss, inaccessibility, data theft, and various other critical issues. Instead of the regular database, we can switch to blockchain where data once entered cannot be deleted or modified, and data security can be ensured. Usually, data-sharing techniques are quite tedious and need a well-defined mechanism to facilitate safe, fast, and efficient data transfer. The algorithm used in sharing data in the case of medical records where data security is the primary concern. After updating the data, the concerned systems accept and generate the hash for the data received. The generated hash and the data are stored on the block, and the block is sent to all the authorized peers on the network [13]. The authorization can be modified or updated anytime by using the update module present in the system. Finally, after completing all the verification and approval process, the data are finally inserted into the chain and is linked to the hash of the previous block.

In this process, the roles could differ based on the use case. All the access rights are manageable, depending on the roles of the administration and the users. In simpler words, the basic idea behind this algorithm is that the data have to be hashed before uploading it into any cloud-based service. The conditions for accessing the data are stored and encoded into the smart contracts. And when the authorized person requests the data, only after validation by smart contracts is the decryption key finally released. The process of safe blockchain is shown in Figure 5.2.

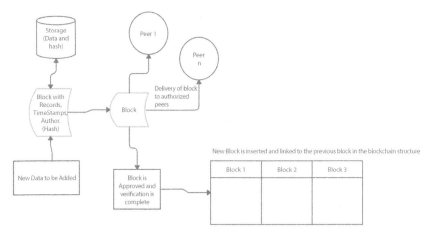

Figure 5.2 The process of blockchain.

5.6.1   Smart Contract

Smart contracts can be described as a piece of code deployed on a blockchain, which gets executed when certain predefined conditions are met [14]. These are highly used in developing blockchain-based innovative/smart applications like financial applications, healthcare systems, and so on, and at the same time ensure security at its best.

- The automated systems used by smart contracts ensure that the transactions are smooth, fast, and accurate at the same time.
- Smart contracts follow a set of predefined rules by the programmer, hence making sure no foul play is involved in the transactions and ensures that only the information should be released when the required conditions are met.
- Smart contracts have removed the need of using intermediaries, thus helping in saving money.
- They are very effective in encrypting blockchain systems.

5.6.2   Algorithm for Fault Tolerance Using Blockchain

Byzantine Problem: According to the Byzantine Generals Problem, how is it possible to find a way to guarantee complete consensus? A very common example for representing is shown in Figure 5.3. You are a general in the Byzantine army planning to attack the enemy city. You have got the city surrounded on all four sides by several battalions of your army, all of the battalions are separated by a distance and led by different generals.

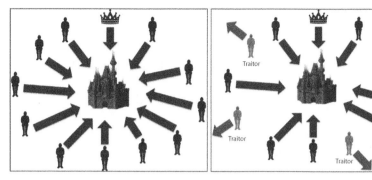

Coordinated Attack Leading to Victory   **Uncoordianted Attack Leading to Defeat**

Figure 5.3 Byzantine generals problem.

There is no way of communication other than sending a messenger from the battalion. Now, the condition here is to win the battle, the generals of the army need to make sure that the attack is coordinated; otherwise, they cannot win the battle. Because the only way to communicate is by sending messengers to other generals, you need to make sure that you receive a reply from each of the generals confirming the situation [9, 13].

The problems arising here are:

1. What if the messenger sent is killed by the enemy and the message remains undelivered?
2. Another possibility is that the messenger gets killed or captured by the enemy and the enemy sends false information to the general.
3. The third possibility could be when the messenger is returning after delivering the information, he gets captured by the enemy and the general receives false confirmation.
4. The fourth possibility could be the generals could be the traitors, and legally send false information.

This problem has remained unsolved for decades. However, bitcoin claims to have solved this problem. It is the world's first distributed ledger that can reach full consensus without requiring any third party to intervene, leading to the creation of the Practical Byzantine Fault Tolerance Algorithm [9].

This algorithm helps a distributed network reach consensus even if some network nodes have failed or are acting maliciously. Byzantine Fault Tolerance Algorithm aims to save the network against failures and help in effective decision making. As discussed earlier, this algorithm has been derived from the Byzantine Generals Problem and hence the name Byzantine Fault Tolerance Algorithm.

In technical terms, Byzantine failures have two types, fail-stop and arbitrary node failure.

Some of the arbitrary node failures are depicted as follows:

1. Failure in returning a response.
2. Deliberately send a misleading response.
3. Send an incorrect response.
4. Send different responses to different parts of the system.

5.6.3   Practical Byzantine Fault Tolerance Algorithm

In a distributed system where pBFT has used the nodes or the peers are ordered sequentially, where only one of the nodes is chosen, based on consensus algorithm, as the master node or the primary node, whereas other nodes in the network are secondary nodes. The first condition here is that any node from the secondary nodes can become primary if the current primary node fails or faces any issue. The ultimate aim is to achieve a state of consensus using the majority rule.

This algorithm works on the notion that the total number of malicious nodes present in the system must not be greater than 33.33% of all the nodes present [15]. This directly means higher the number of nodes present in the system, the more secure it will be. The practical representation of fault tolerance algorithm is shown in Figure 5.4.

The working of pBFT:

1. The primary node receives a request from the client side.
2. Request sent by the primary node to all the designated secondary nodes in the system.
3. The requested action is performed by all the nodes-primary as well as secondary and the reply is sent back to the client.
4. The service request is finally completed successfully after the client receives (faulty nodes allowed + 1) replies from the system.

If the primary node chosen stops responding, the system waits till a predefined timeout is completed. After this, another node in the queue is allowed to become the primary node. Another possible condition can be if the current node is malicious, then the majority of the nodes can vote

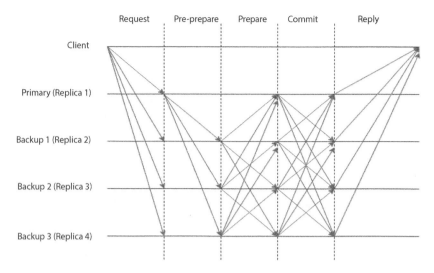

Figure 5.4 Practical byzantine fault tolerance algorithm.

against it, and similarly, the next node in the queue is replaced as the primary node of the system.

Advantages of Practical Byzantine Fault Tolerance Algorithm

- Unlike Proof of Work, practical byzantine fault tolerance algorithm (pBFT) does not require computation of complex mathematical puzzles, which help in saving a lot of energy.
- All the nodes in the p2p network participate in the response request, including the primary node, thus all can be rewarded, hence, allowing users to make better decisions and rewards too.
- The transactions, once finalized, unlike PoW, do not require multiple confirmations.

Disadvantages of pBFT

- The pBFT slows down as the number of nodes increases because it has to communicate with all of them to send a response.
- If the number of nodes present in the system is comparatively less then, pBFT will be prone to Sybil attacks.

5.6.4 Algorithm for Distributed Healthcare Using Blockchain

In today's technological world, remote monitoring of health has become has a necessity. Blockchain can easily be applied to this sector to improve the quality and security of healthcare data. Moreover, using remote healthcare monitoring apps can help both the patient as well as the doctors and researchers, to take proper care of their health and enjoy a healthy life and develop better solutions effectively in a significantly less amount of time, respectively. Because secure sharing of healthcare data is a priority of blockchain-based method, the latest multiple encryption-based cryptographic techniques help enhance security. We can use a private smart contract-based blockchain model to implement such applications. Smart contracts can easily help us keep the data safe and allow only authorized persons to have access to the data. This blockchain-based model will be used in the management of health data, which will allow patients to always retain their ownership of the data and also allowing hospitals to have access when needed. This system is based on **Ethereum services**—a decentralized blockchain-based database that allows applications to use a custom blockchain. The blockchain naturally does not offer sufficient storage, so to store the healthcare data, we use decentralized storage—**Ethereum Swarm**. Every block of data recorded has a unique swarm hash, which is then combined with the decryption key to forming the root chunk. Only the authorized people who are aware of the reference of the root chunk are allowed access to the data. And these root chunks working as decryption

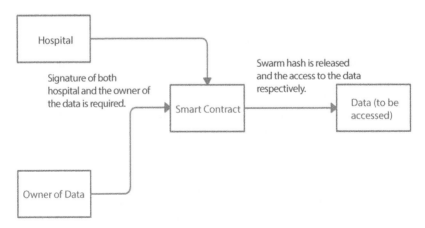

Figure 5.5 Flow diagram of distributed healthcare.

are stored securely using smart contracts through blockchain and released only when the conditions of the contract are met. Figure 5.5 shows the flow representation of distributed healthcare [16].

The ownership problem can be resolved by employing multisignature contracts where both the owner of the data and the hospital have to sign the smart contract to access the data collectively. Using this technique, we are safeguarding both the sides.

1. The patient cannot alter the data without the hospital's signature (permission).
2. The patient has all the control over who can access their data.

Moreover, after accessing the data once the swarm hash will be known to the hospital, they can access it any time even without the patient's permission [17]. To protect this, we need to add a last accessed timestamp to the data every time the data are accessed, this will change the swarm hash of the data, thus making it secure once again.

5.7   Security for Healthcare System Using Blockchain

Maintaining the privacy and security of the health data becomes the primary concern for any organization or individual related to it [18]. According to HIPAA, the policy for controlling abuse and fraudulent transaction within the healthcare system, five essential rules were laid down:

1. **Privacy:** There must be regulations for disclosing and using a patient's health records.
2. **Security:** This rule adds to the privacy rule securing the communication over the network.
3. **Unique identifier system:** Only a standard designated organization can maintain these records and the patients' identity.
4. **Transactions:** All organizations involved in the healthcare system must complete transactions scientifically to ensure simplification.
5. **Enforcement Act:** In case of violations, the violators must be penalized.

The properties attained using blockchain technologies are as follows:

1. **Decentralization:** Blockchain has decentralized the data, thus making sure that no third party is involved.
2. **Immutable:** Data wrote cannot be erased.
3. **Security:** Single-point failures are not possible in the blockchain.
4. **Autonomy:** Using smart contracts the patients hold the right to decide whether to share the data or not.
5. **Auditability:** It becomes more convenient to keep a record of all the medical history.
6. **Pseudonymity:** Every node in the peer-to-peer network is bound with a key, protecting the node's anonymity.
7. **Incentive mechanism:** This blockchain mechanism can be used to promote the development and research sectors of medical science.

5.7.1   Framework for Security Using Blockchain

The methodology used to fetch the data and process it requires a combination of ML and IoT technologies integrated with blockchain to work efficiently. Here, the data recorded by intelligent apps and smart sensors embedded in healthcare devices used by the patients are exported to the blockchain, the devices used by the end-users, i.e., patients, are synchronized with the help of an IoT mechanism. The data are then stored on a blockchain recorded in multiple transactions. Also, the blockchain allows patients to securely manage their data and share the data as required by them. The machine learning model developed facilitates multipurpose in detecting the anomalies in the recorded data and reporting it directly to the patients so that they can take better care of themselves. The ML model will be based on the suggestions and standardized parameters prescribed by the healthcare professionals [19]. Moreover, the ML model can be used in research to quickly detect the problems and help scientists develop a solution in a shorter time. Figure 5.6 shows the data security framework.

IoT in blockchain-based healthcare system: This module of the healthcare system helps synchronize the devices used by a single patient and collect the data recorded with the help of sensors and applications monitoring the patient's health. This system helps doctors to monitor every single second of the data of the patient undergoing some treatment. This IoT-based data monitoring system will effectively reduce heart attacks and other serious deadly diseases, which start from minor basic health complications. Patients will always be aware of their latest health status and will be able

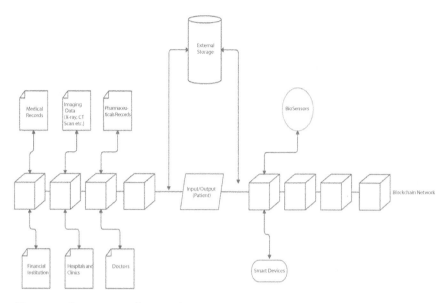

Figure 5.6 Data security framework.

to take action immediately, depending on the data detected and displayed by smart IoT-based devices. More importantly, if the patient is bedridden or has some serious healthcare issue that requires constant monitoring like high blood pressure, blood saturation detection, calorie release, sleep monitoring in case of insomnia or depression, in such cases, IoT-based monitoring systems will prove to be a boon for a patient's life.

Action management and transactions in a blockchain-based health-care system: Because the volume of data generated by the IoT devices will be massive and will be associated with multiple stakeholders, we need to make sure that the data are being managed and processed efficiently managing the time and space complexities and also making sure that the data recorded is 100% secure in the blockchain, which is possible with the help of following implementation technique, i.e., using personal healthcare (PHC) and external record management (ERM) blockchains.

The PHC is primarily used by the patients or the users wearing smart devices like a smart watch, pacemaker, smartphone application for record-ing their basic healthcare data. These data are stored on an external blockchain-based cloud database. Moreover, these data are used by the patients for self-monitoring of their current health status. Other than that, if the patient needs any professional help requirement, the recorded data can also be shared with the healthcare professionals, who can then diag-nose and help the patient accordingly.

ERM blockchain is used to store and manage the data recorded by the healthcare department directly, i.e., when the patient visits the hospital, the data stored can include imagery like X-rays and CT scans, and so on, bills, previous health records, insurance status, prescriptions, pharmaceutical details, and so on. The data generated are constantly added to the blockchain based on the consensus of all the healthcare stakeholders based on the proof of stake consensus algorithm. Using ERM blockchain insurance companies can also validate the data regarding the claims raised by patient.

Machine learning model: The machine learning model's design is entirely inspired by the diagnosis and detections recommended by trained healthcare professionals. This is a fundamental module of any digital healthcare system [19]. The data recorded are immediately analyzed by the model, and if any problems are detected, the system immediately notifies the doctor or the concerned authority regarding the issue raised so that swift action to tackle the issue is taken up as soon as possible, making patient much safer than they are in the current healthcare system.

In the model discussed above, it is observed that the primary aim of the blockchain-based healthcare system is taken care of which includes:

1. maintaining data privacy and ownership,
2. secure data sharing,
3. real-time processing of data,
4. improving healthcare.
5. allow doctors to concentrate on healthcare instead of administrative work,
6. making data immutable and handy for easy access,
7. allowing data to be verifiable and preventing fraud transactions.

5.8   Issues and Challenges in Healthcare Using Blockchain

Despite all the pros of using blockchain as an alternative source in the management of the healthcare system data, on the other side of the coin, there are many issues as well. The major concerns are discussed below:

- **Adopting entirely a new technology:** This is proven to be one of the most significant challenges because most doctors are still used to the old healthcare system where the article is used to record the data. They even are used to the habit of leaving some columns blank, which might be a required field and cannot be skipped when using blockchain. This seems to be a small problem but trying to change a concrete system that has been there for years is not as easy as it seems to be and can hinder the revolution process.

- **Components of the healthcare system are very vast and distributed:** This means the healthcare system involves many organizations, like multiple hospitals, different insurance companies, pharmaceutical companies, governments, and so on. For implementing a blockchain-based system, it is important to have a single, well-maintained, and streamlined system. Also, if any of the components show resistance in adopting the new technology, the entire system would become comparatively inefficient.

- **Hospitals and insurance companies not willing to share the data:** The hospitals always try not to share the data to gain a competitive and financial advantage. If they are forced to share all the data, there are chances that they will not earn as much profit as they are earning now, hence leaving a significant challenge in the path of implementation of the blockchain-based healthcare system.

- **Negligence from the government:** In many developed countries, governments are not approving the new healthcare system proposed, and similarly in smaller developing and underdeveloped countries, where even the old healthcare system is not functioning correctly, it is currently almost next to impossible to convince the government stakeholders for such a huge change in the system.

- **Absence of any central authority:** Because there is no single central control system that would enforce the blockchain-based healthcare system, it is challenging to convince every branch involved in the distributed healthcare system to adopt the new system.

- **Technological shift:** Shifting the healthcare system from paper to blockchain would involve a substantial technological shifting, making the small organizations involved in the healthcare negligent in adapting the system. Moreover, the employees would also require to get trained for using the new system, hence raising another question on the implementation.

- **Finances:** A lot of finances will be required to implement the new centralized system, and the big question here is who will invest in it.
- **Not getting enough opportunities to prove itself:** The bitter truth is that the stakeholders in the healthcare system will not adapt anything new that will influence the whole system so easily, without having any concrete proof of application. And in the current scenario, no one from the healthcare system is willing to come forward and take the initiative.

Despite the fact, real-life application of blockchain-based healthcare systems is currently facing many difficulties and issues for implementation because it is challenging for all the healthcare organizations, insurance companies, and governments to work together in harmony and change the entire system and adopt an entirely new methodology [20].

However, it is believed that pace at which technology is bringing a whole new revolution in the world, the healthcare system will be no exception. Soon, blockchain will be fluently implemented in the healthcare sector and in all the possible sectors of the world. As it is rightly predicted that "data are the future and data are the new money".

5.9   Future Scope

Blockchain is a database that is capable of handling all kinds of data in a single place. These data are impossible to change without leaving a transaction mark in the ledger maintained by the blockchain. A blockchain is a perfect tool for recording and accessing perfect data for personal health management and improved research purposes. In the current scenario, all the data available are not accurate because of some of the factors discussed above in the limitations section. However, in the future, a blockchain-enabled healthcare system can truly revolutionize the world, people will have all the information including time of birth, medical histories, and whatnot stored in a single wallet. This will ultimately make this world a better and healthier place to live in. There are a variety of incurable and deadly diseases which if detected earlier can be easily cured, the blockchain-based healthcare system can help in achieving the same, if applied correctly. Currently, a lot of potential in the blockchain is still unexplored. Other than that, the available potential is also not fully functional in the healthcare system, but in the years to come the industry will boom and change the whole scenario of the healthcare system. Experts even said that, with the successful implementation of blockchain, finding the cure of diseases like the common cold, cancer, AIDS, and so on, will become a thousand times easier.

5.10 Conclusion

The mainstream blockchain has a variety of consensus algorithms that are promising for successful augmentation and a safer and better healthcare plan with absolute transparency of data. Moreover, we conclude that the data stored in the blockchain is safe and immutable, which will essentially help researchers in the better formulation of healthcare techniques, helping people to live a healthier life. Currently, many challenges are being faced by the blockchain in real-world implementation in the healthcare sector. However, it is expected that with time the system will adapt to this technology. Consensus algorithms like pBFT in itself are a great success because the Byzantine Problem was there for years and was considered unsolvable. Using Ethereum and Smart Contract implementation in the blockchain, the main concern regarding the medical data, that is, security and easy access will be ensured. Other than that, blockchain technology is still not completely developed and is growing at a very fast pace, it is expected soon not only implementation of this technology will be possible but it will prove to be a concrete revolution in the healthcare industry, completely changing and securing the way how data storage works. Using blockchain in healthcare would help healthcare professionals stop wasting their time for administrative work and rather work with more dedication toward the patient's health.

References

1. Singh, M. and Kim, S., Blockchain based intelligent vehicle data sharing framework. *CoRR*, abs/1708.09721, 1–4, 2017.
2. Kombe, C., Dida, M., Sam, A., A review on healthcare information systems and consensus protocols in blockchain technology. *Int. J. Adv. Technol. Eng. Explor.*, 5, 49, 437–483, 2018.
3. Al-Joboury, I.M. and Al-Hemiary, E.H., Consensus algorithms based blockchain of things for distributed healthcare. *Iraqi J. Inf. Commun. Technol.*, 3, 4, 33–46, 2020.
4. Prokofieva, M. and Miah, S.J., Blockchain in healthcare. *Australas. J. Inf. Syst.*, 23, 1–23, 2019.

5. Ayeelyan, J., Mohan, S., Maria Manuel Vianny, D., Cognitive cyber-physical system applications, in: *Cognitive Engineering for Next Generation Computing: A Practical Analytical Approach*, pp. 167–187, 2021.

6. Denny, J.C. and Collins, F.S., Precision medicine in 2030—seven ways to transform healthcare. *Cell*, 84, 6, 1415–1419, 2021.

7. Dimitrov, D.V., Blockchain applications for healthcare data management. *Healthc. Inform. Res.*, 25, 1, 51–56, 2019.

8. Shrestha, A.K., Vassileva, J., Deters, R., A blockchain platform for user data sharing ensuring user control and incentives. *Front. Blockchain*, 3, 48, 2020.

9. Castro, M. and Liskov, B., Practical byzantine fault tolerance. *OSDI*, vol. 99, 1999.

10. Fan, K. *et al.*, Medblock: Efficient and secure medical data sharing via blockchain. *J. Med. Syst.*, 42, 8, 1–11, 2018.

11. Lamport, L., Shostak, R., Pease, M., The Byzantine generals problem, in: *Concurrency: the Works of Leslie Lamport*, pp. 203–226, 2019.

12. Chen, H.S. *et al.*, Blockchain in healthcare: A patient-centered model. *Biomed. J. Sci. Techn. Res.*, 20, 3, 15017, 2019.

13. Shi, S. *et al.*, Applications of blockchain in ensuring the security and privacy of electronic health record systems: A survey. *Comput. Secur.*, 97, 1–20, 2020.

14. Cong, L.W. and He, Z., Blockchain disruption and smart contracts. *Rev. Financ Stud.*, 32, 5, 1754–1797, 2019.

15. Batubara Rizal, F., Ubacht, J., Janssen, M., Challenges of blockchain technology adoption for e-government: a systematic literature review. *Proceedings of the 19th Annual International Conference on Digital Government Research: Governance in the Data Age*, 2018.

16. Mackey, T.K. *et al.*, 'Fit-for-purpose?'–challenges and opportunities for applications of blockchain technology in the future of healthcare. *BMC Med.*, 17, 1, 1–17, 2019.

17. Zhu, X., Research on blockchain consensus mechanism and implementation. *IOP Conference Series: Materials Science and Engineering*, vol. 569. No. 4, IOP Publishing, 2019. https://iopscience.iop.org/journal/1757-899X

18. Chakraborty, S., Aich, S., Kim, H.-C., A secure healthcare system design framework using blockchain technology. *2019 21st International Conference on Advanced Communication Technology (ICACT)*, IEEE, 2019.

19. Muthukumarasamy, S., Kumar, A., Tamilarasan, J.A., Adimoolam, M., Machine learning in healthcare diagnosis, in: *Blockchain and Machine Learning for E-Healthcare Sys*, p. 343, 2020.

20. Abdellatif, A.A. *et al.*, ssHealth: Toward secure, blockchain-enabled healthcare systems. *IEEE Network*, 34, 4, 312–319, 2020.

6

Industry 4.0 and Smart Healthcare: An Application Perspective

R. Saminathan*, S. Saravanan and P. Anbalagan

*Department of Computer Science and Engineering, Annamalai University,
Annamalainagar, Tamil Nadu, India*

Abstract

Industry 4.0 makes a revolution in the modern economy globally. Industry 4.0 is the combination of physical and nonphysical systems which uses the state of the art technologies, such as Internet of Things (IoT), big data, cyber security, autonomous machine, artificial intelligence, and so on. It is the current trend in machine automation and data exchange by using information technology. It can be characterized by forming a platform between the physical world and digital world by means industrial IoT through cyber security analysis, performs better automation than the third term revolution, the control systems and data models are in the closed loop, smart products were developed. Industry 4.0 makes a huge revolution toward an efficient and effective way in businesses. It also plays an important role in the healthcare industry. This chapter gives a detailed view about Industry 4.0 and its vision toward how Industry 4.0 plays a major role in healthcare industries. Further, this chapter elaborates the technologies used in Industry 4.0 in terms of application perspective.

Keywords: Industry 4.0, healthcare industry, vision, blockchain, smart grid, augmented reality, big data, embedded systems

*Corresponding author: samiaucse@yahoo.com

T. Poongodi, D. Sumathi, B. Balamurugan and K. S. Savita (eds.) Digitization of Healthcare Data Using Blockchain, (117–136) © 2022 Scrivener Publishing LLC

6.1 Introduction

In the era of modern world, Industry 4.0 plays an important role. Industry 4.0 is termed as fourth term of revolution. Industry 4.0 plays a role in automating the machines using Internet of Things (IoT) technologies, controlling the industry value chain and thereby reducing the labor and expenses [1]. They use a modern control system which is embedded by means of smart embedded devices which can be controlled by means of IoT. It is the current trend in machine automation and data exchange by using information technology. Industry 4.0 is evolved from the German technology and it is globally adopted. It can be characterized by forming a platform between the physical world and digital world by means industrial IoT through cyber security analysis, performs better automation than the third term revolution, the control systems and data models are in the closed loop, smart products were developed [2].

The main vision of the fourth industrial revolution is to enable automated decision making system, real monitoring and analysis, real time connection of smart devices and integration through vertical and horizontal method. This system makes use of the existing data and also collects the additional information to make the data processing more effectively and efficiently. To gain efficiency in multiple levels, replacing the existing old manufacturing process, to provide end to end information across the value chain and to make use of new models and new services, Industry 4.0 model is used. It is referred as the intelligent chain of machines and automation [3, 4]. Industry 4.0 is a collection of technologies including cyber security, IoT, big data, cloud computing and cognitive computing which helps to make a smart industry. It gives a broad vision in creating clear framework and architectures and forms a connectivity from real world to the digital world through technologies. The IoT also have a major role in Industry 4.0 through IoT platforms to Industrial IoT gateways, devices, and so on. In Industry 4.0, the full value chain includes suppliers, customers, and origin of the materials and goods and the final destination of products and goods. The main aim of Industry 4.0 is toward customer centric where the customers' needs are satisfied at high level with value speed, cost effective, and value-added services which in turn increase the customer satisfaction, customer experience, customer life time, customer sales time, and new innovations are added. It provides the highest level of optimization and accuracy in automation. Data optimization is the better process in Industry 4.0. It transfers the partial automated data to the cyber physical devices, machines, and so on. In vertical integration, the traditional method of automation is affected from initial level to the planning level. In vertical integration, the traditional methods were not used. This method of integration starts from floor level to control level, from control level to production level, and from production level to enterprise planning level. In horizontal integration, the flow starts from end to end integration. The flows start from the supplier and the process information flows, from process flows to the development of product, from distribution to the customer. It plays an important role in the society and customers.

6.2   Evolution of Industry 4.0

The term Industry 4.0 is first established on 2011 by the German federal government. Industry 4.0 came from the term of different types of revolution.

Industry 1.0: It is termed as first term of revolution. It was introduced by Britain government on the end of 18th century. Industry 1.0 introduces machines for production in the industry. It uses steam power engines and water as a power source. With the introduction of steam engines, the productivity in machines increased. Businesses were developed because of the invention of steam engines, which lead to the industrial transformation. This industrial transformation leads to the invention of steam engine trains. The advantages of this revolution include invention of new products, the products made are cost effective, and custom-made products, which leads to economic growth. The disadvantages of the revolution includes work condition being very poor, unregulated growth of business, air pollution increased, and overcrowded cities.

Industry 2.0: It is known as the second industrial revolution. It is the period where electricity was introduced. The invention of electricity lead to mass production and automation. The second revolution started at the middle of 19th century. It replaces the old methods like steam engine and water with electricity. This new technology paved the way for two methods: public transports and planes. The second revolution made a global revolution. The existing technology and methods are improved in the second revolution. Steels were replaced by iron. By using iron, the rail lines are built strong and cost-effective. In the 1870s, electric generators were introduced. The major invention of second revolution is internal combustion of engine. Because of the introduction of engines, airplanes and aircrafts came into existence. In the period 1870 to 1890, there is an increase in the economic growth. Advantages of second revolution are modernization in machines, improvement in technology, created a path for digital revolution.

Industry 3.0: Industry 3.0 is also known as third industrial revolution. Third revolution came into an effect of second half at the 20th century. In the third revolution, the emergence of nuclear energy came into existence. In this period, it gives rise to the electronics and telecommunication industry. It also gives rise to programmable logic controllers and robots which gave various dimensions to the technology. The third revolution is also known as digital revolution. It brought a huge revolution in semiconductors, personal computing, and Internet. There is a replacement from analog devices to digital devices. The digital devices are connected through the Internet. The major advantages of third revolution are increase in the use of renewable energy, developing micropower plants to provide energy, storage of hydrogen, and introduction of plugs in fuel engines. It gives rise to various technologies, like artificial intelligence (AI), big data, robots, IoT, drones, and so on.

Industry 4.0: Industry 4.0 is better than Industry 3.0. It is more or less a combination of first and second industrial revolutions. Industrial IoT is the part of fourth industrial revolution. The main goal of the revolution is to make the industries faster, efficient, effective, and customer centric, leading to more innovations. The fourth industrial revolution produces a connectivity between the real and the virtual world globally. The advantages of fourth revolution are greater productivity and more.

6.3   Vision and Challenges of Industry 4.0

The fourth industrial revolution is mainly focused to reduce the cost, improving efficiency and productivity with the help of the automated systems. It improves the speed and flexibility to the producers and manufacturers. The fundamentals principles of fourth industrial revolution are digitalization, controlling, and automation. In digitalization process, real-time data are collected and converted into digital format. It uses embedded systems, sensors and digital systems. In controlling process, the data collected are converted into real-time data-driven actions and control. This process is a full process responsible for tracking, visibility, and decision making. In automation process, the experience for user is improved. Transformation of industrial 4.0 can be carried out in four phases (i) monitoring phase: the sensors and actuators are allowed to monitor the condition of the products. If there is any change occurs, it generates alerts and notifications; (ii) control phase: the functions of the products are allowed to control and the user experience; (iii) optimization phase: the above two phases allow the procedures to uses of the product, which in turn improves the performance. Diagnosis and repair are done if needed. (iv) Autonomy phase: it is the combination of monitoring, control, and optimization phases.

6.4 Technologies Used in Fourth Industrial Revolution

The main technologies used in Industry 4.0 are cyber physical systems, Internet of objects, cloud computing, big data, cyber security, autonomous machine, machine to machine, AI, simulation system, and augmented reality.

Cyber Physical Systems: Cyber physical systems composed of analog, digital, physical components, which are connected through physical and logic. These systems are controlled and monitored by means of computer-based algorithms or procedures [5–7]. Cyber physical systems are the combination of computation, processes, and networking. These systems consist of sensors, communication devices to act in the real time. These systems are used to exchange information, control and start the actions. Applications of cyber physical systems are healthcare monitoring, smart grid, smart manufacturing, smart cities, smart transportation, smart learning environment, aeronautical applications, and so on. Disadvantages of cyber physical systems are cyber threats, wireless exploitation, jamming, remote access, reconnaissance, unauthorized access, GPS exploitation, and so on. Advantages of cyber physical systems are better system performance, scalability, flexibility, faster response time, integration, and so on.

Internet of Objects: It is defined as the network of physical objects which are interconnected with tiny sensors, physical systems, entities, communication devices, which are capable of processing data from the physical world in real time. The IoT devices include smart objects, like smart watch, smart gadgets, smart vehicles, fitness tracker, and so on. It is used to exchange the data from devices over the Internet. The IoT applications use machine learning algorithms to analyze and process the data. Advantages of IoT include accessing information from anywhere, anytime over Internet, good communication is carried between the connected devices, data packets are transferred over the network, and so on. The disadvantages of IoT are as the number of connected devices increases the data transmission over the devices are difficult, data loss happens, corruption of devices, no international standard is maintained, and so on. Applications of IoT are patient monitoring, traffic monitoring, smart city management, smart waste management, environment pollution management [30], and so on.

Cloud Computing: Cloud computing is defined as the data centers where the data can be accessed anywhere. It is used as a data storage center, which helps to store large amount of data. Cloud computing consists of servers, storage disk, software, and analytics over the Internet. Cloud computing can be classified into three types (i) private cloud: private cloud is used by the single organization or single business. In this cloud, the server and database are maintained by a single organization. Some organizations pay for third-party providers to host the cloud. (ii) Public cloud: public cloud is maintained by a third party organization [12].

The computing services are provided by the servers and storage over the Internet. Example of public cloud: Microsoft Azure. (iii) Hybrid cloud: it is a combination of public and private cloud, which combine together to get the data and applications to be shared among them. It offers a higher flexibility by allowing the data to be processed from public cloud to private cloud. It also optimizes the infrastructure and security. The advantages of cloud computing are as follows: used to create cloud based applications, store and backup data, restoring of data, streaming of audio and video, embedded intelligence. Applications of cloud computing are data and backup applications, business applications, entertainment applications, management applications, and social applications. The disadvantages of cloud computing are as follows: data handling is difficult, cloud providers offers limited version, data centers are costly in cloud infrastructure, no data redundancy, issues with bandwidth.

Big Data: Big data deals with large complex data sets without traditional data processing method [24]. It helps to analyze complex data sets to extract the information systematically. It consists of three key concepts, these are volume, variety, and velocity. The challenges of big data are data capturing, data sharing, data analyzing, data storing, data searching, storing, sharing and transferring of data, privacy information, and source of data. It consists of structured, unstructured, and semistructured data. It uses parallel computing method to analyze the data. The size of the data varies from terabytes to petabytes. It is also defined as the collection of huge amount of data, which may be structured or unstructured data.

The data that can be processed and accessed in a fixed format is called structured data. Example for structured data is data stored in the relational database management. In unstructured data, data can stored in any unknown format. Examples of unstructured data: combination of simple texts, images, video, and audio files. Semistructured data are the combination of structured and unstructured data. DBMS is the example of semi structured data. In big data, volume is the major requirement. The name big data itself refers that the size of the data is huge. When the data are out from storage, it determines whether the data are big or not. Variety means collection of structured and unstructured data. Velocity is defined as the speed of the generated data. Variability refers to amount of data handled efficiently and effectively. Application of big data are used in retail industry, healthcare industry, education industry, e-commerce, media and entertainment applications, financial institutions, travel and telecom industry, automobile industry. Advantages of big data are increased efficiency, data redundancy, cost-effective, time effective, and so on. The disadvantages of big data are correlation errors, security and privacy, incompatible tools, lot of unstructured data, speed mismatch, and so on.

Cyber Security: Cyber security is the process of protecting servers, computers, mobile devices, electronic gadgets, networks, and data from malicious activities, like virus, worms, DoS attacks, and so on. It is also known as computer security or information technology security or electronic information security. There are five types of cyber security, these are critical infrastructure security, application security, network security, cloud security, and IoT security. Critical infrastructure security consists of cyber physical systems, such as electric grid, water purification, traffic lights, and shopping centers. These infrastructures are more vulnerable to cyberattacks. In application security, cyber threats are occurred at the development stage of the application. It uses software and hardware to tackle the external threats. Antivirus, firewalls, encrypted programs are used to ensure the unauthorized access [21].

To protect from security threats, firewalls are used. In network security, cyber threats are occur on the network layer. Network security enables security for internal systems by ensuring the infrastructure. Some of the examples of network security are extra login credentials, antivirus software, antispyware software [28], encrypted programs, firewalls, and so on. Cloud security means protection of data in cloud server. It is a software-based tool that protects and monitors the cloud storage data from security threats. By using proper authentication and authorized login credentials, data from the cloud are protected. Internet of things security enables the security of cyber physical systems and noncyber physical systems, like sensors, gadgets, Wi-Fi, routers, and so on. In IoT, security and data aggregation are more important [18]. Cyber threats are the biggest threats to the cyber security. Cyber threats include virus, worms, denial of service attack [9], and so on, which lead to failure of the system, data modifications, leakage of national security data, malicious activities, and so on. The 10 major types of cyber threats are malware, phishing, spear phishing, man in the middle attack, Trojan's, ransomware, denial of service attack, attack on IoT breaches, data breaches, and malwareon mobile apps. Applications of cyber security: network security, sandboxing, back end systems, computer systems, secure coding. Advantages of cyber security: secure by design, secure coding, authentication, authorization, encryption, vulnerability management, defensive management. Disadvantages of cyber security: incorrect configuration of firewalls, difficulty in configuration of firewalls, makes system slow, keeps on updating of software, and so on.

Autonomous Machine: It is also known as auto robot or autonomous robot [17]. An auto robot works on AI, robotics, and information technology. These machines can interact with the environment and surroundings to gain information. It works long term without human resources or intervention. It can adopt to any situations without human interaction. It helps the people from harmful environment and situations. It can operate its own either by wireless or wired mode. An autonomous machine can interact with the environment and make decisions according to the environment and actuates its movement as per the condition in the environment. In the industries these machines are programmed to do repetitive works. In this system, both hardware and software work together to make it function. Autonomous machine can sense the environment using cameras, microphones, scanners, spectrometers, and so on. Benefits of autonomous machine: increased productivity and efficiency, increased safety, reduction in error, work and task, reduce the risk in environment. Limitations of robots: lack of power, lack of employment of people, limited capabilities, maintenance requirement, and cost. Applications of robots: space communication, military applications, medical applications [15], environmental monitoring, and so on. There are three types of robots, these are autonomous-controlled, remote-controlled, and manually controlled robots.

M2M: M2M means machine to machine communication. It is a direct method of communication between the devices, which may be wired or wireless. It is an intercommunication system. It transfers the data to the destination without human interaction. The main components of M2M is sensors, Wi-Fi module, RFID tag, or a cellular communication link. The sensors senses the environment and collects the data from the environment. The sensed data can be transferred to base station. The M2M applications which translates the data, and it starts preprogrammed the automated actions. The communication is carried through two technologies, AI and machine learning. It uses the public methods and access like Ethernet. M2M allows any sensor in the network to monitor the environment and transfers the data and responds to the changes in the environment. A large number of devices are connected in a single network in

M2M technology. They are similar to LAN network which allow the sensor devices communicate with each other.

These devices collect the information from the network and transferred to the another network. M2M is the fastest growing network, which connects the devices with each other. It found a variety of applications in different fields. In the manufacturing field, it alerts the business owners when there is a need of service for the products through smartphones. The network of sensors are connected to the network through which the replacement parts are automatically monitored. In home care applications, M2M alerts the owner through the smart devices which is connected to home appliances once it finished it works. It allows the user to automatically control the devices through internet. Application of machine to machine communication: healthcare monitoring, smart utility management, home care applications, manufacturing applications, security technology, smart application management. Advantages of M2M: improvisation in efficiency, decision making, cost efficiency, quality of services and products, scalability, offers high range and minimum latency, smart connection, large of devices in a network. Disadvantages of M2M: use of cloud computing which limits the flexibility and innovation, security issues, constant internet connection with good speed, interoperability between devices is difficult [8–10].

Simulation System: It is a set of procedures used by the computers to initiate the process of operations through simulation. The complexity of the event is determined by the probability of the event, interaction of the event and difficulty in processing the event. The numerical models, which are created by the computer, are used for the purpose of describing the complexity of the event. There are six different types of simulation, these are process simulation, strategic simulation, functional simulation, concepts simulation, tactic management, and totality simulation. Simulation means representation of system by means of physical process to develop the data to process and make the system to take decision making. Simulation is the decision-making approach to test the process or data and it is a what-if scenario that gives a better response. System simulation helps to develop the control systems [11–13]. Simulation gives the scientific models of the electrical and mechanical systems. In physical simulation, the modeling of system is based on the physical objects by using computer simulation. In interactive simulation, it includes human loop simulation in which the physical simulation is carried out in flight simulator, driving simulation, and so on. Advantages of system simulation: loss of life in danger is avoided, cost effective, better results, behavior analysis is studied, critical situation are analyzed. Disadvantages of system simulation: expensive, although to understand, expensive to build simulation tools. Applications of system simulation: production simulation, personal simulation, logistics simulation, supply chain simulation, and so on.

Artificial Intelligence: Artificial intelligence is similar to human intelligence where the machines are able to think and take decisions. The machines can think like humans, such as problem solving and learning. The main goals of AI are learning, reasoning, and perception. By using AI, the machines can mimic humans. Artificial intelligence can be classified into two types, these are weak and strong. In weak AI, it assigns to do only one particular job. In strong AI, the systems can carried out multiple tasks done by a human being. These machines are more complex and complicated systems. They are allowed to handle the complex situations without human interaction. The characteristics of strong AI are puzzles solving, it takes its own decisions to learn, plan, and communicate. Strong AI are more intelligent and do their works without human intervention. Artificial intelligence is a computer-controlled device or digital computer. Artificial intelligence is a trial-and-error method. Deep learning is the advanced version of AI. Deep learning trains the computer to do its task without human. It performs the tasks like identification and recognizing the images, recognizing sounds, and so on.

The performance of deep learning method is improved by algorithms. The accuracy of the models are improved by new learning approaches. For translation of text and classification of images, neural networks are developed. Neural networks with deep layers are used to stream data through IoT, text data, and data scripts. Computational power is the important source of neural networks. In AI and deep learning, mouse, keyboard are replaced by gestures, swipe, touch and natural language. There are four types of intelligence, these are reactive machines, limited memory, theory of mind, and self-awareness. Reactive machines are the basic type of machines which have the ability to form memories or use past experiences. In limited memory machines, the machines can look into the past. In theory of mind, the machine understands the people and observes the situation. In self-awareness, the machine build self-representationamong themselves. Consciousness is also known as self-awareness. Applications of AI: astronomy, data security, healthcare industry, automotive industry, agriculture, robotics, gaming industry, entertainment, and so on. Advantages of AI: reduced in taking risks, increased lifetime, repetitive jobs, faster decisions, and new applications. Disadvantages of AI: creation cost, laziness in humans, unemployment, out of box thinking.

Augmented Reality: Augmented reality refers to virtual interface between the real world and the physical world. It is the combination of real and virtual world, real-time interaction, and 3D registration of images. In augmented reality, the digital world perception is mixed with virtual world perception. Augmented reality was first introduced for gaming and entertainment purpose. It offers a rich experience of the natural world with enhanced perceptions. It allows the user to give a 3D dimension of the environment without the use of trackers. Augmented reality can be seen on the screens and connected devices. Augmented reality is used as a magic window where the data can be viewed as holograms and 3D models. Augmented reality found applications in variety fields like MRI applications, holography, gaming and entertainment applications. Advantages of augmented reality: it increases interaction and enhances the user experience, it creates innovations, give access to the detailed analytics, increase the engagement toward learning, increased visualization and perception, using Geo Target to find the locations. Disadvantages of augmented reality: lack of privacy, increased cost and takes more time, it is more costly to develop AR device and AR application, huge hardware, and software devices are needed for implementation, lack of security.

6.5   Blockchain in Industry 4.0

Blockchain is a concept of cryptographic chains by blocks in which the information are stored in timestamps. Initially, blockchain uses hash function to create the blocks in the chain [14, 16]. Bitcoins are used to build the network with cryptographic currency recognition. Bitcoins are publicly available to all the transaction records. Bitcoin size varies from 20 GB to 30 GB from 2015 to 2017, later, in 2017, the Bitcoin size varies from 50 GB to 100 GB. To enhance the speed, security, and confidentiality, blockchain is used in finance industry. The first generation of blockchain technology was developed on Bitcoin at the year 2009. It is known as blockchain 1.0. The first crypto currencies were introduced to generate crypto currency. The second generation of blockchain technology was introduced on 2010, which was developed and introduced on smart contract and financial services. In third level of generation, the decentralized applications were introduced. It is used in various industries like health, IoT, supply chain, business, and smart cities were introduced [19, 20].

In fourth level of generation, public services and distributed databases were focused. It eliminates the use of paper contract instead smart contract were used. Some of the requirements of blockchain are (i) smart contracts: In smart contract the performance of transaction are happen without the third party who makes transactions more secure and traceable.

(ii) Tokenization: Tokens are used to represent the digital representation of goods, services and rights. In the absence of central authority, it allows the exchange of values and trust of different users. (iii) Data security: Security is the major requirement of blockchain technology. It gives the legal point of the users. (iv) Decentralized data storage: In distributed system, it is the major requirement. (v) Immutability: The records are stored on the network should not be modified in the shared ledger. It provides the integrity of the data stored in the network. (vi) Consensus: The verified users are updated with their transactions. (vii) Typed blocks: These blocks are used for the smart contract and high speed payment in transactions. (viii) Sharing: It is used for the separation of content from the node subsets where the node does not carry any burden or processing load. (ix) Access rights management: In public and private key cryptography, encryption is carried with user identification to assign and manage access rights. (x) Data formatting: The data formats are standardized to application programming Interfaces. It uses the API interface to communicate within the network. (xi) Updatability: Data updation should be done in distributed ledger. The updated data should be structured in peer to peer network. (xii) Encryption: To make secure transactions, encryption should between the end nodes. It provides better security for the transaction. (xiii) UX: In blockchain technology, user interface is the important protocol. It provides easy and convenient application for users. (xiv) Development Operation: To select the platforms and requires less time, development operation is used. Applications of blockchain includes healthcare, smart city, energy, supply chain and logistics, business, IoT, manufacturing, digital content management, agriculture, and so on.

In healthcare industry, blockchain consists of four blocks, namely healthcare data gateway, MedRec model, MedShare model, EHR. In traditional method, the patient's data are stored in the centralized server. The data stored in the server may be vulnerable to attacks or modification of data content. In conventional healthcare industry, smart healthcare is introduced. In smart healthcare, patient is monitored regularly through wireless communication. The data is collected from monitoring through the wearable devices. Large amount of data is collected from the number of patients. These data are stored in the cloud and secured. The stored data can also be shared to the trusted users like hospitals, doctors, and patients by valid user credentials [22, 23].

6.6   Smart Healthcare Design Using Healthcare 4.0 Processes

Blockchain technology finds its application in healthcare industry by providing transparency, crypto security, immutability, decentralized data network, and data updation. In Healthcare 4.0, the smart healthcare system [12] is combined with blockchain network and Industry 4.0. Industry 4.0 is the combination of physical systems and nonphysical systems, such as IoT, industrial IoT, cognitive computing, cloud computing, AI, fog computing, edge computing, and so on. Healthcare 4.0 provides better transparency, security, efficiency, faster accessibility, high operability, and so on. In proposed system, smart healthcare industry uses blockchain technology. The major features of healthcare Industry are unique identification (UID) system: in proposed system each and every entity is given a UID number. The RFID tag is used for the UID system. The RFID tag is attached to each and every person for unique, secure, and fast communication and identification. The identification IDs are stored in the database using blockchain technology. If the patient is interested to get treatment in various hospitals at different times, the recorded data is transferred through public blockchain. Through blockchain, it is easy to track and update the data [25].

The data are stored in a database in immutable form. The data stored can be updated anytime anywhere by doctors, patients, hospitals, and so on. For a successful treatment, it is mandatory to keep the records of the patients. Most of the treatments are interdependent. The medical records are kept transparency in blockchain [26, 27]. This method is very secure in its way. Security is the major feature to keep the patients records, UID number, account details should be kept secured by blockchain. To secure the data, heavyweight and light weight cryptography are combined. To store, secure and update data, lightweight cryptography is used. The lightweight cryptography are implemented in the scarcity of resources for higher security standards with lighter performance based security algorithms. The information stored in the blockchain can be accessed anywhere anytime because of its decentralized and distributed connectivity. The invented system works on the decision making. This is better to understand the person mind of state before getting into the medical treatment. In Industry 4.0, IoT plays a role where data in the system have UID number and sensors. The records in the network can be accessed through internet.

These systems will generate alert in case of any emergency, like drug expiry, patient health condition fluctuations, failure of equipment, and so on. Industrial IoT makes connectivity globally. So the medical records can be accessed in an easier and efficient way. The availability of the medical records occurred in accurate and faster mode. In this system, patient registration is done at the patient admission cell. The RFID tag from the patients gives the patient information, medical history record, medical insurance, and so on. Once the registration is done, the patient health record is shared through the blockchain technology. When the information is shared, a particular doctor is assigned for the patient. After these process, the patient is given first aid and medical check-up. Under initial scanning process, if there are any abnormalities that occurred in the patient is kept under emergency criteria. In the initial scan process, the blockchain automatically updates the records with timestamps. Once the patient is scheduled meeting with doctor, the patients consults the doctor and explains about the medical situations. After consultation, a specialized doctor is assigned to the patient. The patient is given enough time to decide whether to go through the treatment or stop the treatment. If he/she decides to undergo the surgery, then the patient is moved to the operation theatre. In blockchain technology, the recorded databases are updated with time interval. Once the operation is done, the patient is moved to the recovery room. The patient's records are periodically monitored for a fixed interval of time. If there is an improvement in health, the patient is allowed to move to the ward or room. In some cases, the doctor advises the patient to follow the medicines and take periodical health checkups. To monitor the patient regularly, smart devices or wearable devices are attached on the patient's body. The wireless network in the hospital continuously monitors the wireless signals from the sensors and collects the data from the wearable devices [29, 30]. The records in the blockchain are kept in a prespecified format in the gateways.

From the gateways the information are transferred in form of blocks and sent to records in database. Block miner in blockchain takes care of the transactional fees. Now the blockchain creates blocks and share the information to the residential doctors. When the server is in the idle state, the block is added to the network. The required block is added to the blockchain network, and the blocks are shared to the doctor. The residential doctors should available 24/7 at rotational shifts. If any emergency condition occurs, the residential doctors can call the specialized doctor for treatment. The monitored records are added to the network. In a clinical trial–based smart contract system, the laboratory records and experimentation are taken in advanced.

A sample medicine is trial over the patient in a controlled environment. Once the clinical trial is successful, the research organization prepares the records and presents to the regulatory body. In payment monitoring system, smart contracts are made between the patients, doctors, and hospital. In populated countries, like India, payment monitoring system is introduced to avoid overlook of expenses. To provide better security, lightweight cryptography is used in small contracts system. Lightweight cryptography consists of lightweight encryption and decryption mechanism, hashing mechanism and lightweight trusting mechanism. Lightweight cryptography increases the system efficiency by reducing the time. The overall system is effective and secure. In smart contract system, personal records of the patient is recorded and maintained. These records are directly associated with the hospital and it related people. Hospital-related activities are stored in the hospital contract system. A special list is stored in the memory which have permanent and immutable records of the hospital. The hospital records have the basic information like hospital name, address, staff member's details, phone number, and website. In this system, the surgeon is the important contact where the specialized doctors will not be available all the time.

This technology gives knowledge to the patient whether the specialized doctor is available or not. The basic details of surgeon like name, address, contact details, date of joining, area of specialization, years of experience, working location, and so on, are added in the contract. Apart from this, staff members details are also included. The main and important factor in the contract system is the patient. This system stores the permanent and immutable records like patient id, patient name, location, address, contact details, patient title, gender, date of birth, age, date of admission, type of illness, illness records, allergies list, and any special requirements. With the help of Industry 4.0, drug integrity and traceability is verified. In smart contract system, two types of line codes are simulated. Source of line codes is defined as the number of lines written in the smart contracts for execution. Commented line of code is defined as the number of lines code in smart contract which does go for execution. The integration of blockchain technology with Industry 4.0 gives a better automation, transparency, immutability, fault tolerance, distributed services, data redundancy, and better security. This technology allows the healthcare system of patients to share their data in secure and encrypted form.

6.7   Blockchain Tele-Surgery Framework for Healthcare 4.0

For the overall growth and development of the nation, healthcare is the primary concern. The healthcare industry has grown toward development.

The healthcare industry developed from 1.0 to 4.0 where the data are maintained at manual, data centric, patient centric, and so on. In traditional methods, the patient has to visit the doctor for checkup which increases the time for travel and expenses. To avoid these expenses and to overcome from traditional system, telemedicine smart healthcare system is used. These wireless communication allows the doctor to deliver a real time health services. Telemedicine system consists of medical robots for surgery, faster communication, audio and video equipment, and haptic devices. A traditional telesurgery system consists of master, network, and slave domain. The master domain is operated by the surgeon, who controls the operations of the medical robots, the patients and caretakers are in the slave domain. Generally, the traditional method is the human to machine interaction. This system delivers highly accurate and efficient treatment in remote areas which has expenses in the traveling time and cost of surgeon. The traditional method is a complex method.

The first telesurgery was carried on the fiber optics. These methods are highly vulnerable to attacks. In Europe, the telesurgery system has undergone three types of cyber threats. In first attack, the intruders modify the comments like delete, delay, and reorder; this makes the robot movement uncontrollable. In the second attack, they modified the arm movements, arm rotation, and the force which makes the robot hard to organize and control. In third type of attack, the robot has taken control by hijacking activity. To protect the telesurgery system from attacks, standard encryption like AES, DES, ECC are used. These encryption techniques used different key bits, which varies from 128 bits, 196 bits, and 256 bits. To overcome the cyberattacks and to smoothen the surgical methods, HaBiTs is used. In HaBiTs framework consists of three domain: master domain, network domain, and slave domain. Master domain consists of doctors, and it has a human system interface for passing commands. The doctor can control the robot by giving operational commands through human system interface. It consists of consortium blockchain, which creates blocks.

These blocks contain the information of heart, neuro, and ortho blockchains. Digital smart contract share a trust between the surgeons and healthcare organizations. They share cryptocurrency for security. The other equipment of master domain are master controller, foot paddle, master manipulator, haptic devices, 3D video monitor, position sensor, video de compressor, speakers and microphone. The slave domain consists of robot called teleoperator, which executes the command. It send and receives the data through haptic devices. Slave domain consists of robotic arms, haptic devices, video compression, sensors, and high-definition cameras. To protect the data and commands against security threats, blockchain structures are used. The robotic arm are controlled by the human operators through human user interface. The communication is carried out from master domain to slave domain through AI services, such as the GPS. The tele-surgery system does surgery through AI techniques, like GPS, computer vision, navigation, and learning algorithms. The data within the blocks are secure. In HaBiTs, each block in blockchain contains the procedure for surgery. In this case, middleman for information exchange is eliminated. The records in the blocks are encrypted. Once it enters into the blockchain it can be altered. So it is impossible to alter or hack or modify the data. Without the involvement of a third party, the transaction in the blocks can be executed only if the conditions of the smart contract are satisfied. The advantages of this system are interoperability, security, privacy, authentication, and immutable.

6.8   Digital Twin Technology in Healthcare Industry

Digital twin technology is the advanced technology in industry 4.0. Digital twin makes Industry 4.0 revolution. It integrates AI, machine learning, deep learning, and industrial IoT. Digital twin makes the replication of living and nonliving entity in a digital format. It can manage the integration of IoT and data analytics through the physical and virtual twin. It is a set of virtual information from the microatomic to macroatomic level. The data flows from the physical objects to digital object. These flows happen in both directions and vice versa. It consists of three models: digital model, digital shadow, and digital twin. The data flow from digital model to digital shadow through manually. Automatic data flow happens from digital shadow to digital twin. In digital twin, the connection is established from physical model to virtual model through IoT. The real time can be generated by sensors. Digital twin find variety of applications, such as smart cities, manufacturing, healthcare, and industry. The growth and development in digital twin mark its development in the field of health industry. Initially, healthcare is implemented by IoT. These IoT devices are cheaper and efficient, but in terms of connectivity, digital twining is used.

Digital twin uses AI algorithms to make smarter decisions and predictions. It is used to manage the beds in large-scale wars in hospital. It can be able to stimulate the effect of drugs. It also gives alertness to maintenance and repair medical equipment. The AI algorithms make smart decisions to save life based on real-time data and historical data. Digital twin monitors the patient by day to day and checks the well-being of the patient. It combines data analytics to check the patient healthy. It spots the risk of the patient through the virtual twin of the patient. Data fusion is used to collect and process the data in digital twin. Using digital twin, the doctor can check the presurgery procedure. Digital twin uses data fusion, remote surgery, and modeling for healthcare industries. Security and data privacy are important factors in digital twin.

6.9   Conclusion

This chapter gives a detailed account on the revolution of Industry 4.0. It also summarizes the context of digital twin and blockchain technology used in the healthcare industry and its challenges toward security. The challenges in Industry 4.0 are taken into account, and the challenges were improved for the future. This chapter also discussed about the specific role of each technology and methods in terms of security, policies and implementation. Industry 4.0 also addresses the socioeconomic policies, ecological changes, like resources efficiency, environmental changes, environmental protection, urbanization, new innovations, and business ideas. The clear road map toward the smart healthcare systems and Industrial 4.0 application was given. This paves the pathway to the researchers who are ready to take up the research in this area.

References

1. EL Hamdi, S., Abouabdellah, A., Oudani, M., Industry 4.0: Fundamentals and main challenges. *12th International Colloquium of Logistics and Supply Chain Management*, 2019.
2. Kumar, A., Krishnamurthi, R., Nayyar, A., Sharma, K., Grover, V., Hossain, E., A novel smart healthcare design, simulation and implementation using Healthcare 4.0 processes. *IEEE Access*, 8, 118433–118471, 2020.
3. Fuller, A., Fan, Z., Day, C., Barlow, C., Digital twin: Enabling technologies challenges and open research. *IEEE Access*, 8, 108952–108971, 2020.
4. Gupta, R., Tanwar, S., Tyagi, S., Kumar, N., Obaidat, M.S., and Sadoun, B., HaBiTs: Blockchain based telesurgery framework for Healthcare 4.0, In *2019 International Conference on Computer, Information and Telecommunication Systems (CITS)*, IEEE, 1–5, August 2019.
5. Bhawiyuga, A., Wardhana, A., Amron, K., Kirana, A.P., Platform for integrating internet of things based smart healthcare system and blockchain network. *2019 6th NAFOSTED Conference on Information and Computer Science (NICS)*, Hanoi, Vietnam, pp. 55–60, 2019.

6. Sethuraman, S.C., Dhamodaran, S., Vijayakumar, V., Intrusion detection system for detecting wireless attacks in IEEE 802.11 networks. *IET Netw.*, 8, 4, 219–232, 2019.

7. Yang, K., Liao, H.-M., Zhao, L.-H., Zheng, S.-Z., Li, H.-W., Research on network security protection technology of energy industry based on blockchain, in: *2020 IEEE/CIC International Conference on Communications in China (ICCC Workshops)*, IEEE, pp. 162–166, 2020.

8. Fernández-Caramès, T.M. and Fraga-Lamas, P., Towards post-quantum blockchain: A review on blockchain cryptography resistant to quantum computing attacks. *IEEE Access*, 8, 21091–21116, 2020.

9. Chakkaravarthy, S.S., Sangeetha, D., Cruz, M.V., Vaidehi, V., Raman, B., Design of intrusion detection honeypot using social leopard algorithm to detect IoT ransomware attacks. *IEEE Access*, IEEE, vol. 8, 169944–169956, 2020.

10. Kawahara, R., Verification of customizable blockchain consensus rule using a formal method. *2020 IEEE International Conference on Blockchain and Cryptocurrency (ICBC)*, Toronto, ON, Canada, pp. 1–3, 2020.

11. Ribeiro, S.L. and de Paiva Barbosa, I.A., Risk analysis methodology to blockchain-based solutions. *2020 2nd Conference on Blockchain Research & Applications for Innovative Networks and Services (BRAINS)*, Paris, France, pp. 59–60, 2020.

12. Sethuraman, S.C., Kompally, P., Mohanty, S.P., Choppali, U., *MyWear: A Smart Wear for Continuous Body Vital Monitoring and Emergency Alert*, 2020, arXiv preprint arXiv:2010.08866.

13. Bao, Z., Wang, Q., Shi, W., Wang, L., Lei, H., Chen, B., When blockchain meets SGX: An overview, challenges, and open issues. *IEEE Access*, 8, 170404–170420, 2020.

14. Gourisetti, S.N.G., Mylrea, M., Patangia, H., Evaluation and demonstration of blockchain applicability framework. *IEEE Trans. Eng. Manage.*, 67, 4, 1142–1156, Nov. 2020.

15. Sethuraman, S.C., Vijayakumar, V., Walczak, S., Cyber attacks on healthcare devices using unmanned aerial vehicles. *J. Med. Syst.*, 44, 1, 1–10, 2020.

16. Hafid, A., Hafid, A.S., Samih, M., Scaling blockchains: A comprehensive survey. *IEEE Access*, 8, 125244–125262, 2020.

17. Sethuraman, S.C., Kompally, P., Reddy, S., VISU: A 3-D printed functional robot for crowd surveillance. *IEEE Consum. Electron. Mag.*, 10, 1, 17–23, 1 Jan. 2021.

18. Chakkaravarthy, S.S., Sangeetha, D., Vaidehi, V., A survey on malware analysis and mitigation techniques. *Comput. Sci. Rev.*, 32, 1–23, May 2019.

19. Zhaofeng, M., Xiaochang, W., Jain, D.K., Khan, H., Hongmin, G., Zhen, W., A blockchain-based trusted data management scheme in edge computing. *IEEE Trans. Industr. Inform.*, 16, 3, 2013–2021, March 2020.

20. Qiu, J., Liang, X., Shetty, S., Bowden, D., Towards secure and smart health-care in smart cities using blockchain. *2018 IEEE International Smart Cities Conference (ISC2)*, Kansas City, MO, USA, pp. 1–4, 2018.
21. Chakkaravarthy, S.S., Rajesh, P., Vaidehi, V., Hybrid analysis technique to detect advanced persistent threats. *Int. J. Intell. Inf. Technol.*, 14, Q2, 59–76, 2018.
22. Wang, S. *et al.*, Blockchain-powered parallel healthcare systems based on the ACP approach. *IEEE Trans. Comput. Soc Syst.*, 5, 4, 942–950, Dec. 2018.
23. Siam, J., Abdo, A., Al Ju'beh, M., Integration of smart mobile handset devices in a smart healthcare center organization: A proof of concept. *2016 3rd MEC International Conference on Big Data and Smart City (ICBDSC)*, Muscat, pp. 1–5, 2016.
24. Akshay, T., Chakkaravarthy, S.S., Sangeetha, D., Venkata Rathnam, M., Vaidehi, V., Role based policy to maintain privacy of patient health records in cloud. *J. Supercomput.*, 75, 9, 5866–5881, June 2019.
25. Liang, X., Shetty, S., Tosh, D., Exploring the attack surfaces in blockchain enabled smart cities. *2018 IEEE International Smart Cities Conference (ISC2)*, Kansas City, MO, USA, pp. 1–8, 2018.
26. Jabbar, M.A. and Aluvalu, R., Smart cities in India: Are we smart enough?. *2017 International Conference On Smart Technologies For Smart Nation (SmartTechCon)*, Bangalore, pp. 1023–1026, 2017.
27. Laplante, N., Laplante, P.A., Voas, J., Caring: An undiscovered "Super –ility" of smart healthcare. *IEEE Software*, 33, 6, 16–19, Nov.-Dec. 2016.
28. Arivudainambi, D., Varun Kumar, K.A., Chakkaravarthy, S.S., Visu, P., Malware traffic classification using principal component analysis and artifi-cial neural network for extreme surveillance. *Comput. Commun.*, 147, 50–57, November, 2019.
29. Cook, D.J., Duncan, G., Sprint, G., Fritz, R.L., Using smart city technology to make healthcare smarter. *Proc. IEEE*, 106, 4, 708–722, April 2018.
30. Heo, S., Jeong, S., Lee, J., Kim, H., Development and implementation of smart healthcare bidet. *2019 International Conference on Computational Science and Computational Intelligence (CSCI)*, Las Vegas, NV, USA, pp. 1556–1557, 2019.

7

Blockchain Powered EHR in Pharmaceutical Industry

Piyush Sexena, Prashant Singh, John A.* and Rajesh E.

School of Computing Science and Engineering, Galgotias University, Greater Noida, India

Abstract

Blockchain has been an intriguing area of research for a prolonged period, providing a large number of benefits that are being proficiently utilized by a number of industries in various purposes. One of these is the healthcare sector. Modern healthcare systems exhibit characteristics of being highly intricate and expensive, although factors, like enhanced record management in healthcare, better use of insurance policies and blockchain technology, can be helpful to minimize these problems. The healthcare sector would stand to profit largely from the utilization of blockchain technology because of the privacy, security, decentralization, and confidentiality that it provides. Blockchain technology has proven that it is on the brink of revolutionizing the manner in which we manage healthcare data, both in terms in which we store data and its utilization. Electronic health record (EHR) system is the modern technology that provides an improved way to maintain data in the form of electronic records. However, data security, data integrity, and data management are some areas of difficulty for EHR systems.

Blockchain could reinvent the manner in which a patient's digital records are stored and shared. This can be done by coming up with safer applications for the exchange of information of medical details in the healthcare sector. In this article, we formulate ways in which blockchain technology can be utilized to find solutions for these issues and make the EHR systems more productive. We propose a framework that can be used to implement blockchain technology for EHR in the healthcare sector. The architectural framework even provides the EHR system with benefits of having scalability, security, and essential blockchain-oriented solutions. This architecture helps to handle and share healthcare details among various organizations. The main aim of this architecture is to reduce the amount

*Corresponding author: johnmtech@gmail.com

T. Poongodi, D. Sumathi, B. Balamurugan and K. S. Savita (eds.) Digitization of Healthcare Data Using Blockchain, (137–158) © 2022 Scrivener Publishing LLC

of time required for sharing of data among different institutions and to bring down the overall expenses.

Keywords: Blockchain, electronic healthcare records, security, healthcare systems, pharmaceutical industry, security, privacy

7.1   Introduction

In the simplest terms, blockchain is a way to structure and communicate data among parties. In a more technical definition, it is a cryptographically authentic, distributed ledger that validates, safeguards, and preserves transaction of data. To have a proper grasp of this technology, it is necessary to dissect each of its components. Blockchain technology can be understood as a decentralized, distributed ledger. It records the provenance of a digital data set. Blockchain can be termed as a promising and revolutionary technology as it aims to help reduce the risk, detect fraud and bring transparency in a scalable way for multiple uses. Each block in the chain consists of multiple transactions. Whenever a new transaction takes place, a record of that transaction is appended to the ledger of every participant.

The electronic health record (EHR) systems which were created to merge paper based and digital medical records helped to witness a shift in trend in the healthcare sector. An electronic health record system is a digital means of representing a person's information. It contains a collection of all the confidential and relevant facts of a person's health history. It includes the entirety of previous and ongoing medical conditions, illnesses and treatments, giving appropriate attention on the events affecting the patient during his present condition. Electronic health records are patient-centered records that work on real time principle by making information available immediately and securely to accredited users. A key feature of EHR is that it allows authorized individuals to create and manage the stored healthcare data in digital format. This information can be easily shared among multiple healthcare organizations. EHR systems enable the data to be shared to other healthcare providers as they carry details from all the clinicians employed in a patient's treatment [1].

Nowadays, a large number of hospitals have put EHR systems in use and are reaping the benefits it provides, especially its cost effectiveness and enhanced security. EHRs accommodate highly sensitive information about a patient such as his ongoing diagnose or treatment. These details are precious source of knowledge and are supposed to be kept private. The exchange of healthcare information among organizations is an important step for enhancing system intelligence and improving the service quality. An EHR is a structure that consists of health-related data of a patient, which is created and maintained as long as a person lives on, in a digital format and is generally stored by and distributed among various hospitals, clinics, and health providers. These suppliers basically look to maintain easy access to the records, prevent access to previous data by patients. In circumstances where the patients possess control over their health records, they start to interact with data in an unproductive manner which reflects the nature of how these records are maintained.

Electronic health record provides a vast range of functionality and are thus considered an essential part of healthcare sector. These functionalities may include managing appointments, storage of medical information, finance and bills of a patient, and so on. Their primary aim is to provide security of data which can remain immune to tempering, and could be readily shared across different platforms. Regardless of the fact that EHR systems helped in improving the ways of medical records management they still could not meet the required expectations. There were still some areas in which EHR systems struggled. Blockchain comes up with some prospects which can explore some possible solution regarding these hindrances. In this article, we try to discover ways in which blockchain application can be applied in the healthcare sector to provide better accessibility, security, and integrity in data management.

The paradigm of blockchain can be enlarged to provide an ambiguous framework for the implementation of decentralized computing resources in the healthcare environment. To summarize, the objective of this work is to assess and evaluate the condition of blockchain in healthcare. Blockchain technology makes sharing of information much more convenient while at the same time promising control on its accessibility. The private details of a patient are encrypted and can be accessed by a limited number of authorized personnel, whereas the public information is open and accessible for all participants. Therefore, blockchain-accommodated systems fortify EHRs while also improving the privacy at the same time. Blockchain is immensely effective and efficient in protecting the integrity of medical records pertaining to the fact that the data encrypted by blockchain cannot be deleted or altered.

7.2   Traditional Healthcare System vs Blockchain EHR

The existing healthcare environment cannot be presumed to be complete as several personnel in the ecosystem do not have a system in place for fluent supervised administration. Moreover, it is a general opinion that it needs major modifications as it is considered inadequate for information handling and sharing processes. The improper use of gathered data is restricting healthcare organizations from delivering adequate care for patients and elevated quality of services for the sake of better health. Regardless of being highly efficient in terms of cost efficiency, these organizations are unable to satisfy the patient needs and requirements.

Most healthcare facilities today still rely on the worn-out systems for maintaining records of patients. These systems are responsible for retaining records of the patient's data. These outdated systems make the process burdensome for the doctor to diagnose, which also consumes a lot of time. As a result, the expenses needed to maintain a patient-oriented profession has increased significantly. The healthcare ecosystem still has a lot of prevailing issues to deal with. They have a tendency to grow with high intensity as the time goes on. The requirement for a technically advanced system cannot be denied. Health Information Exchange is a monotonous and time-consuming process which results in higher costs. Because patients have no command over their data, the prospect of financial crimes, identity theft, and data manipulation has been escalating every day. Regardless of having devices like computers and mobiles at every healthcare facility nowadays, we are even now unable to compile, review, secure, and share information smoothly. Thus, the healthcare system presently is not only in need of an enhanced system rather it requires a system that is fluent, offers data transparency and cost-efficient, and is feasible [2].

Blockchain has entirely reinvented the manner of information management and storage by bestowing safer mechanisms for trading of medical information in the healthcare industry and linking it over a decentralized network for person-to-person communication. Blockchain is really an intriguing technology that can completely transform the healthcare sector and bring about massive changes in it. This technology allows the control to rest in people's own hands. This means that the person will attain complete supervision of his data, thereby he will possess the ability to maintain, share, and manipulate his data according to his desires.

The use of blockchain in EHR has helped to improve the quality of care that can be given to the patient while also maintaining the economy. During the process multiple level, authentication can cause a few hindrances, which can be terminated by blockchain. The demand of blockchain in the healthcare sector has been constantly increasing. Even though the technology is still in its infancy, it has been gaining major positive responses all around the world and is being widely acknowledged.

Blockchain also allows formation and exchange of a common database for all information related to healthcare. This system could also be availed by any entity participating in the procedure regardless of the electronic devices or systems they use. This makes the system highly secure and transparent, thus permitting doctors to find extra time to dispense on patient's treatment and his needs. Besides, this enables better exchange of statistical healthcare data which facilitates doctors to look for clinical treatment for any rare disease.

The ecosystem of healthcare is such that a better rate of data sharing among various organizations would result in getting more accurate diagnosis and better treatments within economical budget. The everyday maintenance of a patient's condition demands adequate employment of resources so that the insights discovered can be utilized more effectively.

Blockchain in healthcare also allows various modules of the healthcare environment to stay in sync at all times and transfer data on a commonly distributed ledger. This kind of a system always maintains the security and integrity of data so people can easily keep tracking their data and share it according to their needs.

7.3   Working of Blockchain in EHR

Blockchain has become one of the most popular and in demand technologies that has grasped the world by surprise today. A blockchain can be understood as a distributed ledger. It helps to keep track of transactions that occur throughout the network. One of the most intriguing features of a blockchain is that as soon as a component of data is appended to the ledger, no tampering can be done with it. The stored records on a blockchain remain completely immune. If anyone desires to make a change in any one of the blocks it becomes obligatory to make alterations in each of the blocks succeeding it. The implementation of blockchain basically depends on three principles. Systematic working of these permits blockchain in maintaining safe digital associations [3].

Private Key Cryptography

Private key cryptography is a process which uses any variable as a secret key along with an algorithm to perform encryption and decryption on the data. It is necessary to keep the key secret although the algorithm may be public or not. An open network is created to conduct the transactions after creating a reference of protected digital key.

Distributed Ledgers

A distributed ledger can be understood as a consensus of shared records. Its job is to update the ledger in actual time as no central dominion is held accountable for the maintenance of the ledgers. Instead, the participants in the network keep the ledger updated. Only a few seconds are needed to reflect any updates or changes done in the ledgers.

Authentication

Authentication can be described as a process that establishes genuineness of work. In Blockchain, authentication for all the transactions is conducted before being appended to the chain. Algorithms that check the validity and verify all the transactions are held responsible for carrying out these processes. The information needs to be encrypted and signed digitally before being stored for proper authentication.

Many technology experts, healthcare industries and other parties are on the lookout for ways, which could help determine the current situation of blockchain, its limitations and area which we could improve to make this blockchain technology a success in healthcare sector in the future.

Blockchain is really an intriguing technology that can completely transform the healthcare sector and bring about massive changes in it. This technology allows the control to rest in people's own hands. This means that the person will attain complete supervision of his data, thereby he will possess the ability to maintain, share and manipulate his data according to his desires.

The technology is capable enough to genuinely improve the quality of patient's care while also helping to maintain funds at a very affordable rate. Blockchain can easily eliminate all the hindrances that take place at multilevel authentication. With its increasing rate of adaptation, Blockchain has carved its way into the healthcare sector prominently. Even though the technology is still in its infancy, it has been gaining major positive responses all around the world and is being widely acknowledged.

7.4   System Design and Architecture of EHR

System design is the process of developing a system from its theory hence considerably one of the most important part of a framework. In this section, we highlight the areas such as modules, architecture and many other components which are required to unite together to form a framework. The main intention for designing this framework is to make a system that is entirely based on blockchain so that it can provide a secure, temper proof system for the betterment of healthcare. The proposed system or framework includes three modules or entities. Integrating these modules together would allow to keep our system to function properly [4]. The concept of these entities does not end here and it is vital to comprehend further details as explained ahead. The layered structure of the design is shown in Figure 7.1.

User Layer
An individual who is able to make efficient use of the system and its assets can be defined as a user of the system. A system user needs to attend to multiple responsibilities of a system, which makes the system recognize him particularly.

A system can accommodate and recognize anyone, such as a patient, clinician, or staff members to be the user. The basic aim of these users would

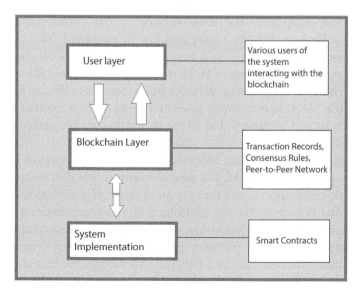

Figure 7.1 Layered structure of the design.

be to make interactions with the system so that they are able to carry out some basic tasks, such as reading, creating, updating, and deleting records. The people operating the system should be capable enough to access the system functions through a browser known as DApp. This DApp browser includes the framework of the system as its graphical user interface (GUI). Each and every function that is accessible by any user is contained in the GUI. In respect to the duties assigned to the user can use the GUI to interact with the other layers present in the system.

Blockchain Layer
The consecutive layer on this system is the blockchain layer. A code is needed for the user to interact with the DApp which functions on blockchain and this layer is responsible to carry out the function. It consists to three components, which are as follows:

- **Blockchain Assets:** Ethereum blockchain is a category of its own. In this, a transaction process is implemented to append or alter any kind of information or records, which are stored in Ethereum blockchain. Ethereum blockchain consider these transactions as resources as they are segment of details, which can be sent to one person to another or be stored to be put in use later.
- **Governance Rules:** In general, blockchain adheres to a few consensus rules so that the transactions can be performed and completed. For these reasons, a few algorithms are needed so that the blockchain can be protected from any kind of tempering and maintained securely. Consensus algorithm like Proof of Work is used by the Ethereum blockchain. The agenda to carry out this process is to ensure that the blockchain is being governed properly in a manner of trust and by approval of all the nodes that are connected to the network.
- **Network:** Ethereum blockchain makes use of person-to-person network. All the modules within this network are linked as peers, and there is an absence of a central node that is responsible for controlling all the functionalities in a network. The idea to use such a network was to create a more spread-out platform rather than one that is centralized. Therefore, to use a network in which all the linked-up nodes attain an equality in status was considered the best option to be undertaken.

Transactions:
Following transactions are included in the system:

- Added records are used for creating medical records for a patient. The record consists of fields, such as identity, id-no, blood group, gender, and so on. The basic medical details, treatment, and diagnosis of a patient are maintained by it along with IPFS hash.
- Update records is used to append any changes or alterations made in the medical data set. It is responsible for changing the ordinary details of a patient without disturbing the IPFS hash. For ensuring the safety of records it is essential to keep the IPFS hash secure.
- View records permits a person to observe the records and medical information of a patient. Patients as well as doctors are both allowed to use this function. An authentication program is applied by the system so that a patient can observe only his own details. Secure functions are carried out to allow only the relevant data to be viewed by the patient.
- Delete records grants access to erase all records and details of a patient. Usually, patients are not entitled to use this function. The doctors alone can make use of this if they need to erase any information regarding a patient.
- Grant access allows a person to implement any of the mentioned functions as he desires. The access is restricted to doctors and staff member only. A patient is allowed to observe his personal details but cannot make any changes to them, neither can he erase any segment of information. Thus, all major functions are not administrative people only.

System Implementation
The system was put into practices by using the Ethereum blockchain and its tributaries. Here, we try to look into deeper details to get insights on various functions of the system.

Smart contracts: Smart contracts are segment of codes used to carry out tasks on blockchain. The execution takes place when a transaction is done by the user. They operate on blockchain directly, so they are immune to any alteration and are temper proof. They usually work on solidity language and can be programmed to perform any function that a user needs to be done on blockchain [5].

Smart contracts perform all the basic operations and are a very vital part of DApp. The framework consists of contracts such as:

- Patient records
- Roles

These contracts give control to the users on the DApps. They also perform CRUD operations on patient's records. The Patient Records smart contract is purely made up to implement functions of presented framework. It is responsible to perform CRUD operation and other important roles as needed.

According to the second contract as stated before roles is a predefined smart contract that exists in the OpenZeppelin smart contract library. Various smart contracts which perform functions like creation of one's own smart contract are included in this library. The motive to make use of these libraries is for the benefits it offers which are too hard to ignore. The Rolessmart contract is a part of the Asset library, that itself is a sub-library under OpenZeppelin. Various contracts lie under the asset libraries to define the access rules, although the role that libraries provide is defining mechanics, which serve as the primary reason for selecting this particular smart contract.

An algorithm that defines Patient Records smart contract is stated ahead. It describes the multiple functions being accomplished in it and the many constraints which are linked with them. It even talks about the duties which are maintained to grant access to specific functions.

7.5   Blockchain Methodologies for EHR

The modules of the architecture are often made up of linked up devices, such as a sensor or collector. They gather data and send them to the network of blockchain for being stored. The quantity of data that originates from mobile or sensor devices has been increasing at a staggering rate [6]. The framework based on commodity hardware offer economical solutions and greater scalability. Blockchains are presently one of the most popular forms of DLT. These are mainly categorized into three types as:

- **Public Blockchains.** It belongs to distributed networks where everybody can take part. It is used for checking the transaction of data and verifying them. They also take part in the procedures of reaching consensus.

- **Consortium Blockchains.** The authoritative node is picked out in advance and generally forms associations, for example business-business partnership. The information stored in blockchain is considered a decentralized network, and the data could be open or private.
- **Private Blockchains.** Here, the modules are under restriction. Everyone cannot take part in the Blockchain. It enforces severe command for managing access of data.

A literature review presents a set of models for proposed architecture. Blockchain is basically considered the central element of such architectures, and it is accountable for the storing, authorizing, and assisting with open standards, as the healthcare architecture is sanctioned. The offered blockchain architecture must be built in such a way that it is able to brace the deposition of healthcare information, consisting medical details and healthcare–related data from smart devices and wearable sensors. They must peruse the user as long as he lives. Other supremacy of distributed architectures of blockchain includes integrated fault tolerance and recoveries in situations of n disasters. The blockchain makes use of address generating mechanics to authenticate and authorize the network employs and a public key cryptography for managing modules within the framework. The public key cryptography then uses some mathematical related public and private keys for creating digitally generated signatures and encrypted data. In computation it is not feasible to generate a private key, which is based on a public key. Therefore, public keys are exchangeable and could be freely shared. This helps to enable users to perform encryption on context and verify digital signatures. Similarly, private keys should be confidential and undisclosed to guarantee that only the person who holds the private key is able to decipher the content and generate digital signatures. Smart contract is one of the other important features of the blockchain. Smart contracts are software programs that are used for execution of programs in a Blockchain. It possesses the ability to comprehend other contracts, take decision, and implement other contracts. A smart contract is capable of storing digital resources into the Blockchain and professes ownership of these resources. These resources are governed by the smart contracts. Their execution is carried out automatically by the program code. Smart contract enforces severe command for managing access of data. In the healthcare sector, smart contracts are used for creating knowledgeable representations of preexisting medical details that remain stored in singular modules of the network. They might also consist of metadata that states about owner records, permissions and integrity of data. In this section, we discuss about few of the conceptual features that make healthcare–related data reasonable and ways in which blockchain can sanction interoperability of data and its privacy. Further, it explains the process flow implemented in blockchain for handling medical details, perform analysis of usability of the implementation, and eventually confer some challenges faced during its implementation.

The lack of common framework and principles that permits safer exchange of sensitive private information has greatly affected the state of healthcare records maintained presently. The permission requirements of a patient to the current EHR are quite limited. Basically, a patient is not able to transfer or exchange their data with researchers easily. Despite all the progress made in medicinal field, different EHR systems are unable to communicate efficiently. The predominant means of exchanging healthcare details among different organizations and institutions are still conducted by means of mails and faxes. Every healthcare institution offers services, tracks them and appends the patient's records every time a medical service is provided. This data set consists of sensitive information, such as the patient's gender, age or date of birth, and so on, or may also include details on the specific service provided like the undergoing treatment, diagnosis, illness, and so on. These kinds of information are generally stored in a database inside a predefined network of healthcare institutions. The flow of data and records starting from the patient through the healthcare institution every time he undergoes a service should not stop at the healthcare network only. Rather, this information which is responsible to represent every interaction with patient should be administered to a national level blockchain transaction layer. Hence, anything that is virtually stored on a blockchain can be easily accessed by a specific individual universally at any given time with the help of his private key. The private key makes exchange of data or information between the patient and organization much more convenient. Healthcare information are very sensitive data that should always be kept confidential. Therefore, every healthcare institution that maintain patient's personal data should enforce privacy policies to make sure that only the patient or authorized personnel who have the permission can access the medical details and personal information of a patient. Additionally, precautions must be taken by all healthcare industries connected to blockchain to maintain update their end of information on the ledgers. For the purpose of increasing security and limiting the risks regarding malicious activities any alteration done on blockchain should be instantly broadcasted to the network. The blockchain helps to keep their copies safe harmful attacks and hacking techniques. The distributed ledgers even protect copies from harmful hacks. Next, we try to analyze the procedure of process flow implemented by blockchain for handling and sharing of data among various healthcare institutions.

Process Flow
The process flow in blockchain could be summed up in a few steps as follows:

- The healthcare institutions are responsible for storing information on the blockchain: Health organization imparts assistance to a patient and store the person's details into an already existing software system. Next, the data fields and public-ID of patients are rerouted to the blockchain through APIs.
- Uniquely identifying and completing a transaction: Encryption is performed on each transaction and given an identity that is stored on the blockchain, containing the patient's public ID.
- Direct query on the blockchain by health organizations: If healthcare organizations need access to information, they require submission of queries through APIs and make use of patient's public-ID on blockchain to get back the encrypted data. Patient's information, such as age, gender, diseases, are now viewable and can be analyzed to uncover new insights.
- Only authorized person can access medical details of a patient: The private key retained by the patient affiliates their identity to the data in blockchain. The patient can allow to share this private key with other organizations to perform decryption on his data. Thus, the property of nonidentifiability remains to any individual who does not have the access to the key.

7.6 Benefits of Using Blockchain in EHR

The application of blockchain technology can aid the healthcare industry in numerous ways, some of which are [7, 8]:

- ❖ **Decentralization:** In blockchain, the information is dispersed across the span of entire network instead of settling at any central point. The blockchain is copied and spread across a network of computers. This makes blockchain's data more difficult to tamper with. The data set which was earlier focused at a particular point is now looked after by multiple trustworthy entities.

❖ **Public Health:** With the use of blockchain, managerial parties are able to create an exchangeable stream of a patient's information. The stream helps the authorities to recognize any threat so that they can proceed with required actions to restrict the difficulties in a suitable fashion.

❖ **Data Security and Privacy:** The use of cryptographic functions is a common way of dealing with problems to provide security to modules connected in a blockchain network. It makes use of SHA-256, algorithm which basically stands for Secure Hashing algorithm, on the hash which are stored on blocks. The hash is used to ensure the security measures implemented in blockchain which also helps in maintaining the integrity in data. Cryptographic hashes are powerful functions which produce checksums for electronic form of data, which cannot be used for extraction purposes. This property makes blockchain platform, which is decentralized in nature. These comfortably make use of cryptographic techniques, which help to maintain privacy of data and protects it from being tempered with by the outsiders.

❖ **Managed Consent:** Patients have the right to grant authority to any person to access their medical details. Patients need to have authority over their own data. The increasing healthcare consumption transforms this requirement into demand. There are some regulations, such as HIPPA and PHi, which poses restrictions on a patient to access EHR and limits their capability to evaluate and exchange their details with other healthcare staff members. Blockchain could eventually allow people to have control over their own data. They enable access to EHRs by implementing a fine-tuned sanctioned system. For every patient, a digital signature can be assigned with the help of both private and public keys and a hash function. This digital signature will act as an authentic id for a patient to access their data. The incorporation of permission layers to these entities and to blockchain allows patients to have command over their information and restricts unauthorized access to their own data. They can decide what they want to share and what they want to withhold. For example, revealing only specific segments of details with a certain medical institution for healthcare.

❖ **Claim Processing:** The technology of blockchain also aids to clarify the complex medical billing process by eradicating the series of validations and various outside parties that try to act on behalf of them.

❖ **Data transparency:** If we want to attain transparency in data in any technology, we should have entities that work on trust-based relationships. The data in consideration should be kept secure and unaltered. Any kind of data which has been stored on blockchain is not only connected at one particular point but is rather spread out across a distributed network. The possession of data is shared. This makes the data secure and transparent from any influence of outside intervention.

❖ **Patient Generated Data:** This allows patients to upload data in a secure manner without having to fear about affecting any previous records.

7.7   Challenges Faced by Blockchain in HER

❖ **Interoperability:** The process in which various information systems try to share and transfer information among them is termed s interoperability. The exchange of information serves a vital purpose and its usefulness should not be underestimated. Health information exchange (HIE) is also one of the essential characteristics of EHR. With multiple EHR systems being implemented in numerous hospitals around the world, they have an inconsistent degree of terminologies, complexities, and functional abilities, which do not have any globally defined standards. Besides, at basic level, the medical details which are interchanged must be understandable, and that understood segment of information can be put into use later [9].

❖ **Storage capability:** The use of blockchain in healthcare would require a significantly large amount of storage as it needs to store medical records, pictures, documentations, reports, and so on. Theoretically, each member who is a participant of the chain would possess a full duplicate of all medical records of each person in the country, and this amount of volume can probably overrun the magnitude of storage capacity of blockchain technology currently. As can be understood, medical records and healthcare sectors produce a humongous amount of EMR. This comes from all kinds of sensor data from a patient and wearable IoT gadgets. In contrast, blockchain framework supports limited amount of capacity for storage of data. Although the decentralized and hash-based architecture of blockchain comes with a very high a cost for storing data. Similarly, blockchain data accessibility, management, and functions can also be quite expensive if the magnitude of data is bigger. Therefore, this is a factor to be kept in mind before designing a blockchain application.

❖ **Asymmetrical information:** Critics define data asymmetry as one of the biggest problems in the healthcare sector. Data asymmetry can be understood as one institution possessing better accessibility to data than the other. The EHR and healthcare sector is a victim of these problems as hospitals retain access to the records of patients, hence, the information becomes central. Any patient who desires to access his details would need to undergo a lengthy and tiresome process to gain accessibility. The information is maintained in such a way that it remains centralized only to a particular healthcare organization. Thus, only the hospital or organization has authority over its data.

❖ **Data Breeches:** Breech of data in healthcare sector points out the requirement of an improved platform. Many healthcare systems are not built to satisfy the demands of the patients and face the issues related to inefficient and bad adaption of these systems. These problems justify the reason to find a platform that is capable enough to help in reshaping healthcare sector to be more patient oriented. A platform that is transparent, secure and is able to impart integrity to data for the medical details of the patients.

❖ **Scalability:** The issue of scalability is considerably less serious in comparison to others due to the decentralized nature of the blockchain architecture. Nevertheless, hospitals, research organizations, clinics, insurance companies, and so on, consist to extremely large number of users with differing infrastructure. Blockchain technology demands a greater computation power, which in return requires high

Table 7.1 Solutions provided by blockchain to major challenges in healthcare.

Factors	Healthcare challenges	Blockchain solutions
Data fragmentation	Fragmented, decentralized data are being produced. Doctors, patients, clinics, and so on, tend to produce data separately.	Computers and the connected decentralized system can create a network among all groups.
Timely access	Timely access and analysis of data can suffer due to privacy policies and negotiations.	Distributed blockchain can be used to carry out analysis on the same data set without involving any risk to manipulation of data.
Scalability	Trust issue creates unrest in collaboration among parties.	Participating nodes are verified by blockchain along with related data, which helps to eliminate all risks.
Sensor (IoT)data handling	Numerous IoT devices are being used to gather and disperse information, that are hard to track and handling is difficult.	Blockchain can make IoT device secure by creating a private blockchain network.
Data access consistency	People handling data must not remain open and emphasis should be given on regulations for distributing data.	Blockchain can use its 3 types of user scope to define data processors and regulators selected by owner.
Cost for Data Processing	Presently, identity of the owner is open and processors are concealed.	Smart contracts can secure permissions and data flow in blockchain. It has a secret way to handle data where process identity is open for all.
Peer to Peer communication	Presently, mediator and outside entities manipulate and disperse data to gain profit.	Blockchain can eliminate all third parties to make a non-dominion open boundary for distributing data in a very secure manner.

electricity consumption by working equipment. Some kind of solution needs to be found to resolve the issue of scalability in healthcare to popularize blockchain.

❖ **Modification:** While on one end blockchain attribute of immutability in data secures the system, on the opposite end, it leaves no choice for modification of data and its deletion hence the alterations needed are unavoidable. We require to fabricate a new block from all modules and entities or generate a new chain. Although these methods are expensive and infeasible. Therefore, the development of blockchain application should be done in manner in which data modification needs are lowest.

The summary of solutions provided by blockchain to major challenges in healthcare represented in Table 7.1.

7.8 Future Scope

Blockchain technology has a great potential for making the healthcare systems of today much more efficient and economical than the previous outdated systems. This can be achieved by augmenting exchange of data in healthcare, allowing transparency of information, providing quality patient-care services, enhancing efficiency and maintaining vigorous medical research. With its improving progress rate, blockchain technology can soon become the center for technology driven care services. EHR systems implemented with blockchain have already proven to be much more effective than the outdated systems, hence, it is very likely that there will be an exponential increase in its adoption rate in the coming future [10]. The future of blockchain in EHR certainly looks bright.

On the basis of our current knowledge, we can be certain that blockchain technology may provide a suitable solution in the future for habitual problems in the healthcare sector. Problems persisting in the EHR include interoperability, lack of trust between data sharing parties in healthcare, privacy and security issues and authorization and authentication requirements. To reach its true potential, blockchain technology would need to overcome these challenges and must have guidelines to allow flexibility to provide better services. Moreover, human factors must be considered instead of relying on technical solutions, which otherwise would limit the use of digital platforms.

In our study, we realize that any scenario that includes data exchange, where multiple stake holders are involved can be a good usage for blockchain.

Sharing health records, medical records, and research data among numerous parties is common in healthcare. Hence, it is believed that healthcare is one of the best application areas for the implementation of blockchain. It can be argued that blockchain is still in its infancy when it concerns healthcare, but it is certain to have a bright future due to the efficient solutions it provides to various EHR problems. If we truly wish to maximize its effectiveness, blockchain platforms should incorporate some guidelines to permit broad use and flexibility to accommodate local practice variations. Furthermore, human factors must be considered instead of relying on technical solutions, that otherwise would limit the use of digital platforms. Maintaining records on digital platforms allows further opportunities for analyzing data more conveniently and improving the quality of care. While information is digitized, they are isolated in local centralized data storages that allows a strong hindrance to further developments. Blockchain-accommodated systems fortify EHRs while improving the privacy and security services and reducing its cost. Blockchain is also immensely effective in protecting the integrity of medical records pertaining to the fact that the data encrypted by blockchain cannot be deleted or altered.

Further research could be carried out on finding out how different types of blockchain types (permissioned, permissionless, or hybrid) can be implemented and what are their pros and cons in regards to prescription management. The technology is very auspicious in terms of managing medical data, stopping data breaches, improving interoperability and observing medical devices for healthcare purposes. Although it is difficult to predict the future of blockchain in healthcare in such an initial stage, the prospects and solutions it offers look very promising. It makes sense to have professional consultation in such matters, although the future of blockchain in EHR in healthcare sectors looks promising.

7.9 Conclusion

Blockchain shows a lot of potential in renovating the conventional healthcare sector. Blockchain has entirely reinvented the manner of information management and storage by bestowing safer mechanisms for trading of medical information in the healthcare industry and linking it over a decentralized network for person-to-person communication. However, if we want to fully integrate the blockchain technology in the EHR systems, we still need to overcome numerous research and operative challenges. In this chapter, we studied and deliberated about a lot of these obstacles and recognized numerous probable opportunities, such as relating to IoT, big data, and machine learning. We are hopeful that this review will contribute to impart better understanding for development and implementation of the next generation EHR systems that would be able to improve and provide better services to the society.

Blockchain is an auspicious technology that not only addresses existing industry pain points, but also offers a framework to integrate healthcare information across participants. While this emerging technology still faces many challenges to adoption in healthcare, its potential to innovate and disrupt is already affecting other industries. The banking and technology industries are the biggest stakeholders in blockchain technology. According to Forbes, blockchain private funding outdid $4.5 billion U.S. dollars this year. Companies, like Airbus, American Express, Change Healthcare, Cisco, Fujitsu, IBM, JP Morgan, Intel, and SAP, are working in aggregation with the Linux Foundation on the Hyperledger project. Hyperledger is a blockchain based on modular architecture that provides flexibility to meet the needs of different industries, and is beginning to be used as the development and blockchain platform for many companies. Microsoft is also placing its bets on blockchain as they work on developing Project Bletchley, a blockchain middleware built for multi-party interoperability.

As this technology continues to be developed, healthcare and pharmaceutical companies should actively become involved, and, like the financial sector, establish a consortium to support the blockchain development and identify early areas of adoption. Additionally, by engaging in early-on experimentation, the industry could provide valuable lessons to help developers in evolving the technology. By cooperating with legislators, experimentation insights can be used to address common grey areas and provide recommendations to this technology without constraining its growth. Ultimately, the promise of blockchain presents numerous opportunities for the healthcare and pharmaceutical industry—from the creation of a blockchain-powered exchange of information, to the audit and verification of supply chain and clinical trial processes. By connecting fragmented systems, it has the potential to save companies millions of dollars and in addition can improve medical treatment and increase patient safety.

References

1. Magyar, G., Blockchain: Solving the privacy and research availability tradeoff for EHR data: A new disruptive technology in health data management. *2017 IEEE 30th Neumann Colloquium (NC)*, IEEE, 2017.

2. Vora, J. *et al.*, BHEEM: A blockchain-based framework for securing electronic health records. *2018 IEEE Globecom Workshops (GC Wkshps.)*, IEEE, 2018.

3. Shukla, R.G., Agarwal, A., Shukla, S., Blockchain-powered smart healthcare system. in: *Handbook of Research on Blockchain Technology*, pp. 245–270, Academic Press, 2020.

4. Wang, S. *et al.*, Blockchain-powered parallel healthcare systems based on the ACP approach. *IEEE Trans. Comput. Soc Syst.*, 5, 4, 942–950, 2018.

5. Radanović, I. and Likić, R., Opportunities for use of blockchain technology in medicine. *Appl. Health Econ. Health Policy*, 16, 5, 583–590, 2018.

6. Khezr, S. *et al.*, Blockchain technology in healthcare: A comprehensive review and directions for future research. *Appl. Sci.*, 9, 9, 1736, 2019.

7. Yaqoob, I. *et al.*, Blockchain for healthcare data management: Opportunities, challenges, and future recommendations. *Neural Comput. Appl.*, 1–16, 2021. https://doi.org/10.1007/s00521-020-05519-w

8. Peters, A.W. *et al.*, Blockchain technology in healthcare: A primer for surgeons. *Bull. Am. Coll. Surg.*, 12, 1–5, 2017.

9. Mayer, A.H., da Costa, C.A., da Rosa Righi, R., Electronic health records in a blockchain: A systematic review. *Health Inf. J.*, 26, 2, 1273–1288, 2020.

10. Carter, G., Shahriar, H., Sneha, S., Blockchain-based interoperable electronic health record sharing framework. *2019 IEEE 43rd Annual Computer Software and Applications Conference (COMPSAC)*, vol. 2, IEEE, 2019.

8

Convergence of IoT and Blockchain in Healthcare

**Swaroop S. Sonone[1], Kapil Parihar[2], Mahipal Singh Sankhla[3]*,
Rajeev Kumar[4] and Rohit Kumar Verma[5]**

*[1]Department of Forensic Science, Dr. Babasaheb Ambedkar Marathwada
University, Aurangabad, Maharashtra, India
[2]State Forensic Science Laboratory, Jaipur, Rajasthan, India
[3]Department of Forensic Science, Vivekananda Global University,
Jaipur, Rajasthan, India
[4]Department of Forensic Science, School of Basic and Applied Sciences,
Galgotias University, Greater Noida, India
[5]Dr. APJ Abdul Kalam Institute of Forensic Science & Criminology,
Bundelkhand University, Jhansi, U.P., India*

Abstract

As the Internet of Things (IoT) is a way of interconnecting computing machines, programmed and digital tools have implemented blockchains to play a crucial function in the prevailing advanced applications in the healthcare sector. Spreading blockchain technologies in the healthcare sector will allow the number of cryptographic materials to be converged in this sector. The convergence of IoT and blockchain technologies in the healthcare sector will revolutionize upcoming goods and services to manage sufferers with therapeutic, precautionary, rehabilitative, and care. The convergence concept of IoT and blockchain in Healthcare is improving remarkably; Combining IoT and Blockchain was never done before. This will lead to the benefit of all services related to healthcare industries. This integration will change the face of Medicare and its facilities. The IoT will combine and manage services collaboratively to achieve a healthier state of life, actuality, energy-saving human health. The current technology in healthcare platforms needs to be integrated all over the world. Convergence IoT and blockchain can be the energy chain that will provide a new model for next-generation healthcare

**Corresponding author*: mahipal4n6@gmail.com

T. Poongodi, D. Sumathi, B. Balamurugan and K. S. Savita (eds.) Digitization of Healthcare Data Using Blockchain, (159–180) © 2022 Scrivener Publishing LLC

services. The potential application of concerning technologies is the new hope for our healthcare field.

Keywords: Blockchain, Internet of Things, healthcare, electronic health records, digital healthcare, smart healthcare

8.1   Introduction

Information & Communication Technology (ICT) portrays a vital part in the application of Digital-Healthcare. Upcoming technologies, like block-chain technology, Internet of Things (IoT), and artificial intelligence, have never been used earlier as mix-tech for the benefits of humans. This integration has numerous complimentary features, such as computerization, trust free, devolution, security, and democracy. Attention in blockchain technology is growing since the Bitcoin has landed up in markets; the tech is attaining consideration and can be supposed as a rampant theme [1]. Internet of Things can subordinate and communicate millions of things in one time. This offers varied benefits to shopkeepers, which will modify the way in which that client's interaction with novelty [2]. Present IoT system relies on combinations bounded server/client appearance, which needs all apparatuses to be linked and confirmed by a server. Therefore, shifting the IoT network in dispersed means might become the correct option. Coordinating IoT with blockchain will have abundant benefits [3]. Integration of IoT and blockchain models is altering Smart Healthcare industries. It escorts industries, administrations, and nations too. Blockchain-IoT technologies is broadly known and extremely appreciated because of its distributed nature and peer-to-peer features. The following chapter points consist of various safety matters and difficulties, which obstruct the implementation of IoT-Blockchain technology, discovering the several difficulties in diverse facets of supportable healthcare systems [4]. Because of the critical part of IoT instruments in detecting the nearby ecosphere and triggering correctly, gathering reliant information has an importance on the exact capability of such instruments. Reliability of data in IoT can be attained by means of distributed signal processing approaches that perform a confirmation procedure among all its contributors to guarantee that information endures unchallengeable and unaltered. These thoughtful characteristics of blockchain technology have helped Bitcoin to evolve [5]. We can instinctively discover the ability of block-chain technology to provide the information dependability difficulty in IoT technology. Although assimilating Blockchain technology in IoT will improve safety, information confidentiality, and consistency of IoT instruments, it generates a novel problem. In modern years, experimenters have extensively reviewed the convergence methods, advantages, and problems in IoT networks and devices [6–8]. The aim of this chapter is to present an integration of Blockchain and IoT and revise diverse facets of these entrenched technologies in the healthcare area. We have attempted to offer tactical and practical visions into IoT limits and challenges, blockchain requirements and weaknesses, blockchain-IoT integration approaching methods and explanations to overcome application problems. This chapter also delivers summarized high-level information about the convergence of IoT and blockchain technologies.

8.2   Overview of Convergence

Currently, IoT technologies are in adoption stages, yet there are many symbols that marketplace is growing and a greater number of IoT devices are flattering a reliable part of our day-to-day living [9–12]. Since the last decade, blockchain concept is being evolving, from the initial key like Bitcoin to the existing versatile multimodal disparities in diverse arenas, although blockchain technology is constantly refining its structures and is determined to discover a progressively effectual application [13, 14]. The design of IoT technology includes of layers, starting from edge innovation layer at the ground to the application layer at the best [15]. The two bottom layers complement to data catching, whereas the two upper layers are in care of information usage in applications. Edge innovation layer is an equipment layer that combines information accumulation parts, as an example, RFID frameworks, remote sensors systems (WSNs), cameras, worldwide situating frameworks (GPS), electronic information interfaces (EDIs), insightful terminals. Access door layer supervises data takes care of message steering, information transmission, and distributing and buying in messages. It directs the data to the middleware layer received from the edge layer, using corresponding novelties, for example, Li-Fi, GSM, Wi-Fi, Ethernet, WiMax, and WSN [16]. Middleware layer is an artefact stage that stretches image to applications from possessions. Similarly, it provides numerous supervisions, for example, device revelation and managing, data segregation, info accumulation, semantic data analysis; get to control, and data disclosure (using Electronic Product Code [EPC], or Object Naming Service [ONS]). Applications layer is the finest layer and is responsible of conveyance of various applications to different IoT customers.

8.3   Healthcare

Healthcare is a decisive industry because it comprises subtle data of individuals' past well-being, which is of chief concern. It requires high security and privacy. Presently, Internet allows distribution of these records, but it offers a novel danger like misapplication of victim information as it is made available easily. One of the key issues faced in healthcare sector is clinical integration of electronic medical/health records (EHR). In this Internet age, the newest technology that aroused is blockchain because of its amazing characteristics like traceability, security, and transparency. Blockchain arises as an astonishing technology, which has huge chances in the upcoming future and is currently executed in numerous commercial industries. Several preceding revisions have applied blockchain in the healthcare sector. The usage of blockchain in healthcare structure, reviewed intensively to understand how this tech can be applied in healthcare system in the digital world and to resolve numerous issues like electronic medical record (EMR) with the features of interoperability, privacy and security [17]. The EMR is still regarded as the prime problem as it does not crack interoperability issues in the worldly scenarios; other issues like every health organization has dissimilar setup in storage of health histories [18]. Viewing all these, blockchain is an eminent technology, which has huge chances in the forthcoming times and can offer a solution to this. Preceeding revisions talked on the usage of blockchain to be implemented in several healthcare establishments. Health facilities supervise the problems of clinical and healthcare suppliers, its inadequacy and their irregular supply. Health problems also increase difficulties, which result into the requirement of adequate healthcare structures. The drift of information technology in the medicinal sector [19] could be clarified as biomedical database, electronic medical records, and public healthiness, which have been enhanced not only in place of accessibility, traceability but also on the wateriness of information [20]. Many nations are addressing critical subjects in healthcare organizations like convenience, superiority, and charge of healthcare [21]. However, researches recognized that EMR sharing is capable to attract healthcare matters [22], maximum healthcare institutes preserve documentation of affecter's histories unreachable to other establishments because of confidentiality. Such valued information is reserved in the organization [23]. Researches revealed interoperability capacity to assimilate the whole excellence of facility in medicinal area [24], these matters are associated to convenience, excellence, and charges. Supplementary problems like data possession fights generally take place due to dissimilar understanding on data value, secrecy, and business domination methods [25].

8.4   IoTs and Blockchain Technology

The IoT defines the system of physical substances, i.e., things which are entrenched with detectors, softwares, and supplementary technology for the motive of linking and sharing information with other devices and structures through Internet. The IoT can subordinate and communicate millions of devices at single time. Present IoT structures rely on certain server-client organizations, which need all devices to be correlated and confirmed by a server. Thus, shifting IoT system in dispersed manner might be the correct option [1, 2]. Blockchain is an advancing list of histories, known as blocks, which are connected through cryptography. It is one of the harmless and utmost dependable kinds of construction for building a settled equivalent intellect carriage organization structure. BC technology is undergoing modification at a speedy rate and has the capability to revolutionize progressively in implementation of Intelligent Transport Systems (ITSs). Utilizing BC tech to create a safe, consistent and dispersed independent transportation system network will enable more effectual usage of present ITS substructure and properties, particularly for crowd sourcing tech. In upcoming times, ITSs would be contained of a massive system of independent automobiles in the smart communities. Even in the enigmatic civilization, the request for ITSs is growing because of the suitability of isolated traffic that comes at the huge price of intense road-resources. Human influences, which are dangerous to ITSs, also portrays a significant part in all arenas of tech that ITSs would alter vividly, which comprise traveller information management and vehicle control design [17, 18].

8.5   IoT Technologies for Healthcare

The IoT technology on the Wireless Body Area Network (WBAN) for healthcare implementations is a functioning situation for IoT gadgets, which has received consideration from massive study arenas in current eons. Internet of Things links all topics and healthcare structures effortlessly [26]. Health-Internet of Things (H-IoT) is the landmark of data arrangement progress. It portrays a key part in informing the individual's health stages and enhances the value of lives. It is multifaceted organization that includes microelectronic networks, health and medical, computer sciences, and several supplementary arenas. Conferring to the general linked healthcare systems, phase from 17s to 22s in 21st century is the development stage of IoT healthcare applications, which will fasten the healthcare businesses and many investors who are pacing up their exertions [27, 28]. So, there is no uncertainty that IoT technologies in converting the healthcare segment by totally revising gadgets, applications and the persons connected and linked with one another in healthcare resolutions. Therefore, IoT tech is continuously offering innovative gadgets, as the competences that make up a combined healthcare part guarantees healthier victim care. It is also discovered that healthcare charges were decreased pointedly and additionally, therapy consequences were enhanced [29]. The tech is having ability of interrelating millions or billions of varied things by Internet. Such an expansion is permitted by newest progresses in smart detectors, interaction techs, and Internet protocols (Ips). Critical requirement for versatile approaches arose. In these conditions, a technology of IoT can be understood with three vital empowering approaches that comprise Social IoT, Human Bond Communication, and People Centric IoT [26]. Internet of Things offers required results to enormous implementations like industrial management, road traffic overcrowding, emergency facilities, and healthcare. To efficiently govern distant patient healthiness, IoT grounded healthcare applications are obtaining thrust everyday [30, 31]. Through the unceasing growth in Information and Communication Technology (ICT), medical detectors offer an explanation to numerous medical implementations like patient action observation at distant side, analyzing long-lasting illnesses, and giving senior healthcares. Furthermore, accessibility of health IoT devices centrals to an improved method for analysis the sicknesses. Correspondingly, the usage of therapeutic devices, detectors, and analytical gadgets can be seen as smart gadgets making a H-IoT/Health IoT atmosphere. Figure 8.1 depicts the usage of IoT technology in varied networks

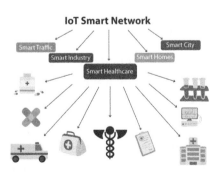

Figure 8.1 IoT network in smart healthcare.

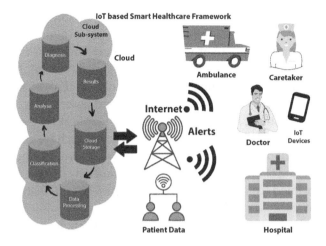

Figure 8.2 IoT-based smart healthcare framework.

which is beneficial for Smart Healthcare. Smart Healthcare network comprises of varied testing services of healthcare, health industries, emergency services, health records, doctors/clinicians/surgeons and caretakers.

Internet of Things supplemented by cloud-computing develops a controlling dais for observing affected ones at distant location offering unceasing health data to clinicians and wardens. Cloud storing provides vast quantity of storage-space and dispensation abilities in a mountable system. Cloud-computing improvements can hold source distribution, corresponding dispensation, information package combination with ascendable information storing, and safety difficulties effortlessly. Additionally, in current situation, observation-based cloud centric structures can be utilized for expansion of apps and facilities beneficial in smart atmosphere [32, 33]. Figure 8.2 showcases the IoT-based Smart Healthcare framework comprising of cloud-computing, its subsystems, its integration with patient data, healthcare facilities, and IoT devices over the Internet.

8.6   Blockchain in Healthcare

There are numerous extents of healthcare and finesses, which can be improved by means of blockchain technology. Blockchain has massive implementations into healthcare. Chief problem in this sector is confidentiality and safety of present histories [34, 35]. Master Patient Identifier or MPI is a sample of Blockchain in healthcare in which a solitary single identifier is utilized for whole healthcare benefactors impeccably. Numerous academics have studied for recognition of affected ones and consent-grounded structures by means of patient verification to exchange information with others through blockchain technology. Others likely the implementation for clearance of dues to the suitable victims and scam recognition deprived of involvement of arbitrators with usages of smart agreements, which is an added characteristic of BC technology. Scam identification could be additional utilization of blockchain. Because of legality, each transaction made is proven. Distribution chain supervision in healthcare can be benefitted from positioning of BC technology by the application of smart agreements, which are printed from crude source to completed item, distribution and subscription particulars [36–41]. One more subtle and utmost significant problem is medication forging in emergent nations in which elements are not at standard mark or nonvigorous elements. Drug forging can be eradicated if confirmation is achieved by the blockchain. There is no well-known noneconomic execution of blockchain, like Bitcoins; a monetary implementation, but a notable contribution of BC tech in healthcare, is an implementation of exact drug and a medical test by means of separate layer of blockchain containing dispersed and corresponding computation architype, storing administration, unidentified supervision, and information distribution managing [36, 42]. Inside medical prosecutions, blockchain could be utilized to get over the glitches of deceitful consequences and elimination of information, that do not back scholar's prejudice or subsidy foundation's purpose. It will apply veracity in medical prosecutions. Additionally, it permits an unchallengeable record to be reserved of experimental patient's permission. With health assurance, several sectors might be benefitted by a reliable record of proceedings round the affected one's path, consisting of enhanced broadcasting around events and mechanizing guaranteeing actions. Health agreements can be evidently helpful in automatic transactions for the patients. The great ability of blockchain usage for EMRs in emerging nations; however, the constructions are immature and is respectable to ponder for upcoming applications. There are still countless chances to discover blockchain use in healthcare network for illustrations, convergence of hospitals, medicinal centers, healthcare start-ups, insurances, and also administrations.

Blockchain found that healthcare structure would permit suppliers to distribute histories with judiciary, brokers, workers, and other sectors with a curiosity in individual's fitness deprived of the significant rise in threat agents, which comes by extending the networks; at last, multidivision organization as safe as the securing at its frail point. Regrettably, blockchain convergence in healthcare is a still long way. Figure 8.3 shows

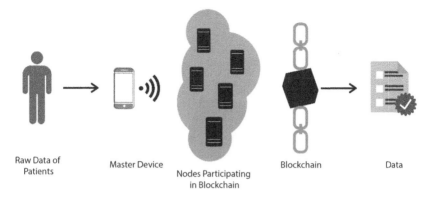

Figure 8.3 Usage of blockchain in healthcare sector.

the process by which a patient's data is passed through the blockchain nodes. On technology-application forepart, there is a necessity to reconstruct database substructure, educate and employ staffs, and to encourage managements that blockchain is valued the economic expense means that networks developed would be restricted to health-based start-ups for predictable forthcoming times [43]. Studies predicted that integration of blockchain with Artificial Intelligence, IoT, and Machine Learning will offer novel chances for digital health economies. Blockchain will give the ability of distributive stage which will disperse the healthcare connections that would safeguard veracity, safety, entree regulation, and legitimacy. It can exhibit new worth-dependent care and settlement structures.

8.7   Integration for Next-Generation Healthcare

Complete exchanges and all the linked information travels over IoT-Blockchain network, to gather an unchallengeable and noticeable documentation of inter-connections. Such a method is beneficial in commercial situations to get consistency and safety but keeping track of all these interconnections enhances bandwidth and information store utilization [44]. Figure 8.4 shows the integration of Blockchain and IoT for next-generation healthcare. Inside pharmacological industries, integration of Blockchain-IoT technology can aid to overcome an expanding threat around fake and illegal unsanctioned drugs. Along with gadget tracing, it is feasible to describe smart agreements for drugs and then recognize capsule vessels, with combined GPS and chain of custody cataloguing [45].

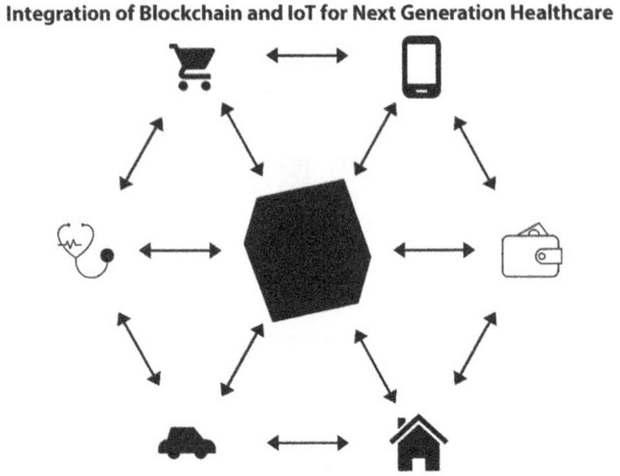

Integration of Blockchain and IoT for Next Generation Healthcare

Figure 8.4 Integration of blockchain and IoT for next-generation healthcare [45].

- ***Clinical Trials***
  Clinical checks, administration of examinations and patient permissions are an arena where the Blockchain-IoT has the capacity to amplify visibility, ascertainability, and answerability of clinical consultants and scholars [46].
- ***Data Distribution***
  Information distribution signifies one of the highest chances for enhancements in healthcare but possess one of the major confidentiality encounters. It is significant to have a countrywide quality for interactions in information technology facilities in healthcare [47].
- ***Drug Tracking***
  Medicine tracing on the IoT-Blockchain integration is added chance as it influences the fixity of the integration to advance tracing and accountability chain from producer to affected one. Benefit of this technology in drug tracing complimentary to outdated form is the regionalization of belief and expert characteristic in values behindhand applications, where fundamental establishments can be corrupted or falsified, it is considerably tougher to induce a compromise of such in the integration. On the condition that medications could be altered and traced using technology's characteristic anti-interfering abilities at the position of production, forged medicines can be totally eliminated from contributing in distribution networks [48]. Drug tracing is a completely dissimilar issue to medicinal gadget tracing, as chief worry is the forging of medicines.

This permits the whole chain of responsibilities to be supervised, guaranteeing that the clinics have accepted the medicines from a genuine basis [13].

- **Patient Records**

  The IoT-blockchain proposes a circumstance for correlations in healthcare networks as taking a dispersed record of recognized statistic in health histories where every healthcare suppliers have entry to these records. It would mean, however, that operator alliances might be dissimilar, its essential record will be indistinguishable crossways to all the suppliers [49].

- **Device Trailing**

  Medicinal gadget tracking is additional chance for IoT-blockchain in disorderly healthcare from producer to withdrawers. Usage of blockchain along with IoT technology provides an option for an absolute record, which showcases not only where the gadget is but also how much it has travelled since manufactured, along with the history of producer, distributor, and sequential quantity that are related with gadget, assisting supervisory amenability. An integral approach serves diverse advantages over localized trailing goods. The utmost understandable of that is perpetuation and interfere-resilient abilities of the integration. It avoids a nasty operator from altering the position antiquity of a gadget or erasing it from record. It is chiefly a vital issue regarding the medicinal gadget robbery and reduction [50]. Evidences of idea have been advanced that brings BC-IoT technologies in healthcare sector though there are numerous barricades for implementations. Important blockade will be the characteristic confrontation of healthcare sector to modify its present usages, particularly connecting to administrative, mechanical, technical, and social agents [51]. Big-Data integration in BC-IoT technology can alter the healthcare sector by quickening worth and novelty, but sector should experience vital variations before shareholders can grab its complete worth. Starting with massively amplified source of data grabbing by web-empowered healthcare data structures, which are currently shared location in maximum present clinic around the world. Since the past 10 years, pharmacological corporations have been amassing ages of studies and growth of information in medicinal records, whereas customers and suppliers have digitalized its affect in one's documents for comfort of victim healthcare administrations and interchangeability. Accordingly, today it is extensively thought that, in upcoming times, the usage of information technology is predicted to decrease the price of healthcare, whereas enlightening its superiority and distribution by creating healthcare more defensive and modified which could effortlessly be adapted to suit more widespread (house-relied) uninterrupted victim observation [52, 53]. Nowadays and in upcoming times, few of the main and important radical efforts are being attach by alliances among clinical and data specialists, with potentials to peer into the upcoming times and recognise health associated issue prior to its occurrence.

8.8   Basic Structure of Convergence

Worldwide smart town systems could assist the healthcare sector as Information Communication Technology carries together Big-data, Smart systems, Blockchain tech, IoT technology, and state-of-art critical study creating it in Smart Healthcare. Healthcare develops as the chief socioeconomic difficulties due to elderly inhabitants although it possesses innovative encounters in old-style health facilities due to inadequate medical supplies. The new SARS-CoV-2 or 2019 novel coronavirus or 2019-nCoV disease has exposed in what way complete countrywide well-being facilities can drive into catastrophe. Fresh improvements into fields of habiliment health gadgets in health information convey chances in advancement of distant health facilities at household or in hospitals. Confidentiality guarding and safety guarantee are critical and still posed difficulties. Safeguarding IoT instruments working on healthcare systems using a blockchain technology can possibly get over such issues. Griggs *et al.* [54] offered a structure in which information produced by therapeutic detectors are accomplished and distributed by use of smart agreements. Through entire process, secrecy can be acquired due to Blockchain technology. A ground-breaking answer has been presented by Rahman *et al.* [55] where a Blockchain-IoT based edge computing outline is utilized for an in-house treatment administration.

- *Robust Atmosphere*
  Integration of urbanization and globalization provides unparalleled encounters to the sector; so, their organization must be robust to outward tremor and guarantee feasibility for healthcare.
- *Interoperable and Versatile*
  To empower the interconnectedness of each bodily item, the ICT would be the interaction. Likely, an IoT stage for smart house

implementations that can be regulated from anyplace and offers home information to the cloud substructure.

- **Decision Support System**
  Smart cities comprised of multifaceted and varied structures that seek to discover equilibrium among financial growth, development, and ecological necessities. It sets off difficulties for strategy creators, so extremely compatible choice making approaches shall be utilized to regulate ideal resolutions.

- **Behavior Monitoring**
  The usage of computerized recreations is mandatory to pretend adaptive behavior. Because of web, mutual association series generate designed conduct information which is demonstrated in intercommunication among financial, communal and corporal structures that represents the systems of structures.

- **Energy Sources and Distribution**
  The superiority of energy distributions and reusable sources has become a significant need which might be undertaken. So, a dispersive technology shall be embraced in the energy network systems and in other arenas too.

- **Smart Infrastructure**
  To create a maintainable smart town, all of the persons require to labor composed permitted by smart structures.

- **Scalability**
  Smart towns comprise of huge quantity of software and hardware apparatuses where numerous facilities offer to its residents the capability of its substructure to gather and proceed real-time information. Consequently, a dispersed IoT-blockchain cloud infrastructure is necessary for supportable towns.

- **Safe Infrastructure**
  In an exertion to defend systems and information from different dangers, keeping a watch on hateful actions, verification, approval of things and supplementary system regulation strategies shall be advanced to shelter and defend the supportable smart healthcare [56].

Distant observation is a significant example for countless real-life implementations. These days, globally, there are countless individuals whose well-being may agonize because of deficiency of operative healthcare observation. Aged, kids, or long-lastingly diseased persons required to be inspected nearly every day. The option of distant observation structure will assist to evade creating circles of clinic for examination. Due to carping position, occasionally their fitness gets ignored till illnesses progress in disaster phase. Distant access detector aids caretakers to have pre analysis and previous interference prior becoming wrongful [57]. Although BC-IoT technology is in its early stages, enthusiasm for probable implementation is rising. Explanations for authenticated distribution of health information, comprising information produced by vestures and other IoT gadgets, would become progressively significant to persons who need superior entree to their own information. Outside the clinic, integration of Blockchain-IoT technology assures a resolution which could authorize affected ones, and sustenance for better clarity among healthcare experts. Evolving and challenging new strategies on real-life cases, like information distribution among clinical structures, offers an initial place in representing the supremacy of BC-IoT to disrupt down information stores in healthcare [58].

8.9　Challenges

Integrating blockchain with IoT will have numerous advantages. As the noteworthy progressions have occurred in the field of the healthcare sector due to IoT, safety, & veracity of healthcare information became giant difficulty for healthcare facilities implementations. Nevertheless, Blockchain-IoT technology is not a faultless archetypal, it has its faults and problems. Figure 8.5 depicts the security issues in the convergence of IoT and Blockchain. These difficulties could be briefed as follows:

A.　Scalability
Scalability matters in BC-IoT might provoke centralism, or, at finishing may overshadow the probable fate of cryptographics. Blockchain balances incompetently as quantity of center opinions

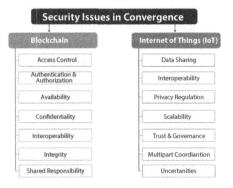

Figure 8.5 Depicting security issues of IoT and blockchain in convergence.

in the context upsurges. The IoT structures are relied on to comprise a substantial amount of center points [59].

B. *Processing Power and Time*

Formulating power and period predicted to achieve encoding for each of the objects combined into the BC-IoT basis. IoT workings have different types of devices that having absolutely dissimilar registration capabilities, and not each of them would have an ability to process same encoding controls at desired rapidity [60].

C. *Storage*

The sole quality favourites of BC-IoT is that it gets free of the requirement for a dominant server to hoard trades and device identities, so far histories should be protected in central nodes. Streamed records would enlarge in dimensions as period passes by and with spreading amount of center points in an outline. As described earlier, IoT machines have little automated sources and short storage opinion of internment [61].

D. *Lack of Skills*

Blockchain-IoT novelty is still innovative. By this pass, two of persons have considerable data and abilities about BC-IoT, chiefly in management of an account. In dissimilar implementations, there is unlimited nonappearance of understanding of in what way BC-IoT technology works. IoT devices occur at all sites, so getting Blockchain along with IoT tech would be remarkably worrying deprived of exposed mindfulness about the convergence [62].

E. *Legal and Compliance*

Integration of Blockchain and IoT technology is other novelty which will be able to subordinate characteristic persons from numerous countries without having any genuine or consistence code to follow or problem for 2 manufacturers and expert administrations which will be the noteworthy obstacle for getting BC-IoT in many establishments and implementations [63].

F. *Naming and Discovery*

Blockchain expansion has not been deliberated for IoT technology, signifying that centers were not predicted to discover one other in context. The classical structure is Bitcoin implementation in that IP positions of a couple of "senders" presented inside the Bitcoin client and used by centers to manufacture the framework topology. Such plan does not function for IoT as IoT gadgets will be always showing movement all time which would alter the network topology endlessly [64]. By means of an instance of a clinic or healthcare suppliers, loosely managed victim information enhances the dangers that an affected one would be diagnosed wrongly, treated erroneously, or which test consequences become lost or tainted. There is also a worry that two touch-points on a victim's therapy trip may have dissimilar data sets for the same individual. Thus, inserting healthcare records on blockchain will make a sole, unalterable source for doctors to usage while serving an affected one [64]. Most noteworthy advantage BC-IoT can provide in healthcare is safety. As an instance, in USA, insurers, such as Anthem, UCLA Health, and numerous others, vanished more than 100m victim histories to hackers in 2015, an opening that kept affected ones at threat of identity theft. Below BC-IoT, even a clinician may need numerous official "signs" or consents from supplementary portions of a system to handle victim histories [65, 66].

8.10   Conclusion

The IoT technologies-blockchain convergence paradigm is changing the smart healthcare industry. Combining blockchain with IoT technology will authorize the shared enlightening, documentation movement, and self-decision co-ordination among IoT gadgets with no requirement for the focused server-client appearance. Blockchain & IoT technology with its dispersed documented novelty has grabbed the marketplace's thought for its data trade with abilities like regionalization and safety. With the normally actual use in the currency associated arenas, diverse undertakings presently comprehend its benefits and are examining the ability of blockchain in its places. Medical facilities are one such sector captivating a look at introducing benefits of this integration. A part of important medical amenities implementations is chattered nowadays. The faultless condition for blockchain-IoT for EHRs is to retain a real-life medical record and be open to group comprising clinicians, laboratory experts, and others for motive of rumination. In present implementations of EHRs, forbearing data are put aside transverse through different connotations through affected life. Blockchain-IoT into medical study is a widespread headway in stirring curative data from documents to electronic accounts, medical facilities business is employed through the problems concerning to distribution of victim data over providers and relations. Affected ones can directly regulate their medical data and propriety to allow or revert info admittance to elderly figures and families. Blockchain-IoT in Drug Distribution Chain Administration is one of the chief encounters in pharmacological corporate and is lacking secure portions in the network.

As a result, IoT-Blockchain convergence will aid in transforming healthcare industry. Integration of uprising technologies will be a good platform for investors and researchers too. Such an integration between varied technologies will be beneficial in the future in terms of different networks.

References

1. Nakamoto, S. Bitcoin: A peer-to-peer electronic cash system. 2008. https://bitcoin.org/bitcoin.pdf

2. Ahram, T., Sargolzaei, A., Sargolzaei, S., Daniels, J., Amaba, B., Blockchain technology innovations, in: *2017 IEEE Technology & Engineering Management Conference (TEMSCON)*, IEEE, pp. 137–141, 2017, June.

3. Devibala, A., A survey on security issues in IoT for blockchain healthcare, in: *2019 IEEE International Conference on Electrical, Computer and Communication Technologies (ICECCT)*, IEEE, pp. 1–7, 2019, February.

4. Singh, S., Sharma, P.K., Yoon, B., Shojafar, M., Cho, G.H., Ra, I.H., Convergence of blockchain and artificial intelligence in IoT network for the sustainable smart city. *Sustain. Cities Soc.*, 63, 102364, 2020.

5. Mohril, S., Sankhla, M. S., Sonone, S. S., Kumar, R. Blockchain IoT concepts for smart grids, smart cities and smart homes, in: *Blockchain and IoT Integration: Approaches and Applications*, pp. 103–122, 2021.

6. Conoscenti, M., Vetro, A., De Martin, J.C., Blockchain for the Internet of Things: A systematic literature review, in: *2016 IEEE/ACS 13th International Conference of Computer Systems and Applications (AICCSA)*, IEEE, pp. 1–6, 2016 November.

7. Reyna, A., Martín, C., Chen, J., Soler, E., Díaz, M., On blockchain and its integration with IoT. Challenges and opportunities. *Future Gener. Comput. Syst.*, 88, 173–190, 2018.

8. Atlam, H.F., Alenezi, A., Alassafi, M.O., Wills, G., Blockchain with internet of things: Benefits, challenges, and future directions. *Int. J. Intell. Syst. Appl.*, 10, 6, 40–48, 2018.

9. Murray, A., Papa, A., Cuozzo, B., Russo, G., Evaluating the innovation of the Internet of Things: Empirical evidence from the intellectual capital assessment. *Bus. Process Manag. J.*, 22, 2, 341–356, 2016.

10. Bahga, A. and Madisetti, V.K., Blockchain platform for industrial internet of things. *J. Software Eng. Appl.*, 9, 10, 533–546, 2016.

11. Pieroni, A., Scarpato, N., Di Nunzio, L., Fallucchi, F., Raso, M., Smarter city: smart energy grid based on blockchain technology. *Int. J. Adv. Sci. Eng. Inf. Technol.*, 8, 1, 298–306, 2018.

12. Orecchini, F., Santiangeli, A., Zuccari, F., Pieroni, A., Suppa, T., Blockchain technology in smart city: A new opportunity for smart environment and smart mobility, in: *International Conference on Intelligent Computing & Optimization*, Springer, Cham, pp. 346–354, 2018, October.

13. Atlam, H.F., Alenezi, A., Alassafi, M.O., Wills, G., Blockchain with Internet of Things: Benefits, challenges, and future directions. *Int. J. Intell. Syst. Appl.*, 10, 6, 40–48, 2018.

14. Reyna, A., Martín, C., Chen, J., Soler, E., Díaz, M., On blockchain and its integration with IoT. Challenges and opportunities. *Future Gener. Comput. Syst.*, 88, 173–190, 2018.

15. Ahram, T., Sargolzaei, A., Sargolzaei, S., Daniels, J., Amaba, B., Blockchain technology innovations, in: *2017 IEEE Technology & Engineering Management Conference (TEMSCON)*, IEEE, pp. 137–141, 2017, June.

16. Bjorklund, M. YANG-a data modeling language for the network configuration protocol (NETCONF). *Internet Engineering Task Force (IETF)*, 2010. Available at https://www.hjp.at/doc/rfc/rfc6020.html.

17. Christ, M.J., Tri, R.N.P., Chandra, W., Gunawan, W., Exploring blockchain in healthcare industry, in: *2019 International Conference on ICT for Smart Society (ICISS)*, vol. 7, IEEE, pp. 1–4, 2019, November.

18. Suksmono, A. and Rahayu, W., Towards sharable and longitudinal medical records for e-health in Indonesia using an Australian-based openEHR standard. *Australia Indonesia Covernance Reserach Partnership 2010*, 2010.

19. Wan, J., Zou, C., Ullah, S., Lai, C.F., Zhou, M., Wang, X., Cloud-enabled wireless body area networks for pervasive healthcare. *IEEE Netw.*, 27, 5, 56–61, 2013.

20. Kim, G.-H., Trimi, S., Chung, J.-H., Big-data applications in the government sector. *Commun. ACM*, 57, 3, 78–85, 2014.

21. Hill, J.W. and Powell, P., The national healthcare crisis: Is eHealth a key solution? *Bus. Horiz.*, 52, 3, 265–277, 2009.

22. Safadi, H., Chan, D., Dawes, M., Roper, M., Faraj, S., Open-source health information technology: A case study of electronic medical records. *Health Policy Technol.*, 4, 1, 14–28, 2015.

23. Aslam, U., Sohail, A., Aziz, H., II, Vistro, D.M., *The Importance of Preserving the Anonymity in Healthcare Data: A Survey.*

24. Cosío-León, M.A., Ojeda-Carreño, D., Nieto-Hipólito, J., II, Ibarra-Hernández, J.A., The use of standards in embedded devices to achieve end to end semantic interoperability on health systems. *Comput. Stand. Interfaces*, 57, 68–73, 2018.

25. Vallette, M.A. and Caldwell, B.S., Activity cycles and information alignment in healthcare information flow, in: *Proceedings of the 2012 Symposium on Human Factors and Ergonomics in Healthcare: Bridging the Gap*, p. 127, 2012.

26. Wang, F.Y., Toward a revolution in transportation operations: AI for complex systems. *IEEE Intell. Syst.*, 23, 6, 8–13, 2008.

27. Sadek, A.W., Artificial intelligence applications in transportation. *Transp. Res. Circ.*, 1, 1–7, 2007.

28. Dhanvijay, M.M. and Patil, S.C., Internet of Things: A survey of enabling technologies in healthcare and its applications. *Comput. Netw.*, 153, 113–131, 2019.

29. Perumal, K. and Manohar, M., A survey on Internet of Things: Case studies, applications, and future directions, in: *Internet of Things: Novel Advances and Envisioned Applications*, pp. 281–297, Springer, Cham, 2017.

30. Atzori, L., Iera, A., Morabito, G., The Internet of Things: A survey. *Comput. Netw.*, 54, 15, 2787–2805, 2010.

31. Baig, M.M. and Gholamhosseini, H., Smart health monitoring systems: An overview of design and modeling. *J. Med. Syst.*, 37, 2, 9898, 2013.

32. Melillo, P., Orrico, A., Scala, P., Crispino, F., Pecchia, L., Cloud-based smart health monitoring system for automatic cardiovascular and fall risk assessment in hypertensive patients. *J. Med. Syst.*, 39, 10, 109, 2015.

33. Xu, B., Xu, L., Cai, H., Jiang, L., Luo, Y., Gu, Y., The design of an m-Health monitoring system based on a cloud computing platform. *Enterp. Inf. Syst.*, 11, 1, 17–36, 2017.

34. Li, S., Da Xu, L., Zhao, S., The Internet of Things: A survey. *Inf. Syst. Front.*, 17, 2, 243–259, 2015.

35. Rizwan, P. and Suresh, K., Design and development of low investment smart hospital using Internet of Things through innovative approaches. *Biomed. Res.*, 28, 11, 4 979–4 985, 2017.

36. Bell, L., Buchanan, W.J., Cameron, J., Lo, O., Applications of blockchain within healthcare. *BHTY*, 1, 1–7, 2018.

37. Ekblaw, A., Azaria, A., Halamka, J.D., Lippman, A., A case study for blockchain in healthcare: "MedRec" prototype for electronic health records and medical research data, in: *Proceedings of IEEE Open & Big Data Conference*, vol. 13, p. 13, 2016, August.

38. Mettler, M., Blockchain technology in healthcare: The revolution starts here, in: *2016 IEEE 18th International Conference on e-health Networking, Applications and Services (Healthcom)*, IEEE, pp. 1–3.

39. Sohaib, O., Solanki, H., Dhaliwa, N., Hussain, W., Asif, M., Integrating design thinking into extreme programming. *J. Ambient Intell. Humaniz. Comput.*, 10, 6, 2485–2492, 2019.

40. N.J. Witchey, . U.S. Patent No. 10,340,038. Washington, DC, U.S. Patent and Trademark Office, 2019.

41. Nath, I., Data exchange platform to fight insurance fraud on blockchain, in: *2016 IEEE 16th International Conference on Data Mining Workshops (ICDMW)*, IEEE Computer Society, pp. 821–825, 2016, December.

42. Sohaib, O., Kang, K., Miliszewska, I., Uncertainty avoidance and consumer cognitive innovativeness in e-commerce. *J. Glob. Inf. Manage. (JGIM)*, 27, 2, 59–77, 2019.

43. Smyth, D., Why blockchain? What can it do for big data?, 2016. Available at http://bigdata-madesimple.com/why-blockchain-what-can-it-do-for-big-data-2/ [Access Date – 11/6/2020].

44. Dagher, G.G., Mohler, J., Milojkovic, M., Marella, P.B., Ancile: Privacy-preserving framework for access control and interoperability of electronic

health records using blockchain technology. *Sustain. Cities Soc.*, 39, 283–297, 2018.

45. Schumacher, A., Blockchain & Healthcare Strategy Guide 2017: Reinventing healthcare: Towards a global, blockchain-based precision medicine ecosystem, 2017.

46. Maroufi, M., Abdolee, R., Tazekand, B.M., On the convergence of blockchain and Internet of Things (IoT), Technologies. 24, 1904-1936, 2019, arXiv preprint arXiv:1904.01936.

47. Bell, L., Buchanan, W.J., Cameron, J., Lo, O., Applications of blockchain within healthcare. *BHTY*, 1, 1–7, 2018.

48. F. Curbera, D. M. Dias, V. Simonyan, W. A. Yoon and A. Casella, "Blockchain: An enabler for healthcare and life sciences transformation," in *IBM Journal of Research and Development*, 63, 2/3, 8:1–8:9, March-May 2019, doi: 10.1147/JRD.2019.2913622.

49. Wachter, R., *Making IT work: harnessing the power of health information technology to improve care in England*, Department of Health, London, UK, 2016.

50. Bacheldor, B., Pfizer Prepares for Viagra E-Pedigree Trial. *RFID Journal*, Feburary 2007, 2007.

51. Azaria, A., Ekblaw, A., Vieira, T., Lippman, A., Medrec: Using blockchain for medical data access and permission management, in: *2016 2nd International Conference on Open and Big Data (OBD)*, IEEE, pp. 25–30, 2016, August.

52. Manyika, J., Chui, M., Brown, B., Bughin, J., Dobbs, R., Roxburgh, C., Hung Byers, A., *Big data: The next frontier for innovation, competition, and productivity*, McKinsey Global Institute, New York, 2011.

53. Gianchandani, E., Can computer science save healthcare?. The CCC Blog, 2011. Available at https://cccblog.org/2011/11/11/can-computer-science-save-healthcare/

54. Griggs, K.N., Ossipova, O., Kohlios, C.P., Baccarini, A.N., Howson, E.A., Hayajneh, T., Healthcare blockchain system using smart contracts for secure automated remote patient monitoring. *J. Med. Syst.*, 42, 7, 130, 2018.

55. Rahman, M.A., Hossain, M.S., Loukas, G., Hassanain, E., Rahman, S.S., Alhamid, M.F., Guizani, M., Blockchain-based mobile edge computing framework for secure therapy applications. *IEEE Access*, 6, 72469–72478, 2018.

56. Executive Report, Healthcare rallies for blockchains, IBM Institute for Business Value survey conducted by The Economist Intelligence Unit. 2016 Available at https://www.ibm.com/downloads/cas/BBRQK3WY

57. Sligo, J., Gauld, R., Roberts, V., Villa, L., A literature review for large-scale health information system project planning, implementation and evaluation. *Int. J. Med. Inform.*, 97, 86–97, 2017.

58. Iqbal, A., Ullah, F., Anwar, H., Kwak, K.S., Imran, M., Jamal, W., ur Rahman, A., Interoperable Internet-of-Things platform for smart home system using web-of-objects and cloud. *Sustain. Cities. Soc.*, 3, 8, 636–646, 2018.

59. Chiuchisan, I., Costin, H.N., Geman, O., Adopting the Internet of Things technologies in healthcare systems, in: *2014 International Conference and Exposition on Electrical and Power Engineering (EPE)*, IEEE, pp. 532–535, 2014, October.

60. Cyran, M.A., Blockchain as a foundation for sharing healthcare data. *BHTY*, 1, 1–6, 2018.

61. Kouicem, D.E., Bouabdallah, A., Lakhlef, H., Internet of Things security: A top-down survey. *Comput. Netw.*, 141, 199–221, 2018.

62. Esposito, C., De Santis, A., Tortora, G., Chang, H., Choo, K.K.R., Blockchain: A panacea for healthcare cloud-based data security and privacy? *IEEE Cloud Comput.*, 5, 1, 31–37, 2018.

63. Kshetri, N., Blockchain's roles in strengthening cybersecurity and protecting privacy. *Telecomm. Policy*, 41, 10, 1027–1038, 2017.

64. Swan, M., *Blockchain: Blueprint for a new economy*, O'Reilly Media, Inc., Sebastopol, California, 2015.

65. Leiding, B., Cap, C.H., Mundt, T., Rashidibajgan, S., *Authcoin: Validation and Authentication in Decentralized Networks*, 2016, arXiv preprint arXiv:1609.04955.

66. Kaushik, A., Choudhary, A., Ektare, C., Thomas, D., Akram, S., Blockchain—Literature survey, in: *2017 2nd IEEE International Conference on Recent Trends in Electronics, Information & Communication Technology (RTEICT)*, IEEE, pp. 2145–2148, 2017, May.

9

Disease Prediction Using Machine Learning for Healthcare

S. Vijayalakshmi[1]* and Ashutosh Upadhyay[2]

[1]*Department of Data Science, Christ University, Bangalore, Karnataka, India*
[2]*Computer Science and Engineering Medi-Caps University, Indore, India*

Abstract

Machine learning has an application in healthcare, one such application is disease prediction. Because of industrialization and construction, the pollution in the cities has been increased, which gave birth to the critical diseases. We could easily identify that the living habits of a human being is changed because of working condition and work pressure. Identification of disease at an earlier stage is a very crucial job. The early prediction of a disease by a doctor is a challenging task because it requires a huge amount of data to make accurate prediction and to take preventive action. The data are collected over time in a hospital utilized to predict disease, and further, we can do mortality analysis to utilize hospital resources. If we could predict a pandemic, like COVID-19 and number of patients who are going to be affected accurately, then accordingly, we can plan resources and suggest precautions to prevent it from spreading. Prediction models are based on analyzing data using k-means clustering, K-Nearest Neighbor (KNN), and Convolution Neural Network (CNN). Disease prediction consists data of living style and routine check-up information of a person. The CNN prediction is recorded to be near about 84.5%. The prediction algorithm, which utilizes the benefits of CNN and big data analytics, reported a 94.8% accuracy.

Keywords: Data analytics, machine learning algorithms, decision tree, random forest, healthcare, KNN, naive bayes, CNN

*Corresponding author: svijisuji@gmail.com
S. Vijayalakshmi: ORCID: 0000-0002-0310-5495
Ashutosh Upadhyay: ORCID: 0000-0003-0771-9459

T. Poongodi, D. Sumathi, B. Balamurugan and K. S. Savita (eds.) Digitization of Healthcare Data Using Blockchain, (181–202) © 2022 Scrivener Publishing LLC

9.1   Introduction to Disease Prediction

Disease is a deviation from the normal functional or structural behavior of an animal. Prediction is the forecasting of any outcome based on history of records; hence, disease prediction is the mechanism of forecasting a potential disease that a person may have, depending on the patient's check-up reports. We can understand disease prediction better with the help of Figure 9.1.

Figure 9.1 shows the steps involved in the disease prediction. We need patient details with check-up information as data sets. It may be X-ray, endoscopy, MRI, ultrasound or any other medical information. All the mentioned information may be in the form of images; hence, image data set is formed. Then features are selected from data sets based on the disease being dealt with. Preprocessing is performed to clean our data sets like noise removal. The prediction model thus formed is used to predict the disease.

Diseases, like diabetes, migraine, jaundice, malaria, and COVID-19, may cause a significant issue on health and sometimes may become the reason for death if not taken as a serious disease.

9.1.1   Artificial Intelligence in Healthcare

Artificial intelligence (AI) is referred to the intelligence of machines. As we use simple word intelligence for human and other living organism. Machine intelligence is proceeding with word artificial as this is imparted by human in machine as opposed to the intelligence of humans or other living species [1]. Artificial intelligence may also be defined as the any

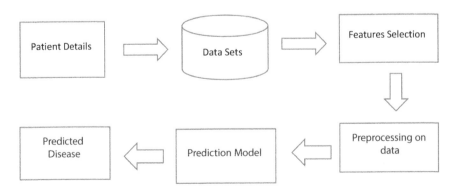

Figure 9.1 Flow diagram of disease prediction.

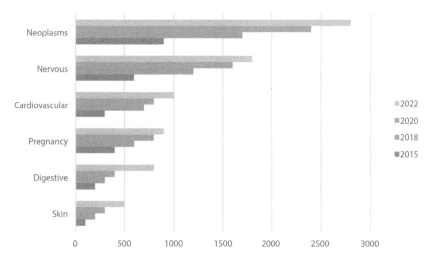

Figure 9.2 AI in disease prediction.

device and agent that has ability to perceive and understand its surroundings and, based on the situation, is capable enough to take suitable action [2]. In simple words, we can say that AI is target that we want to achieve and machine learning (ML) algorithms are ways to achieve AI. Artificial intelligence covers different fields of science and engineering. In this section, the focus is on the use of AI in healthcare sector. Artificial intelligence is used in biomedical information processing, biomedical research, and disease diagnosis and prediction. Although AI literature in healthcare [4–8] is becoming increasingly rich, research focuses principally on a few types of diseases: skin, digestive, pregnancy, cardio, nervous system disease, and cardiovascular diseases and neoplasms as shown in Figure 9.2.

9.1.2 Data Collection and Information Processing

The data collection and its processing are very important in the field of AI. The prediction accuracy highly depends on the data collection and its processing. Data processing is the process of translation of collected raw usable data. This work is generally done by a team of data scientists. Information processing must be done correctly to avoid the negative effect on the final result. Information processing generally starts with raw data and convert into more understandable formats like graphs and documents, making interpretation easier. In Figure 9.3, the steps of data processing are shown.

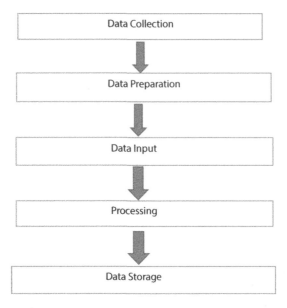

Figure 9.3 Steps in data processing.

a) **Data Collection:** Data collection is the very first step in data processing. Data can be pulled from many sources, for example, company database, organization warehouse, or websites. It is very important that the data collected are from reliable and trustworthy sources.

b) **Data Preparation:** After collecting data, data preparation stage starts, it generally refers to "preprocessing" of data. Data are cleaned and organized for the subsequent stages. During data preparation, data are checked for errors. The purpose of this stage is to remove incomplete, redundant, inconsistent, and incorrect data.

c) **Data Input:** The cleaned data enter into another stage that is data input stage, here we take cleaned data as input to the tools like anaconda, azure, AWS, and salesforce. This is first stage where data start taking usable form.

d) **Processing:** Data are taken as input to the computer in previous steps proceeds to data interpretation. The process is performed using the ML algorithms and statistical data analysis approaches. The technique selected for interpretation may depend upon the type of data sets.

e) **Data Storage:** Storage is the final stage of data processing, after all the steps, data are stored for the future use.

Data should be properly stored to be retrieved quickly and easily whenever needed.

9.1.3   Human Living Standard and Possible Diseases

Lifestyle is referred to the pattern of living shown by people or group of people in specific geographical reason. Life style is considered as the characteristics of living organism of specific place and time.

According to the data presented by the World Health Organization, about 60% factors to health and quality of life is related to lifestyle [3]. Because of work life balance millions of people of country follow unhealthy lifestyle. According to studies it is proved that human life style has significant influence on human health. The parameters like diet and body mass, exercise, sleep, addiction to certain toxic substances, medication abuse, excessive use of modern technology, recreation and study hours. The listed parameter value can be used to predict the probable human disease based on the life style of human being.

9.1.4   Importance of Data in Disease Prediction

The prediction of disease in early stage is very important in healthcare informatics. The disease like diabetes, arthritis, cancer, stokes shows early symptoms and hence detection of these disease before they show actual symptoms becomes very crucial task, and helps in taking prevention and effective treatment in the early stage to save the patient life. At present the storage of patent details and records of the patients related to the test and their life style information at the hospital is very crucial task as the number of patients is very large and each records have several attributes. From the patient data, it becomes very difficult to fetch relevant features becomes very difficult and human effort has limit on analyzing the data. The patient data are very critical and we cannot afford the errors, data must be of utmost quality to avoid the false prediction. The data may contain some useless information that cannot be identified by a human may leads to inconsistencies in the data sets. So, facilitate all these information we need to select proper data preparation techniques and tools. The prediction becomes more accurate and precise if data are relevant and free from redundancy and missing values.

From available data sets selecting features and then reducing the dimension of the features is important [13–15].

9.2   Data Analytics for Disease Prediction

The disease prediction evolves the process of data examination and then infer some conclusions. This is same as the term data analytics. We can apply the tools and techniques of data analytics to find out some patterns and then we can predict the trends [9–12].

Analytics in the field of healthcare gives new information to the health professionals, which is actually processed and managed by expert data scientists. The data analytics future holds more promising predictive analytics. The aim of data analytics is to predict the disease not only detect the disease. The data analysis is first steps of the analytics. The analysis involves the statistical methods to analyse the data but analytics include AI and ML approaches to create a predictive model. These ML tools can be applied to derive inherent meaning of specific patient population data, by considering the factors like gender, lifestyle and geography.

Recent advancement in the field of data science and ML have led to various possibilities to accelerate the process of diagnosis and check whether treatment is working properly and how is impact of the treatment. Collectively we can say the overall aim is to enhance the quality and duration of the patient life with effective and reduced cost. As an example, let's take a tour how the approach of recent technology is used to treat patient well. How these predictive models are prepared and how these models work into more details in upcoming sections.

9.3   Segmentation and Features of Medical Images

The discussion shows that for the predictive model design first we need to clean the data and then select the features. The patient's data are mainly in the form of the image. So, for the feature selection the image needs to be segmented which means breaking the whole image into small meaningful segments. The division of the images into the small regions with similar properties is called segmentation. The accurate segmentation of the medical image is key factor during medical image analysis. Here some segmentation techniques are presented.

The available medical image segmentation techniques are based on the application. Like it depends on the part of human body under consideration. For example, the segmentation of brain image will be different from that of segmentation of the nose and neck because the features that affect the brain image is different from the artefacts that affects the nose and neck. So, while selecting any segmentation algorithm it is important to keep all these into mind.

The different artefacts are mentioned here

- Partial volume
- Motion
- Ring
- Noise, etc.

There is lack of universal algorithm for segmentation which we can use for all type of the images. So, the categories of segmentation techniques for the medical images are shown in Figure 9.4.

As shown in Figure 9.4 the segmentation is broadly divided into two parts based on discontinuity and based on similarity. The edge-based segmentation is based on discontinuity. The edge-based segmentation is applied an edge filter is applied which filters out the edge and non-edge pixels. Region based, threshold based, neural network based, clustering based, and wavelet-based algorithms are based on the similarity among the pixel values.

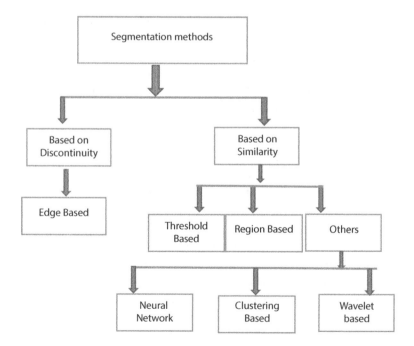

Figure 9.4 Segmentation techniques classification.

Recent research now a day's use model which is based on deep neural networks and which gives better prediction accuracy as compared to traditional approach-based algorithms. Sometimes we can divide the segmentation algorithms based on the features of the grey level.

Methods based on grey Level features

    a) Amplitude segmentation based on histogram features
    b) Region based segmentation
    c) Edge based segmentation

The data set in the field of medical science is generally in the form of images like x-ray, ultrasound, MRI etc. So, most of the time we deal with images to find the features from data set.

9.4   Prediction Model for Healthcare

What is predictive modeling? Predictive modeling uses ML, data mining and statistics to identify pattern in data. The process of building an accurate predictive model involves problem definition and data collection. Predictive modeling is used in nearly every field of science and technology. The models are capable of predicting the sports results, now a days it is used to predict the playing eleven of the team which is very important for the person who make team on various application for bidding purpose. Predictive modeling is also used to predict the ratings of a particular show based on the trailer and history of the actors working in that show and many other factors taken under consideration. Predictive modeling generally uses the terminology like predictive analytics, ML and analysis using statistics. This terminology is used frequently and interchangeably. The analysis is generally referring to the first phase of the data processing means summarizing the data based on the features by using different statistical techniques and then visualizing the data using different visualization tools like matplotlib library in python and other tools. But analytics is more advance term in modeling which consist of analysis as well as use of ML algorithms. Analytics is generally performed at commercial level and predictive modeling term is more often used in academia. In research predictive modeling is more frequently used. Predictive modeling is useful because it gives facility to do more insight of data, which is very large in size. The extraction of any insight from that data is really very difficult by human effort without utilizing machine. Predictive modeling is not only used in the abovementioned areas but also in the field of the healthcare.

In field of medical science nearly all the type of the ML algorithm is used, which also includes the human disease prediction. Just like other application, data are different for disease prediction. Traction data, like customer service data, polling data, and economic data, and so on, are different data used for different types of predictive modeling.

The steps of modeling process are shown in Figure 9.5.

The predictive model is created with the predictor variables, which eventually affects the results. Model can be designed using simple linear equation or it can be designed using complex nonlinear equation. The model can be created using simple neural network or deep neural network. The selection of predictive equation depends on the nature of the data. Data analyst generally use different assessment models to solve the underlying problems and then finally select the model which is giving best solution. The model with the best result validated and tested and then finally executed using real word data.

For example, suppose a patient of certain age group and medical history presents himself/herself with new diagnosed condition then predictive model consider it as a new condition and the patient related will be populated with similar characteristics to develop plan for treatment. Applying

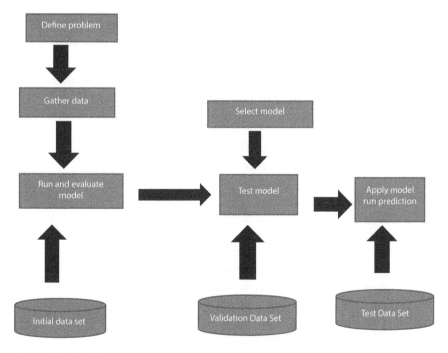

Figure 9.5 Modeling process.

predictive modeling helps doctor, staff, and other workers to receive notification about potential threat and risks, so than they can prepared themselves for future. For example, avoiding readmission, preventing suicide and self-harm, developing precise treatment and recording patient reaction.

The data analytics or predictive analytics and modeling is mainly categorized into four types.

1. **Descriptive Analytics**
   Descriptive analytics is mainly used to describe the data. Descriptive analysis is mainly deals with the questions like how many versus how many? Means it will try to find out the answer in numbers. For example, a car manufacturing company sold out the 2000k cars in first quarter and 45000k in second quarter. Then if we perform the descriptive analytics then we would be able to answer the questions like the how many cars were sold in first quarter versus and how many cars were sold in second quarter.

2. **Diagnostic Analytics**
   If we ask why from predictive analytics, it will become descriptive analytics. For example, in example given above the diagnostic analytics makes a further investigation. The analyst can go further by asking why the sales in the second quarter was greater as compared to the sales in the first quarter. They can analyse the data related to investment in advertisement in first quarter verses investment in second quarter or number of sales men working in first and second quarter and many other factors which may affect the sale. Then they can conclude that the increase in the sale was due to more investment in the second quarter.

3. **Predictive Analytics**
   Third type o analytics is predictive analytics which deals with the ML and data mining-based techniques to build the predictive modeling. Its aims to find out the trends to make a preventive decision so that we can perform the action before it actually happens. It actually cannot predict the future accurately but it can find out the trend but looking at the past data and will able to predict the most suitable outcome which it near to the actual future value.

Data scientist can build predictive models only when they have enough data to generalize predicted outcomes. The company makes a model for investment in the advertisement and the investment in increasing the sales force by analyzing the trends in the data.

4. **Prescriptive Analytics**
This is the last stage of the data modeling that is called prescriptive analytics. In this steps data scientist takes the steps to take decision based on the model suggestion. Once the prescriptive data analytics is in place model starts giving recommendations based on the past data and applied ML algorithms. Now we will explore some of the models used in the healthcare sector.

9.5   Introduction to ML

The brief introduction of ML is presented in this section to get familiar with how we can use ML approaches to form predict model for the healthcare sector. ML becomes a buzzword for the past few years, the reason behind it the large amount of data produces by different sources. ML used in the task of automation and offering intelligent insight and healthcare. Here I am listing some of the applications of ML in brief.

- **Prediction:** ML can be used in the modeling of prediction systems. Considering the stock example, to predict the price of a stock, the model should analyse the trends and predict the future price.
- **Image recognition:** ML is used for face detection and recognition in an image as well as in video. There is a separate category for each person in a database of several people.
- **Speech Recognition:** ML can be used to translate of verbal language to text language. It can be used in voice searches. Voice dialling, Google voice interface for searching, call routing, and appliance control. Nowadays, this is also used for the data entry user interfaces
- **Medical diagnoses:** ML is used in disease prediction, mortality prediction and also recognize different disease like cancer.

- **Financial industry:** Companies use ML in fraud detection, investigations, and transactions checks.

ML can be grouped into three categories:

a) Supervised Learning

In a supervised approach, data are presented to system, i.e., well-levelled data are available for training and testing. As shown in Figure 9.6.

As shown in Figure 9.6, we initially given some data and marked them as original data and some faulty data. The levelled data are used for training, once trained, we can test our model. The supervised models perform two tasks.

- **Classification:** A classification is the process of dividing test data into the category. For example cat, dog, red, black, disease, no disease.
- **Regression:** A problem is said to be regression problem when the output is real values variable, such as weight, height.

b) Unsupervised Learning

In unsupervised learning, the ML system is given unlevelled and uncategorized data and system act on the data without any training.

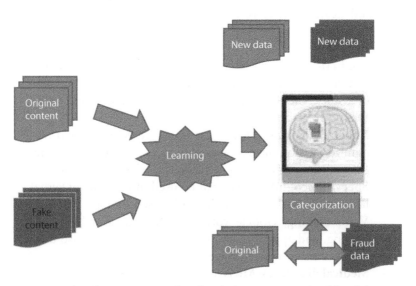

Figure 9.6 Machine learning is trained to classify data into original and fraud data.

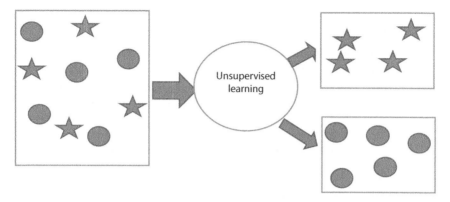

Figure 9.7 Unsupervised learning.

In the above example in Figure 9.7, it shows that the two types of patterns are mixed, say circle and star when these patterns are shown to unsupervised algorithm, it is separating these patterns by analyzing the pattern. There are mainly two types of the unsupervised learning.

- **Clustering:** A clustering is class of problem which deals with the discovery of groupings in the data based on some pattern, for example, grouping online purchase customers based on purchasing behavior.
- **Association:** An association is another type of unsupervised learning problem where one wants to discover some rules that describe association with some other portions of our data, for example, if person x bought some clothes and we want to say that person Y is also more likely to buy the same product.

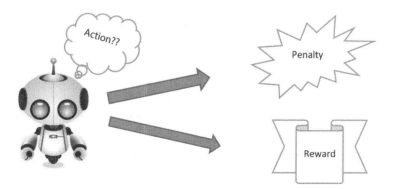

Figure 9.8 Reinforcement learning.

c) Reinforcement Learning

In reinforce learning algorithm, the intelligent agent learns from its surroundings. The agents awarded rewards if right action is performed and receive penalty on every wrong movement as shown in Figure 9.8. The agent learns without human interaction and tries to maximize the rewards points and reduce penalties.

The reinforcement learning involves the following steps:

Step 1. Observe,
Step 2. Select action based on policy,
Step 3. Action,
Step 4. Get reward or penalty,
Step 5. Update policy,
Step 6. Repeat steps 1 to 5 until an optimal policy achieved.

In the next section, some ML algorithms are presented in Table 9.1, which are used for the predictive modeling in healthcare and for other applications.

Table 9.1 Comparison of ML methods: supervised, unsupervised, and reinforcement learning.

Criteria	Unsupervised	Supervised	Reinforcement
Definition	Unsupervised learning is a form of ML in which a model must find patterns in a dataset with no labels and little human supervision.	A class of systems and algorithms known as supervised learning determines a predictive model using data points with known outcomes.	The training of ML models to make a series of decisions is known as reinforcement learning.
Training Data	Unlabeled data	To label data, a domain expert is required.	Learn through interactions with environment
Types of problem	Clustering and association	Regression and classification	Reward based

(Continued)

Table 9.1 Comparison of ML methods: supervised, unsupervised, and reinforcement learning. (*Continued*)

Criteria	Unsupervised	Supervised	Reinforcement
Preference	Discovering data correlation	Routine task	AI
Training	No supervision is required	External supervision required	No supervision is required
Strategy	Rely on the data and the classification algorithm	Rely on the data and algorithm to detect this	Experiment to find the best strategy.
Approach	Predict behavior and discover the results	Identifies and matches the labeled outputs	Trail & error method

9.5.1 K-Nearest Neighbor, Artificial Neural Network, CNN, Decision Tree, and Random Forest

This section presents a brief introduction about the ML algorithms used for the ML approaches.

    a. K-Nearest Neighbor (KNN)

Nearest neighbor (NN) algorithm is based on the NN rule. The KNN algorithm is generalized from that of NN algorithm. The decision making of KNN is very simple that for all samples in set Z, if x is NN of some instance let us say y, then category x will be the result. For any new data sets, KNN will calculate the distance (similarity) from the existing categories, and new data set will belong to the group which is nearest to the existing groups. We can understand it with the help of Figure 9.9

    b. Artificial neural network in healthcare

Artificial neural network (ANN) is suitable to perform predictive modeling of nonlinear equations. Artificial neural network is generally used to develop predictive model for dichotomous in healthcare [16]. In this kind of modeling,

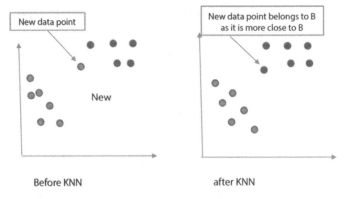

Before KNN   after KNN

Figure 9.9 KNN data points with classes.

less training is required as ANN is capable of detecting the complex relationship among the pattern of data. The advantage of ANN over the other predictive modeling is that is has capability to work properly with somewhat noisy data [17]. The complete ANN model is given in Figure 9.10.

    c. Convolution Neural Network
    Convolution neural network (CNN)-based predictive modeling is suitable for both types of data, i.e., structured and unstructured. In healthcare field, CNN-based modeling is widely used for unstructured data, as well as complex modeling [18–20]. The CNN techniques working flow is given in Figure 9.11. The CNN model suffers from the overfitting problem.

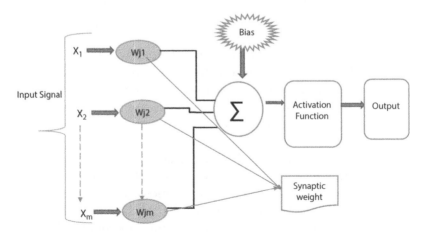

Figure 9.10 ANN modeling.

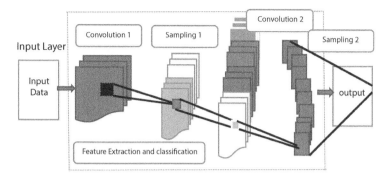

Figure 9.11 CNN architecture.

 d. Decision tree in healthcare

  Decision tree (DT) works on the classification of the data, which is based on the breaking of data set into group on each level and finally making the decision. The division of the data sets at each level is done based on the features of the data. At each level based on the probability of the most likely event, some value is assigned as a basis of breaking up the data. The node in each level is called decision node, and data are divided into subset based on the decision nodes.

 In Figure 9.12, we can see that on each node, we are classifying the data based on some threshold and the final node is leaf node and decision node or we can say the classification node, which cannot be further classified final node can be achieved through any path and final class will decide the state.

 For example, DT is shown in the diagram below.

 The final node is the leaf node, which cannot be divided further. The leaf node is then treated as the final classification, so as that not be divided again into subgroups. The DT algorithms have many variants, for example, ID3, CART, and MARS.

 If we talk about the utilization of DT in healthcare, we have many applications of DT, for example, physicians can make a decision when they face challenges and not able to decide the appropriate treatment, but past data are available.

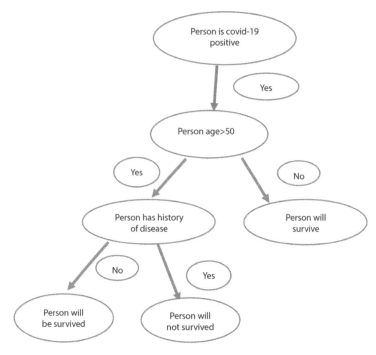

Figure 9.12 Decision tree showing the survival and not survival decision.

9.6   Prediction Model Study of Different Disease

For predicting diseases, like cancer, brain tumor, chronic kidney disease, and heart disease, the same steps are followed, i.e., data collection, data preprocessing, training, and then testing. For example, BraTS 2018 data set is used for brain tumor segmentation. The authors [21] presented an ML over big data for disease prediction. There are predictions that algorithms using regression analysis are very powerful prediction modeling algorithms as explained in Hosmer *et al.* [22]. Support vector machine also uses disease prediction in the modeling that is presented in the study by Joachims [23]. In disease prediction, random forest algorithm is also one of the choices that is similar to DT. This comes under the ensemble classifier which consists of multiple DTs. It gives a very high variation in classification as presented in the study of Breiman [24]. Some of the disease prediction model is also available, which is based on probabilistic model like naïve bays theorem-based model [25]. Some disease models are also based on unsupervised ML algorithm for example KNN [26]. In this model the KNN does not require any probability value assumption. In this algorithm, k represents the number of neighbors.

The model is generally evaluated using the concept of confusion matrix and ROC curve [27]. The confusion matrix is also known as error contingency matrix. True positive rate (TPR), false positive rate (FTR), and false negative rate (FNR) are also used to measure the performance of a model.

9.7 Decision Support System

Decision support system is a computer-based program, which is makes decision making easier and more accurate. Figure 9.13 depicts the healthcare knowledge cycle, demonstrating how AI systems can be used to analyse healthcare information and develop a knowledge representation that can then be used for data and process modelling.

9.8 Preventive Measures Based on Predicted Results

The healthcare industry should always focus on the preventive measure to avoid the disease before it actually happens. The healthcare organization should focus on this important question for the betterment of the patients.

- How can we reduce the number of patients?
- How can we cure or slow down the speed disease progression?
- How can we lower the healthcare cost even providing quality care?
- How can we maximize the use AI in detecting and curing the risk?

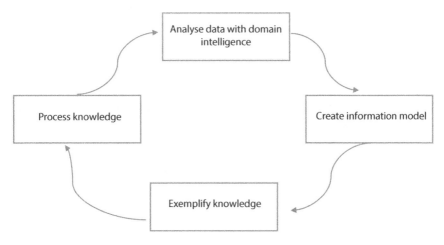

Figure 9.13 Decision support system.

- How can we utilize the benefits of AI to predict the disease in early stages?

Healthcare organization should always try to suggest patient to take preventive measures like changing life style to break the pattern or trends analyzed by predictive modeling.

9.9   Conclusions and Future Scope

From the discussion, we can now clearly say that, in the health sector accurate diagnosis and accurate disease prediction mainly depend on the data collection quality and its interpretation. Data acquisition and cleaning have a lot of advanced techniques to perform its task accurately but the interpretation and modeling accurate prediction model recently gained attention of researcher and have a lot of scope of improvement. Data analytics have a major impact in the development of the predictive modeling and hence enhanced the preventive care. Data analytics helps in identifying the disease before they actually become fatal.

Predictive modeling undoubtedly has numerous applications but it also has some limitations. Predictive modeling mainly works on meeting certain conditions and hence may not predict accurately. Data labeling is a challenging task as we need to label a huge amount of data before it is fed to any ML algorithms. Another challenge is to find the large data set to train and finding unbiased data as data may be biased, which may lead to wrong prediction. In the future, we can utilize the predictive modeling in risk mitigation and study customer behavior and find and predict new diseases.

References

1. Weng, J., McClelland, J., Pentland, A., Sporns, O., Stockman, I., Sur, M. *et al.*, Autonomous mental development by robots and animals. *Science*, 291, 5504, 599–600, 2001.
2. Wooldridge, M. and Jennings, N.R., Intelligent agents: Theory and practice. *Knowl. Eng. Rev.*, 10, 2, 115–52, 1995.
3. Ziglio, E., Currie, C., Rasmussen, V.B., The WHO cross-national study of health behavior in school aged children from 35 countries: Findings from 2001–2002. *J. Sch. Health*, 74, 6, 204–206, 2004.

4. Chen, M., Hao, Y., Hwang, K., Wang, L., Wang, L., Disease prediction by machine learning over big data from healthcare communities. *IEEE Access*, 5, 8869–8879, 2017.

5. Tong, T. *et al.*, A novel grading biomarker for the prediction of conversion from mild cognitive impairment to Alzheimer's disease. *IEEE Trans. Biomed. Eng.*, 64, 1, 155–165, Jan. 2017.

6. Dahiwade, D., Patle, G., Meshram, E., Designing disease prediction model using machine learning approach. *2019 3rd International Conference on Computing Methodologies and Communication (ICCMC)*, Erode, India, pp. 1211–1215, 2019.

7. Kanchan, B.D. and Kishor, M.M., Study of machine learning algorithms for special disease prediction using principal of component analysis. *2016 International Conference on Global Trends in Signal Processing, Information Computing and Communication (ICGTSPICC)*, Jalgaon, pp. 5–10, 2016.

8. Rong, G., Mendez, A., Assi, E.B., Zhao, B., Sawan, M., Artificial intelligence in healthcare: Review and prediction case studies. *Engineering*, 6, 3, 291–301, 2020.

9. Shetty, D., Rit, K., Shaikh, S., Patil, N., Diabetes disease prediction using data mining. *2017 International Conference on Innovations in Information, Embedded and Communication Systems (ICIIECS)*, Coimbatore, pp. 1–5, 2017.

10. Thirunavukkarasu, K., Singh, A.S., Irfan, M., Chowdhury, A., Prediction of liver disease using classification algorithms. *2018 4th International Conference on Computing Communication and Automation (ICCCA)*, Greater Noida, India, pp. 1–3, 2018.

11. Mohan, S., Thirumalai, C., Srivastava, G., Effective heart disease prediction using hybrid machine learning techniques. *IEEE Access*, 7, 81542–81554, 2019.

12. Ali, F., El-Sappagh, S., Riazul Islam, S.M., Kwak, D., Ali, A., Imran, M., Kwak, K.-S., A smart healthcare monitoring system for heart disease prediction based on ensemble deep learning and feature fusion. *Inf. Fusion*, 63, 208–222, 2020.

13. Shardlow, M., *An analysis of feature selection techniques*, The University of Manchester, 2016.

14. Dash, M. and Liu, H., Feature selection for classification. *Intell. Data Anal.*, 1, 3, 131–56, 1997.

15. Tang, J., Alelyani, S., Liu, H., Feature selection for classification: A review, in: *Data Classif: Algor Appl*, p. 37, 2014.

16. Tu, J.V., Advantages and disadvantages of using artificial neural networks versus logistic regression for predicting medical outcomes. *J. Clin. Epidemiol.*, 49, 11, 1225–31, 1996.

17. McGarry, K., Wermster, S., MacIntyre, J., Hybrid neural systems: From simple coupling to fully integrated nueral networks. *Neural Comput. Surv.*, 2, 62–93, 1999.

18. Ismail, W. and Hassan, M., Mining productive-associated periodic-frequent patterns in body sensor data for smart home care. *Sensors*, 17, 952, 2017.

19. Hassan, M.M., Gumaei, A., Alsanad, A., Alrubaian, M., Fortino, G., A hybrid deep learning model for efficient intrusion detection in big data environment. *Inf. Sci.*, 513, 386–396, Mar. 2020.

20. Sahoo, A.K., Pradhan, C., Barik, R.K., Dubey, H., DeepReco: Deep learning based health recommender system using collaborative filtering. *Computation*, 7, 2, 25, 2019.

21. Shirsath, S.S. and Patil, S., Disease prediction using machine learning over big data. *Int. J. Innov. Res. Sci. Eng. Technol.*, 2018.

22. Hosmer Jr., D.W., Lemeshow, S., Sturdivant, R.X., *Applied logistic regression*, Wiley, 2013.

23. Joachims, T., *Making large-scale SVM learning practical*, p. 28, SFB 475: Komplexitätsreduktion Multivariaten Datenstrukturen, Univ. Dortmund, Dortmund, Tech. Rep., 1998.

24. Breiman, L., Random forests. *Mach. Learn.*, 45, 1, 5–32, 2001.

25. Lindley, D.V., Fiducial distributions and Bayes' theorem. *J. R. Stat. Soc. Ser. B (Methodolog.)*, 1, 102–7, 1958.

26. Cover, T. and Hart, P., Nearest neighbor pattern classification. *IEEE Trans. Inf. Theory*, 13, 1, 21–7, 1967.

27. Fawcett, T., An introduction to ROC analysis. *Pattern Recognit. Lett.*, 27, 8, 861–74, 2006.

10

Managing Healthcare Data Using Machine Learning and Blockchain Technology

BKSP Kumar Raju Alluri

SCOPE-VIT AP University, Amaravati, Andhra Pradesh, India

Abstract

Blockchain is one of the interesting inventions that is being applied in various stages of business life cycle like in public sector, infrastructure, agriculture, healthcare, education, and entertainment. In this chapter, our scope is to discuss the impact of blockchain and machine learning in healthcare. Even though blockchain and machine learning are brining disruptive changes in many sectors, it is an exception to the healthcare industry. The work on healthcare using blockchain and machine learning has recently taken special interest by the research community and Industries. In this direction, we will discuss the major works published in SCOPUS Database in the past 4 years. At the end, the outcomes of the study are presented in visual form.

Keywords: Blockchain, healthcare, privacy preserving, machine learning

10.1   Introduction

Transactions can be executed using centralized system or decentralized way. Traditional banks is one of the classical examples of centralized approach. This system is not reliable during multiple node failures. To improve security, a decentralized approach called blockchain was introduced. Blockchain alone cannot exhibit smartness in decision making, and we require data analytics. This includes machine learning, deep learning and artificial intelligence. There is a very close association between one and the other with subtle differences. Artificial intelligence tries to

---

Corresponding author: bksp.kumar@vitap.ac.in

T. Poongodi, D. Sumathi, B. Balamurugan and K. S. Savita (eds.) Digitization of Healthcare Data Using Blockchain, (203–234) © 2022 Scrivener Publishing LLC

mimic the cognitive abilities of human being. In machine learning, feature extraction is a separate step and not embedded into the algorithm whereas in deep learning, this is automatic and part and parcel of neural network architectures.

Integrating both these technologies would benefit healthcare in many ways, and the same are discussed in Section 10.5. In the same section, we represent the outcomes of our study in visual form. The importance of blockchain technology for healthcare is discussed in Section 10.3. The role of machine learning in healthcare sector is briefed in Section 10.4. Finally, we end the chapter with the future opportunities in the hybrid approach for healthcare.

10.2   Current Situation of Healthcare

The evergreen industry, which will not have decreased demand, is healthcare, and this is once again proven with COVID19. Unfortunately, owing to the increased requirement, smart healthcare management still needs extensive work, considering the practical aspects. According to Healthcare 4.0, the expectations are shown in Figure 10.1. Even though, theoretically, the objectives are almost met, practically, healthcare expectation deployment is at nascent stages. One of the main reasons is that data breaches or attacks are being reported very often.

Figure 10.1 Objectives of Healthcare 4.0.

Some statistics of data breaches are listed below:

- 2005–2019: at least 10 Billion Medical records were hacked/accessed illegally.

- 2005–2019: at least 43 % of all data breaches is from Health Sector Alone.
- 2010–2019: at least 256 million people got impacted directly or indirectly from the medical data breaches,
- 2019: at least $150 will be the average loss for a medical breach.

Additional insights of the data breaches are taken from PRC database, and the same are shown in Figures 10.2 and 10.3. Notations used are as follows: Hack—malicious behavior, INSD—attacks within the organization, PHYS—attacking physical assets, PORT—breach on portable device, STAT—not generally movable electronics loss, UNKN—unknown.

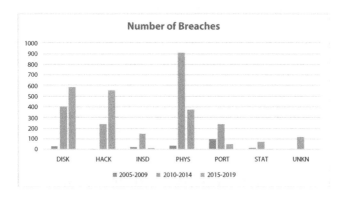

Figure 10.2 Number of breaches for different data breaches.

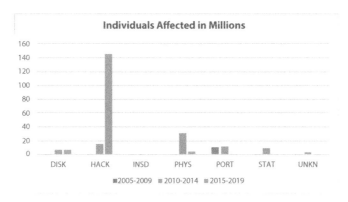

Figure 10.3 Affected people in millions.

The statistics in medical data breaches are extremely high, and it stands second in comprehensive data breaches. For example, as on 2019, more than 249 million users were affected with medical data breach. More than 2000 data breaches were reported from 65 countries. Alone in 2019, more than 41 million health records were illegally accessed. On an average, any data breach would cost less (i.e., $3.9 million) than medical data breach (i.e., $6.4 Million) which is 12 % increase in last 6 years. In the study by Jain *et al.* [1], a time series model to estimate the extent of data breaches in the coming years is built, and the results are promising with simple moving average.

There were many reported incidents even in India and some of them are listed below:

- One of the southern states third-party agency was accused of leaking Aadhar number and other sensitive information.
- In one of the states in India, the data regarding medicines purchases of millions of people from pharmaceutical stores were leaked.

The abovementioned statistics/incidents are extremely in a worrying condition and a big leap toward addressing this problem is "blockchain."

10.3   Introduction to Blockchain for Healthcare

Putting the working process of blockchain in simple terms, the clinical data can be successfully stored in the blockchain only if the validation was successful (Figure 10.4).

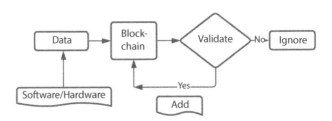

Figure 10.4 High level process in blockchain.

Blockchain has different sets of features (Figure 10.5). Different types of blockchains are available in the literature, and the same is shown in Figure 10.6.

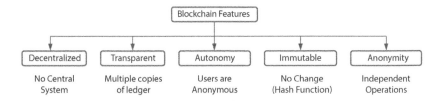

Figure 10.5 Generic properties of blockchain.

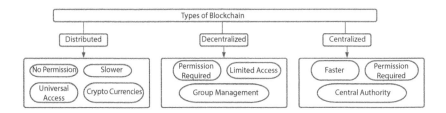

Figure 10.6 Multiple types of blockchain.

However, using blockchain on realistic grounds of healthcare system involves various challenges (Figure 10.7). For some of them, solutions are recently available in the literature and for the remaining, the current solutions will not adhere in the future. For example, in the future, we could break the blockchain using quantum computing and withstanding that situation does not currently have frameworks.

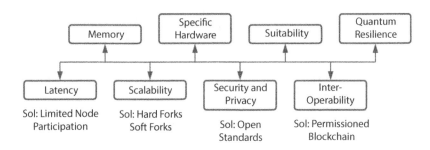

Figure 10.7 Challenges in blockchain.

Table 10.1 Four generations of blockchain.

	Consensus	Speed	Scalability	Cost	Energy
First generation	PoW	Slow	No	Costly	More
Second generation	PoW	Slow	Some issues	Less costly	Moderate
Third generation	PoS	High speed	Highly scalable	Cheaper	Efficient
Fourth generation	PoI	Very high speed	Highly scalable	Much cheaper	Highly efficient

However, observing the area of blockchain from the last few years, the improvements are more than expected. The evolution of blockchain is divided into four generations, and the changes across all of them are listed in Table 10.1.

Blockchain is basically a distributed system which can basically ensure trust for the user. Due to which, Blockchain is used in many applications like,

- **Finance:** for loans, for cross border payments;
- **Healthcare:** record management, drug traceability, clinical trials, and healthcare billing;
- **Media and entertainment:** digital piracy, content crowd-funding, digital advertisements, and royalty payments;
- **Real estate:** property rental, title records, property regulations, and real estate liquidity;
- **Government:** voting, customs and border patrol, transparent budgeting, and national digital currencies;
- **Telecom:** Roaming fraud, low power wide area networks, smart cards, and 5G entertainment;
- **Transportation and logistics:** freight tracking, vehicle performance history, universal transit payment, and payments/dispute resolution;
- **Agriculture:** farm inventory, fair pricing, and food traceability.

Among all applications, applying blockchain for healthcare is much more challenging and the major work in this direction is summarized in Table 10.2.

Table 10.2 Contributions by the researchers for blockchain in healthcare.

Ref.	Blockchain architecture	Objective (blockchain + healthcare)	Cons
[2]	Hyperledger Fabric	Low energy wireless wearable device with blockchain storage	Not scalable
[3]	Ethereum	Secured data transfer using blockchain	Hardware architecture should be customizable
[4]	Not Mentioned	Security aspects related to blockchain based data transfer is discussed.	Lack of standards
[5]	Ethereum	Collaborative decision making of treatment	Privacy aspects were not discussed
[6]	Multichain	Interoperability healthcare data analysis	May not be accepted by the user.
[7]	Hyperledger Fabric	Effective drug delivery system to address fake entries.	Speed of transaction can be optimized
[8]	Multichain	Blockchain network on small training data with improved predictions	Topology varies basic
[9]	Permissioned blockchain	Secure key exchange protocols between devices and blockchain	Security assessments were not extensive

(Continued)

Table 10.2 Contributions by the researchers for blockchain in healthcare. (*Continued*)

Ref.	Blockchain architecture	Objective (blockchain + healthcare)	Cons
[10]	Public blockchain	Cohesive data collection from multiple data regulators	Cost is high
[11]	Not mentioned	Human activity recognition based alarm system	Not scalable
[12]	Permissioned blockchain	Secured personal health record management	Scalability aspects were not discussed.
[13]	Not mentioned	Proposed privilege based access system using blockchain	-
[14]	Hyperledger fabric	Reduce the complexity involved in data transfer between various stakeholders	Privacy aspects were not discussed extensively
[15]	Not mentioned	Provide effective communication between before and after surgery.	-
[16]	Hyperledger	Secured sharing of data to and from blockchain	Not scalable
[17]	Ethereum	Store medical data in less time with reduced retrieval times	Cost of deployment is high

(*Continued*)

Table 10.2 Contributions by the researchers for blockchain in healthcare. (*Continued*)

Ref.	Blockchain architecture	Objective (blockchain + healthcare)	Cons
[18]	Etherum	Sharing health records without ignoring security and privacy	Not greatly scalable
[19]	Ethereum	Framework for effective decision making	Not free
[20]	Private ethereum	Scalable and secured data sharing systems	Costly
[21]	Nem blockchain	Patient data management	Not scalable

10.4   Introduction to ML for Healthcare

Machine learning is not new for healthcare and extensive process is followed for an ML application to get deployed to the real world. The same process is briefed below:

a. Gathering requirements: The medical personnel should be convinced of automating a certain process and should feel the need of using ML for solving the problems being faced by users. This is possible only when the requirements collection is unbiased and comprehensive.

b. Collect and anonymize: Identify the type of the data for the underlying healthcare problem and collect such that noise and incompleteness is reduced since healthcare data are so sensitive and applying the ML algorithms without anonymization is not acceptable. There are many privacy preserving techniques, like homomorphic encryption, differential privacy, and federated learning.

c. Annotate: All the collected data will not have right labels or sometimes will not have label itself and those instances need to be corrected. While performing this, check for class imbalance and data biasedness.

d. Feature extraction: All the features may not be significant and identify the relevant variables for the target ML task and ensure they are appropriately transformed to suit the requirements of predictive analytics.

e. Model building: The model built should be approved by external technical and nontechnical members. For example, algorithmic audit will be performed with the test data on the model built, and if they are satisfied, it will be sent to the Regulatory Approval. Upon extensive experiments, the model will be integrated to the clinical process. Then, user reviews are given the highest importance based on which the model can be upgraded.

f. Robust ML: Since the data collected from many sources is stored in remote locations, there is a chance of data breach in terms of modifying data, changing the model, and adding the auxiliary model (Figure 10.8).

i) Modifying data: To ensure the data modification by the adversary does not reveal much sensitive important information, we can do the following:

- Squeeze the inputs: Reduce the n-dimensional space to t-dimensions such that t<<n.
- Adversarial training: The model is retrained to stabilize with adversarial activities.
- Feature masking: The attributes, which are prone to modification, are hidden or changed, such that they can be reconstructed later.
- Develop nonuseful features for adversary: Convert the existing features into high-dimensional feature space, such that the interpretation of all of them is not meaningful for the adversary.

ii) Adding auxiliary model: The adversary instances should be identified for increasing the robustness of model built.

- Add binary classifier: Generate a binary classifier, which is trained to identify adversarial and nonadversarial instances.

- Construct ensemble models: To increase the strength of detection, ensemble algorithms can be employed.

iii)   Modifying model: The adversary can change the built models, and we need to circumvent those trails.

- Build masked model: The model parameters can be masked enough to reduce the chances of adversarial attacks
- Generate interpretable models: The adversarial model modifications can be easily identified if we employ interpretable models like decision tree. Even for black box models, explainable artificial intelligence (XAI) is used to increase interpretations.
- Knowledge sharing: Use multiple mini models, and the knowledge is spread across multiple functions, and it would be difficult to attack all those models.

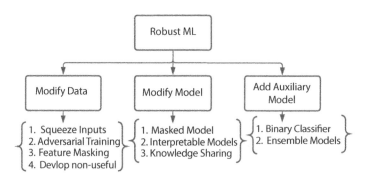

Figure 10.8 Robust ML increases the trust of analytics on healthcare.

g.   Monitor the model: On a continuous basis, monitor the performance of the model so that corrective actions can be taken when benchmarking results are not observed.

10.4.1   Open Issues in Machine Learning for Healthcare

1.   Interpretable ML: In healthcare, decisions cannot be completely based on the suggestions given by the model. Instead, if the model is interpretable even to a non-ML practitioner, then

214 DIGITIZATION OF HEALTHCARE DATA USING BLOCKCHAIN

it would increase the chances of being used in real time. One of the ground breaking technology in this direction is XAI.

2. Edge-based ML Computing: Traditional ML models cannot be built in Edge devices as they have low computational capabilities and less memory.

3. Annotation: The collected data may not have labels by which the classification task becomes difficult. The medical reports need to be analyzed and then radiologists need to manual annotation which is highly time consuming. Instead, automated approaches like Active Learning can be used.

4. Distributed ML: The collected data may not be available in single location, and we need to customize the existing models to run at different subsources and finally combine all the model parameters to build wholistic model. Also, distributed models are also used for preserving privacy of the data.

5. Fairness in ML: The data should not be biased and if so, it will impact drastically as they are life critical situations. Also, misinterpreting the models would reduce the accountability on machine learning.

Among all the open issues, we are interested in distributed ML. We collect healthcare data and store in different blockchain nodes, and in this context, distributed and robust ML would increase the accountability.

10.5 Using ML and Blockchain for Healthcare Management

In this chapter, we focus more on the work in healthcare based on both blockchain and machine learning. Even though the individual work on ML and blockchain is very extensive, the combination of both on healthcare is still at nascent stages. We have taken the popular SCOPUS database, and the search criteria are as follows:

Machine Learning and Blockchain and Healthcare or Deep Learning and Blockchain and Healthcare or Artificial Intelligence and Blockchain and Healthcare

The search results gave 45 articles with a filter of 4 years and conference/journals. We divide all of them into two categories: theory centric and result-oriented.

10.5.1   Bucket 1: Theory Centric

Many research challenges were discussed for applying blockchain and ML in healthcare [22]:

- Security of the device
- Cost and maintenance issues
- Tradeoff between energy and security especially in the case of wearable devices
- Applying machine learning for authentication instead of relying on traditional approaches.

Industrial revolution 4.0 is changing many industries, and healthcare is one of them. Integrating cloud computing, blockchain, machine learning, and Internet of Things (IoT) would open the doors for many problems in comprehensive automation. Al-Jaroodi *et al.* [23] proposed optimized service-oriented middleware (SoM) for increasing the quality and reducing the cost in healthcare services; however, SoM did not touch many aspects like privacy and resource management.

In the study by Banerjee *et al.* [24], the authors have used the combination of fog computing, blockchain, and machine learning to assist the intensive care unit (ICU) patients. Initially, the fog devices will collect psychological features of patients, and they were processed for anomaly identification based on which the right medical personnel will be alerted. The data gathered are very sensitive, and it was secured using blockchain.

Patient monitoring is very crucial especially in the case of ICU and completely involving humans for the same cannot be effective. So, an additional automated monitoring and assessment system is required, which is possible through the use of IoT and machine learning. Also, the data collected is stored in blockchain for secured processing and predicting the patient outcomes. Any abnormal activity from patients can be recognized and informed to the appropriate medical personnel [25].

Al-Emran *et al.* [26] developed an app called MedTravel. It can not only give basic information about health services but also facilitate the effective communication between patients and medical practitioners. In Khan *et al.* [27], the authors discussed the role of hybrid combination (machine learning and blockchain) for various applications, like healthcare, unmanned aerial vehicles (UAVs), smart cities, and smart grid; however, they have given more emphasis on other applications and not on healthcare.

In Jain *et al.* [1], the authors proposed hybrid blockchain using permissioned and nonpermissioned blockchains. The existing data were trained with machine learning model, and the new data were filtered automatically, such that privacy is ensured. The authors also suggested the huge possibility of integrating artificial intelligence (AI) and IoT for extending the capabilities of blockchain in healthcare.

The study of Priya [28] discussed various terminologies involved in blockchain and healthcare. They have developed a model for alerting the diabetes patients by storing and processing the data in secured environment, like blockchain, healthcare benefits with blockchain, and machine learning [29]:

- Patient data privacy preserving system
- Transparency and integrity in the transactions
- Multilayered security
- Remove the interdependency on the server/parent node.
- Efficient retrieval of patient data by medical personnel after getting right to view permission.

Jain *et al.* [30] used combination of multiple technologies to assist the Healthcare Stakeholders in comprehensive way. For example, they suggested the use of Blockchain, IOT and Machine learning would give dynamic predictions by ensuring security.

Implementation of technological improvements in Blockchain and Machine Learning in healthcare is very less in realistic grounds because of several reasons. One of them is laws like General Data Protection Regulation (GDPR). After this law was released in Europe, many research papers discussed this law in the context of opportunities and challenges to move further in the area of Predictive blockchain for Healthcare [31].

The authors proposed secure data transfer using blockchain and backing up with the cloud services. Also, several machine learning algorithms were deployed in Data Quality engine to measure the usefulness of the data. Adhering to the General Data Protection regulation is very crucial to extend the framework to real applications and this was accomplished by the proposed method [32].

Clinical Research Informatics (translational science) study was conducted by mentioning various sub-domains like, AI, machine learning, big data, blockchain, cognitive computing, causal inference, and ethical, legal issues [33]. E-health is improved using blockchain and machine learning. The authors discussed the e-health system using blockchain and the main capability of the model is health monitoring taking the aid of different architecture layers [34].

In the study by Memari *et al.* [35], the authors emphasized on difficulties in detecting the diabetes and addressed the same problem using machine learning. Initially, the statistical properties of an image at different levels can be extracted and then followed by feature extraction using various deep learning architectures. Finally, the authors suggested that features can be further refined using machine learning algorithms, like AdaBoost.

The impact of blockchain on healthcare was assessed for COVID19. The proposed model can be used for tracking the virus spread and taking the precautionary measures to reduce the impact [36]. The study of Hoosain *et al.* [37] assessed the sustainable development goals implementation using blockchain. One of them is health management, and they discussed various strengths, threats, weakness, and opportunities. In Hiwale *et al.* [38], they surveyed use of blockchain for evaluating the patient disease and then, they discussed the use of distributed machine learning in data processing, such that security and privacy is preserved.

The study by Khatoon [39] proposed pseudo unique identifier for ensuring quick access to the medical records across heterogenous environments. This identifier has multiple entities like base record, sequence storage, and leak proof verification. The data were even then used for performing machine learning by ensuring the user privacy and without ignoring the fact of owner controls in terms of data integrity. The proposed method is different from other systems in terms of monetary value as this is offered with no costs, and it can be deployed easily by ensuring quick response time. The study of Hiwale *et al.* [40] proposed health-chain framework, which can collect the data from the cross-sectional units ensuring the privacy. This is achieved by the use of differential privacy in the stochastic gradient descent.

Different healthcare records are available like digital health records and personal health records. Healthcare data can be dynamic, especially in the case of wearable devices. Identifying the right storage component is crucial for ensuring security and privacy along which the response time will differ [41].

Threats in IOT are increasing day by day, and many approaches were developed in the literature. Classification algorithms are used to identify the hybrid patterns in various android malware activities. The extracted information is stored in blockchain for secure transfer and to detect new malware entities effectively and efficiently [42].

Data were not interoperable across multiple data regulators because of the competition in the market. However, the ultimate solution is to provide healthcare analytics on comprehensive anonymized patient history. This can be achieved from data hiding to advanced techniques like homomorphic encryption. Even blockchain markers are used to preserve privacy of user data during its transmission [43].

The role of big data increased extensively in the healthcare domain. It is used for fraud analysis, genomic analysis, electronic health records, and patient profile analysis. Various organizational, technological and legal challenges in this direction are discussed [44]. The study of Lobo *et al.* [45] discussed the role of blockchain in increasing the security of machine learning aspects. On the other side, they discussed the usage of machine learning to understand the blockchain and estimate future statistics. The owners even cannot modify the recorded blockchain transactions, and the authors considered this as a setback as human entry is involved, and there is a high chance of committing mistakes. Also, the database of blockchain transactions increased drastically, and this would urge the research community to come up with better retrieval techniques, such that the response time is minimized by keeping the privacy intact.

The role of AI agents is not just assessing the physical health status of a patient, it can even track the stress levels. This evaluation would help the patient in the right automated guidance through multimedia education [46]. The study of Shen *et al.* [47] discussed the role of both blockchain and machine learning for healthcare domain. Using the hyperledger architecture is one of the ways to ensure data privacy, and we can apply machine learning algorithms for better predictions by complying organizational and ethical standards.

The study of Tanwar *et al.* [48] restructured the organization of blockchain by embedding the decentralized AI. This would increase the feasibility in automating various healthcare management activities, and they specifically emphasized on virtual progress of the patients after discharge. They also discussed the challenges of blockchain in healthcare in terms of scalability, interoperability, security, and latency.

In Kim *et al.*[49], the authors have discussed the need for blockchain and machine learning in individual levels. Then, usage of both technologies in healthcare was structured and justified with real-time examples. The study of Syed *et al.* [50] discussed the importance of blockchain, machine learning and watermarking in managing the UAVs. This paper discussed the challenges and opportunities in each of these:

    a.   Watermarking:
          i)   need approaches for improving the pixel values;
         ii)   processing big files and generating interpretations are crucial tasks, and UAVs should work irrespective of the environment.

   b. Blockchain:
- i) 51 % attack is still possible and require efficient approaches to address
- ii) need to develop secured smart contracts
- iii) Passing the entire data to all the nodes involved in distributed transaction is costly process and require partial information sharing. This is difficult as deciding the filtering conditions is dynamic and costly process.
- iv) Storing the Gigabytes of data is not practically feasible
- v) Resources of UAVs are limited
- vi) Lack of standards and regulations

   c. Machine Learning:
- i) UAVs should be resilient to various attacks
- ii) ML can be used to control the data in blockchain.
- iii) Better decision making is possible with ML integration into the blockchain, and there is a lot of scope of improvement in this direction.
- iv) Appropriate reaction to the unknown environments is still a challenge

In this recent survey, the authors just referred to only one paper in blockchain for healthcare using ML. In other surveys, the discussions are very basic on secure predictions on healthcare data in blockchain [51].

In the study by Alfandi *et al.* [52], the authors proposed blockchain–based IOT framework to ensure security and privacy. The model is multi-layered following dedicated services at blockchain layer, network layer and perceptron layer.

10.5.2   Bucket 2: Result Oriented

The study by Singh *et al.* [53] proposed "Lifepounds" using which the users can store the data very securely, and it also provides the feasibility of selling the user medical data with right levels of anonymization. The customer who buys the data validates the transaction and decrypt the data at his end with the aid of key keepers. The work focused on individual rights in data sharing and getting incentives with right level of granularity. This is further added with a data quality check using Autoencoders and RNNs. However, this requires huge amount of data, which can be addressed using few shot learning.

Distributed data vending approaches for secure data sharing require a strong balance between risks in indexing and effectiveness in information retrieval. Involvement of third parties is avoided such that data producer can use existing blockchain and the consumer perform credible transaction to complete the purchase [54].

The applications of blockchain were extended to veterinary healthcare using machine learning. The proposed models are compared with classical model-Hyperledger Caliper and evaluated based on response time, throughput and success rate [55]. There are five pillars of trust: (i) reliability, (ii) privacy, (iii) security, (iv) resilience, (v) safety. The authors proposed trustworthy model satisfying all these parameters using blockchain, machine learning and federated learning without ignoring differential privacy aspects [56].

The study of Ismail *et al.* [57] discussed the importance of personalized healthcare, which can be improved when cohesive data are collected across multiple data servers. They proposed a blockchain–based model for retrieving the health records from different hospitals and achieved a performance increase to 11.5 times when compared with traditional systems. However, they did not evaluate the security and privacy of their model.

In Abbas *et al.* [58], they proposed a model focused on improving the supply chain process of drugs. Many counterfeit drugs are added into the cycle, and it is difficult to track all of them. The embedded blockchain of the model would recognize all those entities and alert the user during purchase. Also, the model can recommend the best-rated medicines by combining local and global information (Figure 10.9). They have used publicly available data set to test the model observed to improved reliability in drug purchase.

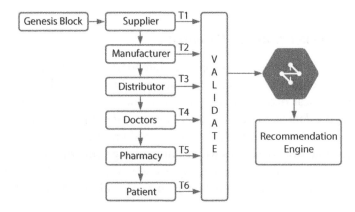

Figure 10.9 Identify the fake drugs and recommend the best medicine.

In Kuo *et al.* [59], explorer model based on blockchain and AI was proposed. The model is compared with centralized server frameworks and identified that the proposed model is equally performing well with additional benefits like improved security and enhanced interoperability parameter quantification.

Distributed decision making is proposed by the authors using both blockchain and machine learning. Interoperability is the main issue for collaborative decision making especially in the case of heterogenous data regulators. The authors developed patient-oriented model and this ranks the relative importance of each criteria using which the right medical personnel will be selected ensuring low cost and high quality [60].

In Kunickaitė *et al.* [61], they have chosen problem of fraud detection in healthcare specifically in insurance claims. They identified the drawbacks of the basic classification and clustering techniques at an individual level and used the combination of evolving clustering methods and support vector machine with advanced hyperparameter tuning.

In Rachakonda *et al.* [62], smart pillow using the blockchain was proposed. This edge device collects EEG data from the user and processed to predict the next day stress. In this process, a lot of sensitive data will be transferred to the cloud environment for pattern analysis. However, this involves, various threats and the authors discussed the solutions for each of them. For example, it will restrict the illegitimate user to add/tamper psychological data by performing encryption with edge device private key and admin node public key.

The study of Le Nguyen *et al.* [63] discussed the role of AI in various stages of healthcare management. Most of the smart healthcare work focused on disease prediction. However, this is very menial, and the healthcare industry needs a reliable automation approaches as they deal with human lives. This critical context requires assistance at every stage of patient management. First, the patients need to be diagnosed at the right time automatically using the hand-held devices and with minimal manual intervention considering the cost efficiency and accuracy. Then, the doctors should also be assisted in the surgery and the best medication based on the similar cases handled across the globe. Finally, post disease monitoring the patient is a difficult and costly process. This can be better managed with the involvement of the technical mobile agents. These can record and analyze the activities and accordingly have a mutual system approach.

Patient over a period will have treatments across multiple hospitals in the same location or different locations. Gathering them and processing require a separate approach called distributed machine learning. The study of Patil *et al.* [64] proposed stochastic gradient descent with DML implemented on permissioned Blockchain-Hyperledger Fabric.

Many blockchain approaches ignore the role of server, and this in turn effects the performance of the blockchain system. In Li *et al.* [65], they proposed a decentralized privacy preserving model, which considers role of both client and server to enhance the correctness in the predictions.

10.5.3   Outcomes of the Study

Based on the work that we have discussed till now, the outcomes are discussed in this section in visual form:

Outcome 1: We summarized the work in ML using blockchain using various parameters like most commonly used ML algorithms, average performance and limitations (Figure 10.10).

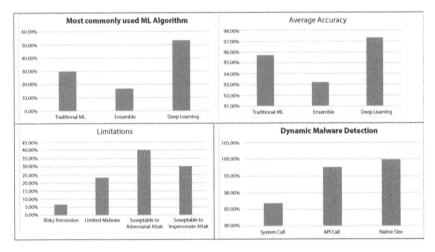

Figure 10.10 Summarizing the work of ML with blockchain in terms of algorithms and limitations.

Outcome 2: Challenges of applying Blockchain and ML in Healthcare (Figure 10.11).

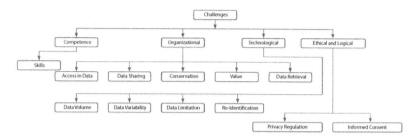

Figure 10.11 Blockchain-based predictions for healthcare challenges.

Outcome 3: Different Technologies for Privacy Preserving (Figure 10.12).

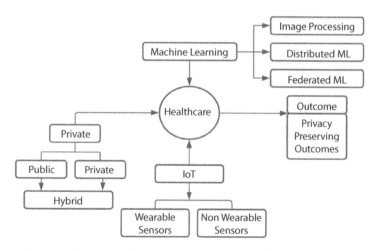

Figure 10.12 Hybrid approach for preserving privacy of healthcare data.

Outcome 4: Consolidated different Healthcare Stakeholder benefits upon using ML and Blockchain (Figure 10.13).

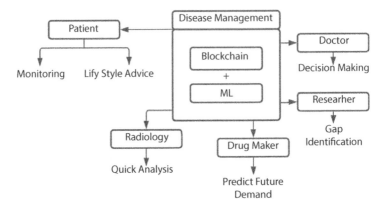

Figure 10.13 Stakeholders and their benefits with blockchain and ML.

Outcome 5: Decision making with blockchain and ML (Figure 10.14).

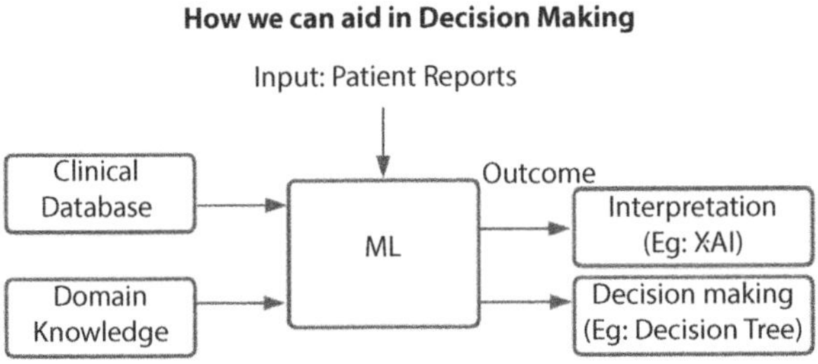

How we can aid in Decision Making

Input: Patient Reports

Clinical Database → ML → Outcome

Domain Knowledge → ML

Interpretation (Eg: XAI)

Decision making (Eg: Decision Tree)

Figure 10.14 Effective and secured decision making with blockchain and ML.

Outcome 6: Summarized benefits of integrating blockchain and machine learning (Figure 10.15).

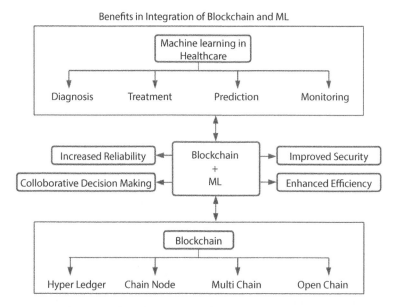

Figure 10.15 Advantages of combining ML and blockchain in healthcare.

Outcome 7: Smart Blockchain application development model for healthcare (Figure 10.16).

Developing an application using Blockchain and Healthcare

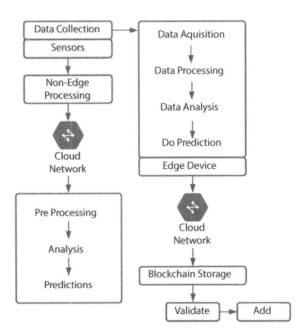

Figure 10.16 Process for developing a smart blockchain application integrated with ML.

Outcome 8: Based on the extensive, we classified the work into two buckets. a) Articles based on pure theory (does not have result-based justification), b) articles focusing on justifying the proposed approach with results (Figure 10.17).

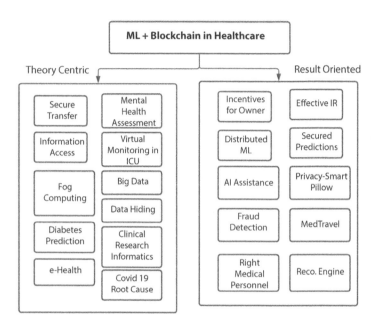

Figure 10.17 Summary of topics focused in blockchain + ML in healthcare.

10.5.4   Why are Most of the Current Blockchain + Healthcare Papers Theory-Based?

There are various practical reasons for the delay in implementing the blockchain in Healthcare.

- The government has to still frame standard laws for ensuring the safety of electronic health records.
- Even the individuals are not aware of the significance of the blockchain in healthcare sector.
- Certain medical conditions of the patients will not allow to have an agreement on smart contracts.

- Data gathering process was not standard, and it drastically varies from one hospital management to the other.
- Comprehensive data collection from multiple data regulators is not possible as of now because of the interoperability issues.

10.6   Conclusion

Healthcare is one of the rarest domains that will not have decreased demand. Considering this, adding smartness and automation would reduce the costs involved and increase the accuracy. On the other side, it should not violate the privacy of the user. One of the key technologies to ensure this is blockchain. The predictions generated from machine learning will be robust and reliable when blockchain is used for healthcare data. In this chapter, we have discussed the individual role of Blockchain and ML for healthcare domain. Then, we have discussed the benefits and contributions of hybrid approach on healthcare in two categories (theory centric and result oriented). Based on this, we could highlight the work which needs validation to get approved by multiple personnel in healthcare life cycle. Finally, the outcomes from the study are represented in the visual form.

References

1. Jain, S. *et al.*, Blockchain and machine learning in healthcare and management, in: *2020 International Conference on Mainstreaming Blockchain Implementation (ICOMBI)*, IEEE, 2020.
2. Wang, Y., Zhang, A., Zhang, P., Wang, H., Cloud-assisted EHR sharing with security and privacy preservation via consortium blockchain. *IEEE Access*, 7, 136704–19, 2019.
3. Lee, H.-A., Kung, H.-H., Udayasankaran, J.G., Kijsanayotin, B., Marcelo, A.B., Chao, L. R., An architecture and management platform for blockchain-based personal health record exchange: Development and usability study. *J. Med. Internet Res.*, 22, 6, e16748, 2020.
4. Girardi, F., De Gennaro, G., Colizzi, L., Convertini, N., Improving the healthcare effectiveness: The possible role of EHR, IoMT and blockchain. *Electronics*, 9, 6, 884, 2020.
5. Celesti, A., Ruggeri, A., Fazio, M., Galletta, A., Villari, M., Romano, A., Blockchain-based healthcare workflow for tele-medical laboratory in federated hospital IoT clouds. *Sensors*, 20, 9, 2590, 2020.

6. Kuo, T.-T., Gabriel, R.A., Cidambi, K.R., Ohno-Machado, L., EXpectation prop-agation logistic regression on permissioned BlockCHAIN (ExplorerChain): Decentralized online healthcare/genomics predictive model learning. *J. Am. Med. Inform. Assoc.*, 27, 5, 747–56, 2020.

7. Abbas, K., Afaq, M., Khan, T.A., Song, W.-C., A blockchain and machine learning-based drug supply chain management and recommendation system for smart pharmaceutical industry. *Electronics*, 9, 5, 852, 2020.

8. Kuo, T.-T., Kim, J., Gabriel, R.A., Privacy-preserving model learning on a blockchain network-of-networks. *J. Am. Med. Inform. Assoc.*, 27, 3, 343–54, 2020.

9. Garg, N., Wazid, M., Das, A.K., Singh, D.P., Rodrigues, J.J.P.C., Park, Y., BAKMP-IoMT: Design of blockchain enabled authenticated key manage-ment protocol for internet of medical things deployment. *IEEE Access*, 8, 95956–77, 2020.

10. Chen, X., Wang, X., Yang, K., Asynchronous blockchain-based privacy-preserving training framework for disease diagnosis, in: *2019 IEEE International Conference on Big Data*, Los Angeles, CA, pp. 5469–73, 2019, doi:10.1109/BigData47090.2019.9006173.

11. Islam, N., Faheem, Y., Din, I.U., Talha, M., Guizani, M., Khalil, M., A blockchain-based fog computing framework for activity recognition as an application to e-healthcare services. *Future Gener. Comput. Syst.*, 100, 569–78, 2019.

12. Zhou, T., Xiaofeng, L., Zhao, H., Med-PPPHIS: Blockchain-based personal healthcare information system for national physique monitoring and scien-tific exercise guiding. *J. Med. Syst.*, 43, 9, 305, 2019.

13. Alnemari, A., Arodi, S., Sosa, V.R., Pandey, S., Romanowski, C., Raj, R., Mishra, S., Protecting infrastructure data via enhanced access control, block-chain and differential privacy, in: *Critical Infrastructure Protection XII. IFIP Advances in Information and Communication Technology*, vol. 542, J. Staggs and S. Shenoi, (Eds.), pp. 113–25, International Publishing, Springer, Cham, 2018.

14. Tanwar, S., Parekh, K., Evans, R., Blockchain-based electronic healthcare record system for healthcare 4.0 applications. *J. Inf. Secur. Appl.*, 50, 102407, 2020.

15. Lee, S.-J., Cho, G.-Y., Ikeno, F., Lee, T.-R., BAQALC: Blockchain applied loss-less efficient transmission of DNA sequencing data for next generation med-ical informatics. *Appl, Sci.*, 8, 9, 1471, 2018.

16. Nortey, R.N., Yue, L., Agdedanu, P.R., Adjeisah, M., Privacy module for dis-tributed electronic health records (EHRs) using the blockchain, in: *2019 IEEE 4th International Conference on Big Data Analytics (ICBDA)*, Suzhou, China, pp. 369–74, 2019.

17. Vora, J., Nayyar, A., Tanwar, S., Tyagi, S., Kumar, N., Obaidat, M.S., Rodrigues, J.J.P.C., BHEEM: A blockchain-based framework for securing electronic

health records, in: *2018 IEEE Globecom Workshops (GC Wkshps)*, Abu Dhabi, United Arab Emirates, IEEE, pp. 1–6, 2018.

18. Wang, J., Han, K., Alexandridis, A., Chen, Z., Zilic, Z., Pang, Y., Jeon, G., Piccialli, F., A blockchain-based EHealthcare system interoperating with WBANs. *Future Gener. Comput. Syst.*, 110, 675–85, 2020.

19. Talukder, A.K., Chaitanya, M., Arnold, D., Sakurai, K., Proof of disease: A blockchain consensus protocol for accurate medical decisions and reducing the disease Burden, in: *2018 IEEE SmartWorld, Ubiquitous Intelligence Computing, Advanced Trusted Computing, Scalable Computing Communications, Cloud Big Data Computing, Internet of People and Smart City Innovation*, pp. 257–62, 2018.

20. Zhang, P., Jules White, D.C., Schmidt, G.L., Trent Rosenbloom, S., FHIRChain: Applying blockchain to securely and scalably share clinical data. *Comput. Struct. Biotechnol. J.*, 16, 267–78, 2018.

21. Cichosz, S.L., Stausholm, M.N., Kronborg, T., Vestergaard, P., Hejlesen, O., How to use blockchain for diabetes healthcare data and access management: An operational concept. *J. Diabetes Sci. Technol.*, 13.2, 248–253, 2018.

22. Tariq, N. *et al.*, "Blockchain and Smart Healthcare Security: A Survey.". *Proc. Comput. Sci.*, 175, 615–620, 2020.

23. Al-Jaroodi, J., Mohamed, N., Abukhousa, E., Health 4.0: On the way to realizing the healthcare of the future. *IEEE Access*, 8, 211189–211210, 2020.

24. Banerjee, A. *et al.*, A secure IoT-fog enabled smart decision Making system using machine learning for Intensive Care unit, in: *2020 International Conference on Artificial Intelligence and Signal Processing (AISP)*, IEEE, 2020.

25. Hu, N. *et al.*, Wearable-sensors based activity recognition for smart human healthcare using Internet of Things, in: *2020 International Wireless Communications and Mobile Computing (IWCMC)*, IEEE, 2020.

26. Almansoori, *et al.*, Critical review of knowledge management in healthcare. *Recent Adv. Intell. Syst. Smart Appl.*, 99–119, 2021.

27. Khan, M.A. *et al.*, A Machine learning approach for blockchain-based smart home networks security. *IEEE Netw.*, 35.3, 223–229, 2020.

28. Priya, C., Enabling the efficiency of blockchain technology in tele-healthcare with enhanced EMR, in: *2020 International Conference on Computer Science, Engineering and Applications (ICCSEA)*, IEEE, 2020.

29. Tripathi, G., Ahad, M.A., Paiva, S., S2HS-A blockchain based approach for smart healthcare system. *Healthcare*, 8, 1, 100391, Elsevier, 2020.

30. Jain, P. *et al.*, A prototype proposal for AI based smart integrated platform for doctors and patients, in: *2020 8th International Conference on Reliability, Infocom Technologies and Optimization (Trends and Future Directions) (ICRITO)*, IEEE, 2020.

31. Fatehi, F. *et al.*, General data Protection Regulation (GDPR) in healthcare: Hot topics and research fronts. *Stud. Health Technol. Inform.*, 270, 1118–1122, 2020.

32. Rajput, A.R., Li, Q., Ahvanooey, M.T., A blockchain-based secret-data sharing framework for personal health records in emergency condition. *Healthcare*, 9, 2, 206, Multidisciplinary Digital Publishing Institute, 2021.

33. Daniel, C., Kalra, D., Section editors for the IMIA yearbook section on clinical research informatics, Clinical research informatics, *Yearb. Med. Inform.*, 29, 1, 203, 2020.

34. Liu, W. *et al.*, Smart e-Health security and safety monitoring with machine learning services. *2020 29th International Conference on Computer Communications and Networks (ICCCN)*, IEEE, 2020.

35. Memari, N. *et al.*, Computer-assisted diagnosis (CAD) system for diabetic retinopathy screening using color fundus images using deep learning. *2020 IEEE Student Conference on Research and Development (SCOReD)*, IEEE, 2020.

36. Fusco, A. *et al.*, Blockchain in healthcare: Insights on COVID-19. *Int. J. Environ. Res. Public Health*, 17, 19, 7167, 2020.

37. Hoosain, M.S., Paul, B.S., Ramakrishna, S., The impact of 4IR digital technologies and circular thinking on the United Nations sustainable development goals. *Sustainability*, 12, 23, 10143, 2020.

38. Hiwale, M., Phanasalkar, S., Kotecha, K., Using blockchain and distributed machine learning to manage decentralized but trustworthy disease data. *Sci. Technol. Libr.*, 10, 1–24, 2021.

39. Khatoon, A., A blockchain-based smart contract system for healthcare management. *Electronics*, 9, 1, 94, 2020.

40. Hiwale, M., Phanasalkar, S., Kotecha, K., Using blockchain and distributed machine learning to manage decentralized but trustworthy disease data. *Sci. Technol. Libr.*, 10, 1–24, 2021.

41. Ashraf Uddin, M. *et al.*, Dynamically recommending repositories for health data: A machine learning model. *Proceedings of the Australasian Computer Science Week Multiconference*, 2020.

42. Amrutha, N. and Balagopal, N., Multimodal deep learning method for detection of malware in android using static and dynamic features. *CSI J. of*, 13, 2020.

43. Santos, J.A., Inácio, P.R.M., Silva, B.M.C., Towards the use of blockchain in mobile health services and applications. *J. Med. Syst.*, 45, 2, 1–10, 2021.

44. Javid, T. *et al.*, Cybersecurity and data privacy in the cloudlet for preliminary healthcare big data analytics, in: *2020 International Conference on Computing and Information Technology (ICCIT-1441)*, IEEE, 2020.

45. Lobo, V.B. *et al.*, Convergence of blockchain and artificial intelligence to decentralize healthcare systems, in: *2020 Fourth International Conference on Computing Methodologies and Communication (ICCMC)*, IEEE, 2020.

46. Conard, S., Best practices in digital health literacy. *Int. J. Cardiol.*, 292, 277–279, 2019.

47. Shen, M. *et al.*, Blockchain-based incentives for secure and collaborative data sharing in multiple clouds. *IEEE J. Sel. Areas Commun.*, 38, 6, 1229–1241, 2020.

48. Tanwar, S., Parekh, K., Evans, R., Blockchain-based electronic healthcare record system for healthcare 4.0 applications. *J. Inf. Secur. Appl.*, 50, 102407, 2020.

49. Kim, S.-K. and Huh, J.-H., Artificial neural network blockchain techniques for healthcare system: Focusing on the personal health records. *Electronics*, 9, 5, 763, 2020.

50. Syed, F. *et al.*, A survey on recent optimal techniques for securing unmanned aerial vehicles applications. *T. Emerg. Telecommun. T.*, 7, e4133, 2020.

51. Lv, Z. and Qiao, L., Analysis of healthcare big data. *Future Gener. Comput. Syst.*, 109, 103–110, 2020.

52. Alfandi, O. *et al.*, A survey on boosting IoT security and privacy through blockchain. *Cluster Comput.*,1, 1–19, 2020.

53. Singh, S. *et al.*, Convergence of blockchain and artificial intelligence in IoT network for the sustainable smart city. *Sustain. Cities Soc*, 63, 102364, 2020.

54. Adate, D.B. *et al.*, Efficient handling of distributed data vending through blockchains, in: *Proceeding of First Doctoral Symposium on Natural Computing Research: DSNCR 2020*, vol. 169, Springer Nature, 2021.

55. Iqbal, N. *et al.*, A novel blockchain-based integrity and reliable veterinary clinic information management system using predictive analytics for provisioning of quality health services. *IEEE Access*, 9, 8069–8098, 2021.

56. Arachchige, P.C.M. *et al.*, A trustworthy privacy preserving framework for machine learning in industrial iot systems. *IEEE Trans. Industr. Inform.*, 16, 6092–6102, 2020.

57. Ismail, L. and Materwala, H., Blockchain paradigm for healthcare: Performance evaluation. *Symmetry*, 12, 8, 1200, 2020.

58. Abbas, K. *et al.*, A blockchain and machine learning-based drug supply chain management and recommendation system for smart pharmaceutical industry. *Electronics*, 9, 5, 852, 2020.

59. Kuo, T.-T. *et al.*, Expectation Propagation LOgistic REgRession on permissioned blockchain (ExplorerChain): Decentralized online healthcare/genomics predictive model learning. *J. Am. Med. Inform. Assoc.*, 27, 5, 747–756, 2020.

60. Badré, A., Mohebbi, S., Soltanisehat, L., Secure decentralized decisions to enhance coordination in consolidated hospital systems. *IISE Trans. Healthc. Syst. Eng.*, 10, 2, 99–112, 2020.

61. Kunickaitė, R., Zdanavičiūtė, M., Krilavičius, T., Fraud detection in health insurance using ensemble learning methods, in: *IVUS 2020, Information society and university studies*, Kaunas, Lithuania, 23 April, 2020, vol. 2698, CEUR-WS proceedings, Aachen, 2020.

62. Rachakonda, L. *et al.*, SaYoPillow: Blockchain-integrated privacy-assured iomt framework for stress management considering sleeping habits. *IEEE T. Consum. Electr.*, 67.1, 20–29, 2020.

63. Le Nguyen, T. and Do, T.T.H., Artificial intelligence in healthcare: A new technology benefit for both patients and doctors, in: *2019 Portland International Conference on Management of Engineering and Technology (PICMET)*, IEEE, 2019.

64. Patil, A.S. *et al.*, Efficient privacy-preserving authentication protocol using PUFs with blockchain smart contracts. *Comput. Secur.*, 97, 101958, 2020.

65. Li, Z. *et al.*, CrowdSFL: A secure crowd computing framework based on blockchain and federated learning. *Electronics*, 9, 5, 773, 2020.

11

Advancement of Deep Learning and Blockchain Technology in Health Informatics

Anubhav Singh[1], Mahipal Singh Sankhla[2]*, Kapil Parihar[3] and Rajeev Kumar[4]

[1]School of Forensics, Risk Management & National Security, Rashtriya Raksha University, Gujarat, India
[2]Department of Forensic Science, Vivekananda Global University, Jaipur, India
[3]State Forensic Science Laboratory, Jaipur, Rajasthan, India
[4]Department of Forensic Science, School of Basic and Applied Sciences, Galgotias University, Greater Noida, U.P., India

Abstract

Sensor-based well-being information assortment, far off admittance to well-being information to deliver continuous counsel, has been the key focal point of brilliant and far off human services. Such well-being checking and uphold are getting monstrously famous among the two patients and specialists as it does not need physical development, which is consistently impractical for older individuals who lives generally alone in current financial circumstances. Social insurance Informatics assumes a key job in such conditions. The gigantic measure of crude information exuding from sensors should be handled applying AI and profound learning calculations for helpful data extraction to build up a canny information base for giving a proper arrangement as and when required. The genuine test lies in information stockpiling and recovery saving security, protection, dependability, and accessibility prerequisites. Well-being information spared in electronic medical records (EMR) is commonly spared in a customer worker information base where the focal organizer gets to regulate like make, admittance, bring up-to-date or erase of well-being records. Yet, in shrewd and distant social insurance upheld by empowering innovations, for example, Internet of Things, Cloud, Sensors, Deep learning, Big information, and so forth. Electronic medical record should be gotten to in a disseminated way among various partners including, for example,

**Corresponding author*: mahipal4n6@gmail.com

T. Poongodi, D. Sumathi, B. Balamurugan and K. S. Savita (eds.) Digitization of Healthcare Data Using Blockchain, (235–256) © 2022 Scrivener Publishing LLC

emergency clinics, specialists, research labs, patients' family members, protection suppliers, and so on.

Keywords: Sensor, informatics, artificial intelligence (AI), Internet of Things (IoT)

11.1   Introduction

Brilliant and Far-off healthcare for old consideration [1] and patient role observing are receiving progressively well-known between analysts because of its relevance and acknowledgment in the present financial situation where the normal lifetime of person has expanded prompting living with age-associated sicknesses and deprived of customized care. Electronic medical record (EMR) [2] has customarily been spared in circulated information bases, which generally follow customer worker engineering. It has a focal controller called executive to administer or oversee authorization of end-clients to make, update, accessor erase well-being records. Well-being information detected by the devices are inclined to safety assaults and weaknesses [3]. In the detecting unit, a few little devices wearable, embedded or encompassing, and so on gain information. These gadgets are inclined to harm by fall while manual taking care of prompting loss of information or incorrect information, moreover gadgets might be undermined by the foe for taking or altering information, may be supplanted by an ill-conceived one and so forth In the correspondence sensor, unit information transportable through heterogeneous correspondence connections, for example, short-range correspondence joins for example Wi-Fi, Bluetooth, Zigbee, WiMAX having differing join security, quality measures, and so forth, away and preparing unit, information gets put away in cloud workers for added access, preparing, information building, criticism or guidance age, and so on [4]. The main period of this cycle includes detecting of information, the broadcast of information and sparing the information in the cloud. The subsequent stage involves admittance of information from the cloud, dissect or adjust information, refresh or erase information at cloud by numerous partners in medical care. Presently, for medical services information, protection and trustworthiness are two significant properties to be guaranteed so individuals do not stress over uncovering their delicate information through unapproved access. Trustworthiness of well-being information is significant as guidance age is mistaken in the event that it depends on wrong information. Hidden safety efforts and standards of Internet of Things (IoT) and cloud empowered medical care structure assists with evading extra computational multifaceted nature, bringing about more asset utilization because of execution of encryption calculations independently. As there are multiparties associated with well-being information access, if information should be scrambled at the sender and afterward decoded at relating beneficiary, then it would build idleness which is not alluring in time basic application like medical care. Also, gadgets in IoT-empowered shrewd medical services frameworks are varied having changing asset level, e.g., sensors to tablet/Smartphone/ PC to very good quality workspace/worker. Thus, one-sided encryption-unscrambling calculations similar to Data Encryption Standard (DES), Rivest-Shamir-Adleman (RSA) or Advanced Encryption Standard (AES) cannot be practical at all degrees of brilliant medical services design. In this way, direct classification may have a usage issue, yet privacy might be guaranteed by actualizing verification and honesty. Also, in blockchain [5], there is a regionalized organization where partners (clinics, specialists, labs for research, and protection supplier) are associated with one another called as blockchain hubs. Huge well-being information [6] put away in cloud database requires further investigation utilizing AI strategies for information extraction. Profound learning procedures are presently generally utilized in medical services; a portion of the mainstream applications incorporate early malady discovery, deoxyribonucleic acid (DNA) investigation, forecast of new medication viability, customized medicines, and so forth. One of the large difficulties of utilizing profound learning strategies in well-being informatics is the requirement for a tremendous measure of marked information. In any case, EMR may contain distinctive unlabeled information, for instance, X-beam pictures with no ailments like malignant growth and fibrosis. In this type of cases, unaided knowledge procedures can be utilized for marking of the information utilizing information drawing out. For named information, managed learning can be utilized. For a mix of marked and unlabeled information, semimanaged knowledge have to be taken inpractical. Convolution neural network (CNN) is profoundly affected by deep knowledge strategy among others, like deep auto encoder, deep neural network (DNN), deep belief network (DBN), recurrent neural organization (RNN) as well-being information are preoverwhelmingly picture-constructed these days. Deep neural networks in ongoing submissions, for example, medical care has effectively been executed with correspondence backing of the graphical processing units (GPU) [7].

11.2   Associated Works

The segment portrays a portion of the works identified with enormous well-being information and problems associated to insightful preparing of them utilizing profound knowledge procedures. Likewise, the security of well-being information regarding protection, verification, and uprightness is most extremely significant, so proficient security procedures to guarantee the security of large well-being information taking consideration of associated issues and difficulties are centered essentially. In the study of Ravì *et al.* [7], the creators had also introduced a thorough survey of profound knowledge procedures and execution topics in dealing with enormous well-being information as far as preferences, downsides and future extension. Utilization of profound knowledge in both sensor-based well-being information and picture-based information is additionally engaged. In well-being information science, EMR comprises the clinical antiquity of a patient, for example, determined to have and without clinical test, remedy exhortation and follow up, inoculation information, inclination to sensitivity, time-differing signals, for example, electrocardiogram (ECG) or electroencephalogram (EEG) or electromyogram (EMG) signals, tactile information utilizing unavoidable sensors, for example, pressure, temperature, beat rate, pulse, and so on. Well-being information in well-being informatics is not generally complete and named. Such information may likewise be incorrect. Also, as detecting or information procuring gadgets are mixed, information is not in a similar organization. Rate, size, and arrangement of information obtaining likewise change representing an incredible test to handling of such informational index. Certified difficulties in the utilization of profound learning procedures, for example, DNN, CNN, and so on in huge well-being information handling lies in the idea of this method itself. Insufficiency of right and complete preparing information may prompt helpless preparing of DNN model. Additionally, restricted preparing named information might be proper to get low blunder yet lead to gigantic mistake while trying with new database. Frequently, scientists put on profound knowledge methods, for example, CNN typical as black box deprived of having appropriate translation of shrouded coats, loads, and so on. Right and effective preprocessing, separating, standardization of preparing informational index is most extreme significant as clamor may prompt misclassification of information in AI strategies, for example, calculated relapse, and so forth. Notwithstanding all, if knowledge and suitable translation of hyperactive boundaries can be developed, the assemblies of DNN, most of the channels in CNN, can be skilful and predefined. In this specific circumstance, a blockchain-based clinical information distribution among untrusted different parties guaranteeing classification, validation, and admittance control has been projected [9]. To take out unlawful alterations by interlopers, exchange demands among real gatherings to get to information by the formation of cloud that is sure about with cryptographical keys. Also, a danger model has been shaped distinguishing safety assaults and dangers of well-being information just as clinical reports. At the point when demands for information access originate from a substance, signature-based validation is completed first, and afterward information is recovered. This information is scrambled and shipped off the requestor. The reason for the information access demand is additionally thought of. Execution assessment regarding inactivity as quantity requestor increments is done depending on genuine test situations. In Hölbl et al. [10], the creators have introduced a thorough and sensible survey of connected takes a shot at blockchain and its submission in medical services. The method deliberately discovers attributes of blockchain innovation that makes it appropriate to guarantee safe and confided in exchanges among numerous partners on the common clinical data base of patients. Countless distributions have been investigated and assessed depending on significant boundaries, for example, blockchain stage utilized, agreement calculation actualized, sort of blockchain network, brilliant agreements, and so on This work includes a thorough inquiry of blockchain papers in medical services during the length somewhere in the assortment of 2008 & 2019 to find that a decent excellence work deserving of investigation have been distributed just 2015 onward and actualized works have just been dispersed in 2017, 2018 demonstrating that enthusiasm for blockchain-based secure medical care is expanding. Despite the fact that blockchain is a hopeful and proficient method to deal with public clinical records between various invested individuals guaranteeing verification, classification, uprightness, access control, and so forth, it has a few restrictions and difficulties with regard to genuine medical care situation. In Shen et al. [11], the creators have recognized numerous difficulties, e.g., extra overheads as far as correspondence, capacity, delay in executing solicitations to get to information, versatility issues. In addition, the execution assessment of the planned blockchain-based calculation has been finished. A fascinating survey of the use of profound learning strategies in medical care has been introduced in Faust et al. [12]. It has arranged profound knowledge strategies practical to explicit physiological indications, for example, EMG, ECG, EEG. A nitty gritty and savvy representation on techniques for profound learning both numerically and engineering savvy will pull in growing or remaining specialists in connected regions. Creators in Griggs et al. [13] planned a remarkable safe far off medical services framework utilizing brilliant agreements by actualizing personal blockchain dependent on Ethereum convention. Its guarantees that the solitary verified clients can get to patient role well-being information. In this effort, just the occasions, for example, information detecting in sensors, preparing in keen gadgets utilizing savvy agreements, caution or alert age and shipping off guardians, and so on, are put away in the blockchain record. Genuine secret data identified with clinical database are spared in the EMR, and planning is kept up among blockchain and EMR record to get or recover information. A few restrictions while creating and actualizing this work have likewise been recognized for example proficient key administration, idleness, and so forth. In IoT-empowered frameworks, the number of sensors is high and will increment quickly after some time, subsequently, key age, circulation is a trifling issue. The extent of such framework to offer help to crisis well-being situation by decreasing idleness in blockchain record preparing is additionally a genuine test. An ongoing examination effort [14] is planned and CNN found a way to deal with anticipate persistent illness hazard. Creators have gathered genuine medical clinic information for a local persistent illness from focal medical clinics of China, since well-being information are generally unlabeled and comprises absent information, they have utilized a dormant feature model to recreate the absent data. They have actualized their proposition and contrasted and other infection expectation calculations. Their trial outcomes show the precision of 94.8% and a combination rapidity which is similarly improved. In Mozaffari-Kermani et al. [15], the creators have indicated that a portion of the AI calculations are inclined to a safety assault named as harming assault. In this sort of assault, the assailant increases the preparation database utilizing malevolent information, which are the sources of incorrect outcomes than anticipated. This can be perilous while diagnosing a diseased. At long last, creators have introduced anticipation procedures for these sorts of assaults [16–29].

11.2.1   Preliminaries

In this segment, the examination of the big data, IoT, different profound knowledge procedures, and blockchain innovation quickly. At that point, the proposed engineering has been examined in subtleties.

11.3   Internet of Things

Internet of Things associates the web with people, which can be accomplished over associating apparatuses and other bodily things with web [30]. This innovation is quickly developing and embraced in medical services.

Utilization of IoT built innovations has facilitated doctors and diseased a great deal. For instance, a diseased can accept guidance from specialists without truly go to see facilities or diseased who need constant observing, do not have to visit emergency clinics. Utilizing organic sensors and web, specialists can watch the physiological boundaries of patients. Remote body territory organization (WBAN) is one of the center advancements to help distant medical services. It essentially comprises of about battery-fuelled light-weighted remote sensors, which is wearable, furthermore, implantable. These sensors are associated with a passage utilizing short-range correspondence and that passage advances the information to a clinical office, for example, facility, clinic. These IoT frameworks produce monstrous information, which can be qualified as "large data". This information should be dealt with in a sure and proficient way, so that it may be provided by every partner.

11.4   Big Data

Enormous information is a huge database that comprises of information in an organized, formless, and semiorganized configuration. Organized information are essentially put away in various data sets or, on the other hand, in spreadsheets in an even organization. Picture, video, sound have a place with unstructured class, and these information are extremely hard to be dissected. Semiorganized information does not adhere to any exacting norm, for example, XML. This information can be utilized in rising applications, for example, clinical choice help, sickness expectation, and so forth, through different AI innovations. Medical services area creates an immense measure of information, for example, sensor information, past well-being records, drug records. This gigantic information is hard to oversee utilizing conventional programming or equipment frameworks. Utilization of cloud stage decreases the expense for proficient putting away and sharing.

11.5   Deep Learning

Profound learning is a noticeable solo component learning strategy, which is utilized to separate elevated level highlights from low-level information. Since include recognizable proof is laborious and costly, deep learning (DL) is utilized. The primary preferred position of solo knowledge is that it does not require named information for learning reason. In most of the cases, clinical well-being information does not contain a mark, similar to X-beam pictures without any ailment. Named information can likewise be utilized in DL methods, it is known as a regulated knowledge. It is a different sort of DL procedures. This segment, the examination of some well-known DL methods. Overfitting issue may happen if an excessive number of layers or perceptrons are included, subsequently, too many commotion information is caught rather than the genuine element. This declines the precision. The design of artificial neural network is appeared in CNN perceptron's are associated and throughout preparing, loads are allocated and changed in each cycle. After every emphasis, misfortune work is utilized to decide the mistake at that point back spread is done to change the loads. Meanwhile indications are transmitted in one heading, for example, input coating to the yield coating, it is known as a feed-forward organization.

11.5.1   Common Deep Learners

Diverse significant learning strategies are available; we need to shrewdly choose the best methodology for a specific issue.

11.5.1.1   *Convolutional Neural Network*

Convolutional neural networks are well-known profound knowledge systems that are excited by the human visual cortex. It is such a feed-forward framework that contains various coatings, and is also an arrangement of interlaced feed-forward coatings having convolution channels. Exactly when input data are gone and have done the coatings, the critical one next to the other characteristics is isolated in every covering. Therefore, CNN strategy is uncommonly useful in the hour of clinical imaging. For example, from tissue morphology, we can gather tumors (due to its irregularities). Convolutional neural network is applied to scrutinize plan, which is a problematic endeavor by human subject matter experts. For example, starting periods of various sicknesses can be perceived from tissue tests.

11.5.1.2   *Recurrent Neural Networks*

Repetitive neural networks (RNN) are alternative valuable method for medical services on the grounds that it underpins streaming information and can be examined. Determinate information vectors are utilized here likewise information, for example, discourse, text, or DNA arrangements can be given as information where yield relies upon past information. In the design of RNN, perceptrons are interrelated with each other, which go about as a recall for back to back inputs. For medical care situation, RNN can be functional for the investigation of clinical content similar to anamnesis. For example, a pool of diseased has a similar infection with various side effects. Repetitive neural network can filter a lot of text documents to discover the similitudes; this can aid a doctor for diagnosis of the disease.

11.5.1.3   Deep Autoencoders

Ongoing investigations depict that there is no general arrangement of highlights where everything is precisely on a different database. This is a solo procedure. Commonly, the covered-up layer is not exactly the information/yield layers. To separate the applicable highlights, it encodes the information in low dimension space, yet in the event that the information has higher dimensionality at that point, a solitary shrouded layer is not adequate.

11.5.1.4   Deep Boltzmann Machine

This is an unaided knowledgeable method, which the associations among the unique coatings are directionless and it comprises of different concealed coatings. In the event that we treat indeed, even coatings on one of the side and odd coatings on the other side, it might be called as a bipartite outline. There is no intralayer affiliation available in Profound Boltzmann Machine, only the sections of adjoining layers are related. Markov secures are used to choose the tendency of the likelihood turn out anyway in every way that really matters, it is moderate.

11.6   Restricted Boltzmann Machine

A well-known variation of Boltzmann Machine is Restricted Boltzmann Machine (RBM), which is hypothetical in nature. A particular appropriation work in random variable units is utilized to demonstrate an organization. It has a few stages in the knowledge cycle known as Gibbs Sampling, which change the loads with the goal that the remaking mistake can be limited. Hubs are undirected in RBM and subsequently, qualities can be proliferated in two ways. To plan as it is the standard methodologies is the usage of Contrastive Uniqueness (Cd) count, it is an independent information system. The two phases in album estimation implied negative and positive stages. The planning set is copied by changing the association course of action in the constructive stage; and the destructive stage, facts/data are replicated subjects to the current association arrangement.

11.7 Profound Conviction Organization

Profound Conviction Organization (DBN) it is used as a piece of Limited Boltzmann Machine (RBM). In DBN, hid covering of each subnetwork is related with the conspicuous covering of the accompanying RBM. Affiliations are aimless for the best lower layer's associations are coordinated. Coating-by-coating eager knowledge strategy is utilized to introduce DBN and step by step changes are done to accomplish the objective yields [31–40].

11.8 Application and Challenges of Deep Learners

Simulated intelligence has diverse compelling entries in the zone of prosperity informatics while Profound Learning (DL) techniques are later and its gathering is moderate. In any case, DL has quick progression and results can be cheerful paying little heed to the different issues. We can isolate clinical uses of DL in three classes.

- Predictive healthcare, for ex. the effectiveness of treatment estimation for various diseases.
- Medical Decision Support.
- Modified treatments, for ex. Designing of drug as per requirement of the patient.

11.8.1 Predictive Healthcare

This is proposed for acknowledging the sicknesses at the starting stages with the goal that the therapy should be started before the infection goes into the rudimentary stage. All around, area of Alzheimer is incredibly irksome in its starting state. Various locales of farsighted clinical benefits join anticipating the sufficiency of treatments. Significant learning (PL) can be used to recognize irregularities that is tricky to be perceived with the common binocular vision, for models Modernized hub tomography (Feline) yields or radiographs. DL are particularly fruitful in anomaly acknowledgment then it can distinguish little assortments which remains unseen by the individual in starting states. Clinical pictures might be used as planning data which can deal with the meager data issue and there is no extra difficulty in getting clinical pictures. Social records of patients can be moreover used for the early acknowledgment of affliction. Using these particular clinical data DL can collect an assumption model. Another huge of judicious clinical consideration can be figure of the capability of new drugs. New improvement strategies can be planned because results are not confident so far.

11.8.2 Medical Decision Support

The most significant uses of Deep Knowledge in well-being information science in clinical choice help which is particularly moving these days. Profound Learning methods can benefit the specialists in each phase of a clinical finding like recognition of the sickness, suggesting customized treatment, post treatment, and so on account of malady expectation from picture investigation, Deep Knowledge strategies it is more exact than people. Biomedical content examination should be possible through deep knowledge due to field independent nature, any sort of information can be examined just as connected utilizing DL. Relationship examination should be possible utilizing an alternate sort of electronic well-being database of patients to give a superior finding. Likewise, from a solitary informational collection, relationship examination should be possible, for instance, cerebrum areas can be connected from various X-ray pictures. For relationship investigation, CNN strategies are broadly utilized. CNN can make deliberations of the info information even information are gathered from heterogeneous sensors. A clinical specialist will be unable to experience a major clinical database of a patient; consequently, Deep Knowledge can take care of that work and can give clinical choice help.

11.8.3 Personalized Treatments

Customized therapies are firmly identified with clinical choice help. In view of the forecast Deep learning methods can uphold dynamic and consequently customized medicines can be given too medications can be planned. Electronic well-being records put away at cloud information base are generally multimodal and unstructured and because of the ongoing progression of advancements, DL can offer a conclusion dependent on the information. Customized medicines can be obtainable dependent on different information. For instance, biomarkers that can be controlled by deoxyribonucleic acid examination and genome drawing out. Biomarkers which is a natural state (infection) marker which can be estimated. Each illness is created inside the body of human itself. Biomarkers they can decide this likelihood of improvement and that can assist the clinical specialists with giving better forecast also, analyse. Genomics assists with distinguishing quality allele which is liable for the advancement of a disease. When the medication is practical its viability can be controlled by assessing the contrast in its qualities, it is called as Pharmacogenomics. This assists with decreasing the dose levels just as the symptoms of the medication. Profound Learning procedures perform very well in malignant growth arrangement from quality articulation information. For instance, to anticipate joining design, highlights taking out from Ribonucleic Corrosive and Miniature ribonucleic Corrosive data can be viably done using Profound Information. Along these lines, profound information help us research data from EMR and can idea redid drugs.

11.8.4 Difficulties

Essentially, in the space of prosperity data there are various challenges of Profound Information. In case of possibility of solutions there is a need of well-being, openness, dependability, effectiveness. For example, only emergencies can be dealt with prosperity sensors as they work with no impedance. Some progressing works portrays that weight channels can be is used in CNN for removing from raised level features yet the entire information component may create non-interpretable. By far the majority of the investigates utilize Profound Information techniques shy of knowing the opportunity of accomplishment; in case misclassification issues occur, by then they do not have the option for backup or modification. We have inspected in the past sections that immense datasets are required for efficient and strong getting ready model. Now a times massive clinical consideration data is open yet infirmity unequivocal data is at this point limited. In this way, DL is not suitable for applications including remarkable diseases. A different customary matter in getting ready of Profound Neural Organization is over fitting issue when the little planning information base is used. This happens when the total amount of tests in the arrangement set is comparative with the amount of limits in that association. Overfitting issue can be avoided by abusing guideline strategies, for instance, idler during the planning measure. DNN does not maintain rough data authentically as data; in this manner, a couple of pre-handling is required or the information territory ought to be modified. Designing of a DNN is managed by hyper limits, for example, the amount of directs in CNN, is an outwardly weakened examination measure and accurate endorsement is a ton of obligatory. Result of an ideal plan of hyper limits and right pre-handling of rough data is a troublesome endeavor and this can incite the long planning measure. Another critical issue in profound learning is that various DNNs can be deceived adequately; if the minor alteration is done in input data (including impalpable clamor in a picture) at that point, the examples will be misclassified [41]. It tends to be noticed that the vast majority of the AI calculations can be influenced by this issue. In the event that the estimation of a specific component is set, exceptionally high or low issues will most likely emerge in strategic relapse. In choice trees, if a solitary double include is exchanged in the last layer, at that point it will item mistaken outcomes. Along these lines, we can state that any AI strategy is defenceless for security assaults likewise, as a basic modification will lead the framework to deliver wrong outcomes.

11.8.5   Blockchain Technology

The blockchain is an assortment of decentralized CPU/hub where the information that can be put away in blocks. It is otherwise called a decentralized record where information blocks are also refreshed persistently. Information squares may comprise arrangements, contracts, deals, monetary exchange, well-being information, and so forth Blockchain was presented by a Japanese named Satoshi Nakamoto in 2008. Fundamentally, this was created to make sure about the digital money (Bitcoin) exchanges. In any case, these days this shared innovation has been received by different areas like fund, transportation, instruction. medical services, administration, and so forth Cryptographic calculations make the framework sealed; these calculations make the framework computationally difficult to adjust the information/exchange put away in this blockchain. A gate crasher requires to bargain 51 Percent of CPU/hubs to beat the amount of hashing intensity is focused on the blockchain network. The square comprises a heading and a message.

11.8.6   Types of Blockchain

As a rule, there are different sorts of blockchains that rely upon oversaw information, accessibility of the information and activities done by a client. It is arranged in there

- The Public Blockchain (permission less)
- The Conglomerate (public permissioned)
- The Isolated Blockchain.

Categories of blockchain, unmistakably blockchains which are available furthermore, noticeable to people in general are the public blockchain. Notwithstanding, the whole information is not available by people in general, meanwhile few aspects of the information it is in a scrambled organization to allow members secrecy [43]. In the open blockchains, anybody is allowed to join this blockchain and go about as a hub, or can turn into an excavator; consequently, endorsements are required. Digital money networks come in this class where a digger increases some monetary motivating force. For example, Bitcoin, Ethereum, Litecoin are digital money organizations in view of this public blockchain. In Syndicate sort of the blockchains, just chose hubs they are permitted to partake in this conveyed agreement measure [43]. This blockchain can be used by any industry, at some point syndicate blockchains are technologically advanced for a specific industry (e.g., medical care area), yet it is open for the public to utilize depending on the endorsement. The Private blockchains are decentralized organization [43] where only allowed hubs are joining the organization. The assignment of the hubs, for example, to accomplish exchanges, to implement shrewd agreements or to go about as a digger, it is controlled by the private blockchains. Essentially, a believed association deal with the blockchain. Stages like the Ripple [44], Hyperledger Fabric [45] just help the isolated blockchain network.

11.8.7   Challenges of Blockchain in Healthcare

Coordinating blockchain in the medical care frameworks is testing. Difficulties like the executives, specialized issues should be dealt with. Here we have talked about a few rational difficulties.

11.8.8   Interoperability

To share information among various medical care suppliers in a quick and successful manner is a testing job. Because of non-joint effort and absence of synchronization, it turns into a obstruction for powerful information distribution [27]. Patients and different partners of medical services may confront issues in information distribution and recovery measure.

11.8.9   Management, Privacy, and Anonymity of Data

The executives of huge well-being histories and distribution it over the medical care suppliers is not a simple undertaking while at the same time incorporating blockchain. Since well-being information is touchy in nature, it ought to be imparted distinctly to confided in parties. It must be guaranteed that an unapproved element does not gain admittance to the information. Public guidelines and security of information must be clung to receive blockchain in medical services.

11.8.10   Quality of Service

Movement period is the greatest concern in getting blockchain clinical consideration; data ought to be passed on inside the essential term. if the fundamental data is not passed on time than patient's life would be in the great risk. Since blockchain configuration is astounding in way, combining blockchain it may make computational deferrals. The huge load of investigation necessities be done, such as to diminish delay and keep up quality of service (QoS) to the extent relentless quality beforehand joining blockchain in clinical consideration.

11.8.11   Heterogeneous Gadgets and Traffic

Normal sensors are critical bits of clinical consideration and these kind of sensor contraptions make diverse kind of traffic. Emergency traffic, and normal traffic are two unique classes in which data is gathered. Emergency traffic is defined as the traffic gathered from the patients in an emergency situation and the data collected by sensors in standard noticing are called as would be normal traffic. Subsequently, despite the fact that executing blockchain in clinical benefits, a need instrument is a great deal of required, so the emergency traffic experiences a base deferment stood out from standard traffic.

11.8.12   Inertness

Inertness is a huge limit of clinical benefits. Some clinical benefits applications are considering ceaseless seeing to make investigation measure speedier. Blocks are affirmed before they are incorporated/normal to different accomplices in different blockchains; this cycle delays the delivery of data and assessment. Along these lines, when arranging a blockchain based clinical consideration system this concede should be considered.

11.8.13   Asset Imperatives and Energy Proficiency

Meanwhile, blockchains incorporate computational intricacies, cryptographic methodologies are the weight for these sensors [46]. Natural sensors are those asset compelled gadgets as far as computational force, battery reinforcement, and so on along these lines, this huge computational burden leads to an ascent of rise and fall of temperatures. This creates uneasiness in the understanding. As sensors are battery controlled therefore energy could be another test.

11.8.14   Storage Capacity and Scalability

Huge size of information is produced by well-being sensor; the hubs of the blockchain ought to be skilled to stock this enormous information. Well-being data may comprise of these medical pictures, lab information, drug history information, these all are required for a lot of capacity space. This issue could be explained if distributed storing stages are utilized.

11.8.15   Security

One more significant problem for fusing blockchain in medical services is the unwavering quality of information accumulated. Despite the fact that blockchain is famous in light of the fact that information put away in the blockchain is permanent, at times information that originate from the sensors might be ruined; thus, the information will stay degenerate. Information got in the blockchain hubs might be adjusted furthermore, it may be conceivable in light of various security assaults like phony information infusion, snooping, and so forth Thus, a compelling security instrument is also taken in consideration to guarantee the trustworthiness of the information.

11.8.16   Data Mining

The Blockchain depends on approval of information block; every information that originates by the sensors is well thought-out as a square of information and information is being sent by the sensors every time should be approved before allowing it to add to the chain. Thus, the difficult will emerge when the quantity of patients is expanded; all things considered; it will take more effort for time for mining on the grounds that the calculation burden will increment. Along these lines, proficient mining is likewise an exceptionally testing issue while coordinating blockchain in medical services.

11.8.17   System Model

Also, the regular IoT-based medical upkeep framework comprises of different layers (Three), the principal layer comprises of various well-being sensors like pulse, ECG, blood pressure, and so on. Normally, sensors, like pulse, ECG, blood pressure, are put on the patient's body. They help recognize exceptional physiological limits of the patient body, and thereafter, this information is transported to the personal digital assistant contraption. In the subsequent coating, PDA gadget advances the information to the clinical worker through a web association and also in third coating specialist/clinical office get admittance of the information. In any case, information in send is powerless for different digital assaults. Along these lines, it is required to receive identical privacy, confirmation, uprightness, entree control. The four boundaries are notable safety prerequisites for medical care requests [47].

11.8.18   Attack Model

Customary IoT-founded applications predominantly aspects two sorts of assaults: assault in contradiction of privacy and assault against respectability. Secrecy implies non-divulgence of isolated data of patient which is inclined to various dangers. Some normal safety assaults on secrecy are like Eavesdropping, pantomime assault, parcel sniffing, side channel assault and so on. Consequently, it is essential to deal with security assaults against secrecy. Trustworthiness guarantees the soundness of information during correspondences. These days, information of IoT-based natural sensors amass physiological information from a patient is sent to clinical offices since and this information is through some shaky wired/remote connections, therefore it is simple for a foe to truly/distantly catch the sending gadget and control the data assembled by sensors. Accordingly, it might prompt some unacceptable finding. A portion of the basic assaults against trustworthiness are information adjustment assault, counterfeit information infusion assault, replay assault, and so on In this projected structure it is well thought-out blockchain, which can shield assaults compared to honesty because it its tendency of at work and to deal with assaults compared to secrecy different cryptographic plans are utilized for encoding of information at these gadget and information can be unscrambled utilizing the mystery key of clinical specialist organizations.

11.9   Open Research Issues

This Particular Chapter, it has been portrayed the part of this blockchain and profound knowledge in well-being information science. Both of the rising advancements accept few difficulties, this research region, legitimate exploration can relieve these problems. As examined before, one-sided cryptographic calculations, like DES, 3-DES, AES, are not a decent decision to put on a blockchain for medical services submissions, putting these calculations will increment the inertness as far as information sharing. So low unpredictability encryption-unscrambling calculation configuration is a significant exploration territory. Key age and key sharing ought to be done in a productive manner with the goal that it does not build the multi-faceted nature of a blockchain based well-being information sharing stage. Additionally, as the quantity of partners may go on expanding in IoT-empowered keen and distant medical care, correspondence directly above issues, stockpiling directly above issues to be dealt with while planning a blockchain founded protected medical services framework. Well-being information put away in EMR are to a great extent unlabeled, missing information, boisterous information, and so forth So analysts ought to contemplate the remaking of information from the absent information, information separation is expected to eliminate the commotions. Likewise, well-being information is a huge information because of the enormous example size and volume of information. Sprouting scientists can investigate setting up own information base depending on their own examination setting other than utilizing existing benchmark information base thinking about demography, geological area, concerned illness, and so on of target subjects to accomplish more sensible canny information preparing outcomes. A lot of examination issues are there in this field, appropriate investigation is expected to embrace profound education and blockchain innovation in well-being information science is a wasteful technique.

11.10   Conclusion

This particular time is the time of keen and distant requests in different zones, medical care in explicit, where various partners are included identified with enormous well-being information which should be procured, put away, recovered in a dispersed way utilizing security strategies, for example, blockchain and prepared wisely by put on profound knowledge strategies. Problems and difficulties stay put on profound learning procedures as a clinical well-being best ever are consistently incomplete, perhaps wrong are not labeled. Likewise, as well-being best ever is huge in size and different parties are included, to perform all procedure of blockchain strategy may prompt extra stockpiling overhead, correspondence overhead, and inactivity to handle a submitted solicitation to get to information in this manner making IoT-empowered ongoing medical services uphold unreasonable. This book section examines all important profound learning calculations, and instruments, presents essential and central ideas identified with large information, medical services, security, IoT, and so on, and the outlines are blockchain-based engineering and characterizes assault model for a total opinion and investigation for the specialists are in this area.

References

1. Majumder, S., Aghayi, E., Noferesti, M., Memarzadeh-Tehran, H., Mondal, T., Pang, Z., Deen, M.J., Smart homes for elderly healthcare—Recent advances and research challenges. *Sensors*, 17, 11, 2496, 2017.

2. Bahga, A. and Madisetti, V.K., Healthcare data integration and informatics in the cloud. *Computer*, 48, 2, 50–57, 2015.

3. Movassaghi, S., Abolhasan, M., Lipman, J., Smith, D., Jamalipour, A., Wireless body area networks: A survey. *IEEE Commun. Surv. Tutor.*, 16, 3, 1658–1686, 2014.

4. Zhang, Y., Qiu, M., Tsai, C.W., Hassan, M.M., Alamri, A., Health-CPS: Healthcare cyber-physical system assisted by cloud and big data. *IEEE Syst. J.*, 11, 1, 88–95, 2015.

5. Nakamoto, S., Bitcoin: A peer-to-peer electronic cash system. *Decentralized Bus. Rev.*, 21260, 2008.

6. Andreu-Perez, J., Poon, C.C., Merrifield, R.D., Wong, S.T., Yang, G.Z., Big data for health. *IEEE J. Biomed. Health Inform.*, 19, 4, 1193–1208, 2015.

7. Ravì, D., Wong, C., Deligianni, F., Berthelot, M., Andreu-Perez, J., Lo, B., Yang, G.Z., Deep learning for health informatics. *IEEE J. Biomed. Health Inform.*, 21, 1, 4–21, 2016.

8. Karmakar, K., Saif, S., Biswas, S., Neogy, S., WBAN Security: Study and implementation of a biological key based framework, in: *2018 Fifth International Conference on Emerging Applications of Information Technology (EAIT)*, IEEE, pp. 1–6, 2018, January.

9. Xia, Q., II, Sifah, E.B., Asamoah, K.O., Gao, J., Du, X., Guizani, M., MeDShare: Trust-less medical data sharing among cloud service providers via blockchain. *IEEE Access*, 5, 14757–14767, 2017.

10. Hölbl, M., Kompara, M., Kamišalić, A., Nemec Zlatolas, L., A systematic review of the use of blockchain in healthcare. *Symmetry*, 10, 10, 16–17, 2018.

11. Shen, B., Guo, J., Yang, Y., MedChain: Efficient healthcare data sharing via blockchain. *Appl. Sci.*, 9, 6, 1207, 2019.
12. Faust, O., Hagiwara, Y., Hong, T.J., Lih, O.S., Acharya, U.R., Deep learning for healthcare applications based on physiological signals: A review. *Comput. Methods Programs Biomed.*, 161, 1–13, 2018.
13. Griggs, K.N., Ossipova, O., Kohlios, C.P., Baccarini, A.N., Howson, E.A., Hayajneh, T., Healthcare blockchain system using smart contracts for secure automated remote patient monitoring. *J. Med. Syst.*, 42, 7, 130, 2018.
14. Chen, M., Hao, Y., Hwang, K., Wang, L., Wang, L., Disease prediction by machine learning over big data from healthcare communities. *IEEE Access*, 5, 8869–8879, 2017.
15. Mozaffari-Kermani, M., Sur-Kolay, S., Raghunathan, A., Jha, N.K., Systematic poisoning attacks on and defenses for machine learning in healthcare. *IEEE J. Biomed. Health Inform.*, 19, 6, 1893–1905, 2014.
16. Sun, W., Zheng, B., Qian, W., Computer aided lung cancer diagnosis with deep learning algorithms, in: *International Society for Optics and Photonics Medical imaging 2016: computer-aided diagnosis*, vol. 9785, p. 97850Z, 2016, March.
17. Esteva, A., Kuprel, B., Novoa, R.A., Ko, J., Swetter, S.M., Blau, H.M., Thrun, S., Dermatologist-level classification of skin cancer with deep neural networks. *Nature*, 542, 7639, 115–118, 2017.
18. Abdel-Zaher, A.M. and Eldeib, A.M., Breast cancer classification using deep belief networks. *Expert Syst. Appl.*, 46, 139–144, 2016.
19. Fakoor, R., Ladhak, F., Nazi, A., Huber, M., Using deep learning to enhance cancer diagnosis and classification. *Proceedings of the international conference on machine learning*, vol. 28, ACM, New York, USA, 2013, June.
20. Ramsundar, B., Kearnes, S., Riley, P., Webster, D., Konerding, D., Pande, V., Massively multitask networks for drug discovery, arXiv preprint arXiv:1502.02072, arxiv.org, 2015, https://arxiv.org/pdf/1502.02072.pdf
21. Li, R., Zhang, W., Suk, H., II, Wang, L., Li, J., Shen, D., Ji, S., Deep learning based imaging data completion for improved brain disease diagnosis, in: *International Conference on Medical Image Computing and Computer-Assisted Intervention*, Springer, Cham, pp. 305–312, 2014, September.
22. Mohsen, H., El-Dahshan, E.S.A., El-Horbaty, E.S.M., Salem, A.B.M., Classification using deep learning neural networks for brain tumors. *Future Computing Inform. J.*, 3, 1, 68–71, 2018.
23. Amin, J., Sharif, M., Yasmin, M., Fernandes, S.L., Big data analysis for brain tumor detection: Deep convolutional neural networks. *Future Gener. Comput. Syst.*, 87, 290–297, 2018.
24. Bar, Y., Diamant, I., Wolf, L., Lieberman, S., Konen, E., Greenspan, H., Chest pathology detection using deep learning with non-medical training, in: *2015 IEEE 12th international symposium on biomedical imaging (ISBI)*, IEEE, pp. 294–297, 2015, April.

25. Ronao, C.A. and Cho, S.B., Human activity recognition with smartphone sensors using deep learning neural networks. *Expert Syst. Appl.*, 59, 235–244, 2016.

26. Zhang, P., White, J., Schmidt, D.C., Lenz, G., Rosenbloom, S.T., FHIRChain: applying blockchain to securely and scalably share clinical data. *Comput. Struct. Biotechnol. J.*, 16, 267–278, 2018.

27. Azaria, A., Ekblaw, A., Vieira, T., Lippman, A., 2016, August, Medrec: Using blockchain for medical data access and permission management. *2016 2nd International Conference on Open and Big Data (OBD)*, IEEE, pp. 25–30.

28. Peterson, K., Deeduvanu, R., Kanjamala, P., Boles, K., A blockchain-based approach to health information exchange networks, in: *Proc. NIST Workshop Blockchain Healthcare*, vol. 1, pp. 1–10, 2016, September.

29. Patel, V., A framework for secure and decentralized sharing of medical imaging data via blockchain consensus. *Health Inf. J.*, 25, 4, 1398–1411, 2019.

30. Tsai, C.W., Lai, C.F., Chiang, M.C., Yang, L.T., Data mining for internet of things: A survey. *IEEE Commun. Surv. Tut.*, 16, 1, 77–97, 2013.

31. Puri, M., Pathak, Y., Sutariya, V. K., Tipparaju, S., Moreno, W., Artificial neural network for drug design, delivery and disposition. Academic Press, 2015.

32. Puri, M., Solanki, A., Padawer, T., Tipparaju, S. M., Moreno, W. A., Pathak, Y., Introduction to artificial neural network (ANN) as a predictive tool for drug design, discovery, delivery, and disposition: Basic concepts and modeling. In *Artificial neural network for drug design, delivery and disposition*, pp. 3–13, Academic Press, 2016.

33. Siddique, K., Akhtar, Z., Kim, Y., Researching apache hama: A pure BSP computing framework. In *Advanced Multimedia and Ubiquitous Engineering*, pp. 215–221, Springer, Singapore, 2016.

34. Goodfellow, I., Bengio, Y., Courville, A., Deep learning. MIT press, 2016. Available online: http://deeplearning4j.org.

35. Chung, Y., Ahn, S., Yang, J., Lee, J., Comparison of deep learning frameworks: About theano, tensorflow, and cognitive toolkit. *J. Intell. Inf. Syst.*, 23, 2, 1–17, 2017.

36. Tan, J., Lungu, M., Avgeriou, P., Towards studying the evolution of technical debt in the python projects from the apache software ecosystem. *In BENEVOL*, pp. 43–45, 2018.

37. Wachter, S., The GDPR and the Internet of Things: A three-step transparency model. *Law. Innov. Technol.*, 10, 2, 266–294, 2018.

38. Kossaifi, J., Panagakis, Y., Anandkumar, A., Pantic, M., Tensorly: Tensor learning in python. arXiv preprint arXiv:1610.09555, 2016.

39. Paszke, A., Gross, S., Massa, F., Lerer, A., Bradbury, J., Chanan, G., ... Chintala, S., Pytorch: An imperative style, high-performance deep learning library. *Adv. Neural Inf. Process. Syst.*, 32, 8026–8037, 2019.

40. Bergstra, J., Bastien, F., Breuleux, O., Lamblin, P., Pascanu, R., Delalleau, O., ... Bengio, Y., Theano: Deep learning on gpus with python. In *NIPS 2011*,

BigLearning Workshop, vol. 3, pp. 1–48, Microtome Publishing, Granada, Spain, 2011.

41. Fawaz, H., II, Forestier, G., Weber, J., Idoumghar, L., Muller, P.A., Adversarial attacks on deep neural networks for time series classification, in: *2019 International Joint Conference on Neural Networks (IJCNN)*, IEEE, pp. 1–8, 2019, July.

42. Bahga, A. and Madisetti, V.K., Blockchain platform for industrial internet of things. *J. Software Eng. Appl.*, 9, 10, 533–546, 2016.

43. Zheng, Z., Xie, S., Dai, H., Chen, X., Wang, H., An overview of blockchain technology: Architecture, consensus, and future trends, in: *2017 IEEE international congress on big data (BigData congress)*, IEEE, pp. 557–564, 2017, June.

44. Koens, T. and Poll, E., What blockchain alternative do you need?. In *Data Privacy Management, Cryptocurrencies and Blockchain Technology*, pp. 113–129, Springer, Cham, 2018.

45. Androulaki, E., Barger, A., Bortnikov, V., Cachin, C., Christidis, K., De Caro, A., Muralidharan, S., Hyperledger fabric: A distributed operating system for permissioned blockchains, in: *Proceedings of the thirteenth EuroSys conference*, pp. 1–15, 2018, April.

46. Zhang, J., Xue, N., Huang, X., A secure system for pervasive social network-based healthcare. *IEEE Access*, 4, 9239–9250, 2016.

47. Saif, S., Gupta, R., Biswas, S., Implementation of cloud-assisted secure data transmission in WBAN for healthcare monitoring, in: *Advanced Computational and Communication Paradigms*, pp. 665–674, Springer, Singapore, 2018.

12

Research Challenges and Future Directions in Applying Blockchain Technology in the Healthcare Domain

Sneha Chakraverty* and Sakshi Bansal

Physiotherapy Department, School of Medical and Allied Sciences, Galgotias University, Greater Noida, UP, India

Abstract

The world has got digital revolution with the ease of storing and sharing data with the help of information technology, every sector is getting digitalized, and the healthcare sector is one of them. After the pandemic hitting the globe dangerously, people understood the need for digitalization of the healthcare domain better, either be it for consultation with healthcare practitioners to the delivery of medicines we need everything to be digitalized. However, one of the major challenges in this digitalization is the safety of data and here blockchain technology leads the role. Blockchain technology is a chain of blocks that maintains trust and information between different users and hence plays an important role in providing privacy of data to the users. Blockchain can resolve one of the major concerns of the healthcare domain that is interoperability. With the emergence of technology, blockchain will be a boon in the healthcare industry. In this chapter, we will discuss the application of blockchain across healthcare domain, such as data storage, management, and security on the Internet of Medical Things (IoMT) along with their challenges and its future directions, like in health education, clinical trials, drug delivery, claims, and bill management, and so on.

Keywords: Blockchain, healthcare, telemedicine, decentralized database

*Corresponding author: snehachakraverty84@gmail.com
Sneha Chakraverty: ORCID: https://orcid.org/0000-0002-8575-6274
Sakshi Bansal: ORCID: https://orcid.org/0000-0003-4353-9287

T. Poongodi, D. Sumathi, B. Balamurugan and K. S. Savita (eds.) Digitization of Healthcare Data Using Blockchain, (257–284) © 2022 Scrivener Publishing LLC

12.1   Introduction

Blockchain is a decentralized database solution that is gaining popularity over centralized databases because of its property of providing more security and privacy to the users. In this database, data are stored in blocks, and each block is linked with a previous block, thus making a chain. It is decentralized, which means it does not involve any third-party organization in the middle [1]. For every transaction ever done in Blockchain, the record is available only to participants, and the participants decide whom to share the data with. This feature provides the participants more transparent and secure transaction than centralized transactions involving a third party. Blockchain seems to address major technical problems of storing and sharing data, but before its implementation in various sectors, we need to go for in-depth analysis to avoid any shortcomings of its application [1]. In this chapter, we will discuss the application of blockchain across healthcare applications along with their challenges and its future directions like in healthcare education, clinical trials, drug delivery, and so on. Blockchain-based patient care applications include medical information systems, electronic health records, mobile health applications and telemedicine, health information and various lab tests done, and medical research systems. These applications may improve patient engagement and permission, improve healthcare provider access to information, and improve the use of healthcare information for medical research.

After the pandemic hitting the globe dangerously people understood the need for digitalization of the healthcare domain either be it for consultation with healthcare practitioners for the delivery of Medicine, we need everything to be digitalized. However, one of the major challenges in this digitalization is the safety of data and here blockchain technology leads the role. Blockchain technology gives the patients access to their medical data, for example, allowing researchers to use their data with consent for a static period. So, we can say that blockchain gives the patient the complete authority to handle their data. With blockchain technology, people can connect to hospitals and collect their reports automatically. Its application is not only limited to medical record-keeping and transactions but these data can be used in education also by different medical schools as the students need case history of different medical conditions during their course of study. Hence, we can say that the application of blockchain can be proven to be a boon in the healthcare sector because it has the potential to overcome some of the major difficulties in the management and delivery of healthcare data. The world is also taking this technology solution seriously as an IBM study states that around 56% of healthcare executives are planning to adopt blockchain by the year 2020 [2].

12.2   Healthcare

A country's growth is dependent on its healthcare because it ensures the well-being of its people. India is a developing country but in the healthcare domain, it loses its pace. The wave of COVID-19 in 2020 had awakened the status of healthcare in every country and it showed how we are lacking in the healthcare domain in terms of bed availability to healthcare workers [3]. However, if we observe the scenario of COVID-19 deeply, we can find the solution for improving our healthcare domain also. COVID-19 had made the world digitalized, it showed the importance of telemedicine [4], it showed the partnership between technology and healthcare can prove to be a boon in healthcare. We cannot create hospitals and increase the number of healthcare workers in a single day but by embracing technology in healthcare we can provide all the services to the needy in a short period. So, we can say that the future of healthcare lies with technology.

12.2.1   Stakeholders of Indian Healthcare Ecosystem

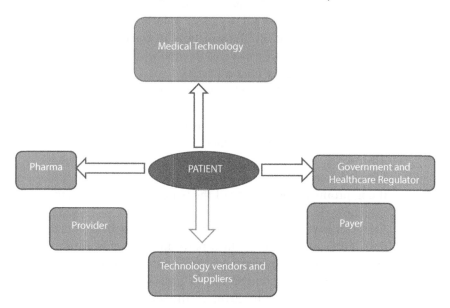

Figure 12.1 Flowchart showing some of the important stakeholder in Indian Healthcare Ecosystem.

Here, medical technology includes medical devices and equipment and diagnostics, Pharma includes retail pharmacy, pharma manufactures and suppliers, Provider includes hospitals, healthcare centers, and diagnostic labs, Payer includes different health insurance and third-party administer, government and health regulator include the ministry of health and family welfare, national digital health authority, and technology vendors and suppliers include hospital information system, electronic medical record, and lab information system [5].

12.2.2   Major Data Related Challenges in Indian Healthcare System

After review of the literature, the following are the points [5] that hold importance in healthcare data:

- Patient identification—a key challenge in the healthcare ecosystem in India is the unique identification of patients as different healthcare service providers have their way of unique identification although AADHAR is being linked to each service in India its implementation in healthcare is still a challenge [6].
- Scattered and disjointed data—a well-defined health information includes two parts-patient identification information and patients' health information. At the provider level, it is scattered in different departments, which creates difficulty in analyzing the data collected.
- Data ownership and duplication—currently, medical care providers are the owners of patient data, not the patients themselves making it easy for falsification, fabrication, and duplication by the care provider.
- Third-party interference—healthcare system of India relies on various third parties mainly for any data interchange, and it compromises the privacy of the patient and increases the total cost.
- Data security and privacy—not being the owner of their data and due to interference of third-party apps, patients' data are at a greater risk of cyberattack. There are reports of various cyberattacks in different sectors of India like banking, telecommunication, etc. In 2018, an Indian hospital was also

targeted by a ransomware attack that questions the data security and privacy between its users [7].

- Data exchange and policy—health policy planners find it difficult to collect, analyze, and exchange meaningful health information in a secure manner because of the lack of unified healthcare industry standards.

12.3 Need of Blockchain in Healthcare Domain

With the wave of digitalization, everything is getting digitalized and the healthcare domain is among one of them. From putting all the medical records to ordering medicine everything can be done through a single system ensuring patients' privacy through blockchain. With blockchain, every person can get their public address and it will be easy for a medical practitioner also to go through all the previous medical records, helping them in better diagnosis. Around the world, many cases are misdiagnosed, and the reason is the communication gap between practitioner [8], also when a patient switches his or her practitioner, they have to go for the entire medical diagnostic test all over again due to poor medical record keeping and its authentication, blockchains seem to reduce the burden of these challenges. For example, suppose a group of physicians and healthcare professionals is working on a critical cardiac case. Every member of the group used to discuss regularly the case and make a case progress report. Now, in 1 day that a patient got critical and they had to admit him/her to the ICU. If all of their previous detailed case progress reports are there in a database then it will be easy for any surgeon to operate the patient at that critical stage by only going through his/her previous records.

In medical practice, there is a continuous need for medical data sharing [9], be it referring a patient to some other practitioner or asking the patient to go for a diagnostics test. However, the ways of transferring these data via paper records or hard drives are not safe and ineffective because of the following reasons:

- It is slow and time-consuming because it takes at least 1 to 5 days to prepare the data and deliver it to patients, and data pickup by patients or their caregivers is also burdensome [10].
- It is insecure and cannot be kept for long times because there is a chance of tempering these paper copies or losing data from hard drives, etc.

- Because these do not contain the patient's whole data, the patient is wholly responsible for keeping a rack of his/her medical history records, and if some of these copies are spoiled, it is very difficult for the patient to retrieve the required data.
- It is not safe and confidential, because the whole data are not shared only between practitioner and patient, other parties have control over them, and also, the identity of the patient is easily identifiable here [11].

During, the COVID-19 pandemic, the world has better understood the need for digitalization and telemedicine in the healthcare domain. Nowadays, some apps like PRACTO gives the freedom to patients to have a video consultation with their practitioner and the system keeps a record of all the previous prescription and advice between the practitioner and patient, making it easy for the patient, as well as the practitioner. Telemedicine had been accepted by many countries, but in India, its growth is still slow. If blockchain is combined with telemedicine, it can bring a revolution in the healthcare domain.

12.4   Application of Blockchain in Healthcare Domain

Looking at the need, we can say that blockchain can be applied to the following sectors in the healthcare domain [12]:

- Prescribing medicine to a patient,
- Telemedicine,
- Prescription tracking,
- Clinical trials in healthcare,
- Medical data sharing,
- Registration tracking,
- Patient digital identity management,
- Keeping personal health records,
- Health insurance claim adjunction,
- Drug provenance,
- Organ registry,
- Pharma track and trace.

These applications will only be possible if the governments of various nations provide proper infrastructure and funding in the implementation of this solution. The proportion of national healthcare expenditure of GDP is the most important indicator for the overall population health of a nation. The current spending of India's total GDP on healthcare is very less (<4%), compared with the top nations of the world, which spends on an average >10% of the total GDP. From the data, it is clear that India needs to work on its national healthcare expenditure by bringing new technology for its growth and development. A report by World Economic Forum anticipation also states that 10% of the global GDP will be stored on the Blockchain by 2025 [13], which indicates the need for blockchain implementation in healthcare for the near future.

In India, healthcare share in blockchain usage is 12%, some of the states that are using or planning blockchain in the healthcare sector are Andhra Pradesh, Tamil Nadu, and Maharashtra [14]. Some of the start-ups in the healthcare sector are Kare4u, Sofocle Technologies, Pipra, Zebi, and their focus area include Insurance and medical loan, medical record keeping and maintenance, medicine prescription and supply chain, fake drugs, and fake prescription identification, secured healthcare data sharing. Many start-ups like CallHealth have successfully incorporated global blockchain technology like ChainTrail by the partnership with ThynkBlynk to enable the sharing of different healthcare data secure [13].

For providing quality healthcare services to its citizens Government of India has drafted a National Health Policy (NHP) in 2017 [15]. Under this, the Digital Information Security in Healthcare Act (DISHA) was drafted in 2017 [16], and its main aim was to ensure the patient's privacy and security of health data and implementing blockchain for the same purpose can meet the objectives of this policy. India is also planning to achieve the United Nations' Sustainable Development Goal of providing Universal Healthcare (UHC) by 2030 [17], and to achieve this, India needs a strong technology solution like blockchain to make the healthcare data readily accessible at the time of emergency, reduce frauds on insurance claims, and provide security and privacy to stored healthcare data.

12.5   Methodology

By looking at the importance and need of blockchain in the present scenario, we carried out a systematic literature review to identify major research works and proposed application of blockchain technologies in various sectors, including healthcare. To achieve this aim, we framed the following research question. What is the current status of research and what are the major challenges in the application of blockchain technologies in the healthcare sector?

12.5.1   Review of Literature

We had screened approximately 149 papers from different databases like PubMed, ResearchGate, Google Scholar, etc. Of those, only 54 papers matched our eligibility criteria, out of which some were press releases or blog articles as there are very few studies on blockchain in healthcare that is why we were able to include only 24 papers for the study.

12.5.2   Interviews

This research chapter aimed to go into the roots of blockchain applications to find its real challenges and comment on future directions, and for this, we had prepared an online interview [18] form in the form of

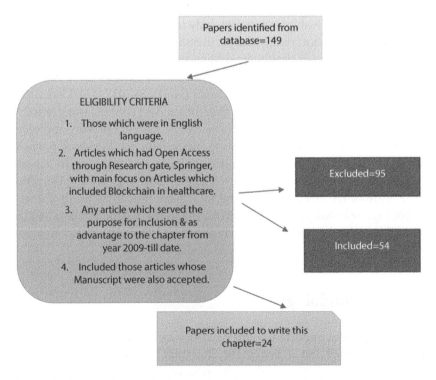

Figure 12.2 Layout of our methodology adopted to write this chapter.

Table 12.1 Overview of respondents.

Respondents	Occupation	Designation	Organization	Country
Respondent 1	IT	Blockchain Developer	Accenture private limited	India
Respondent 2	Software Engineer	Sr. Software Engineer	Sophos Technology pvt. Ltd	India
Respondent 3	Software Engineer Mobility	Tech Lead	1 tab	India
Respondent 4	Student	Independence Researcher	IGNOU	India

Google forms and circulated it among all the experts that have worked with blockchain technology. The interview form consists of 13 questions with a focus on different areas like the status of blockchain in healthcare industries, application of blockchain, potential benefits of using block-chain, challenges, and future directions. Our target population for this interview form was IT professionals, software engineers, data, and research analysts. We had circulated this form among 100 potential experts but got only four responses, which show the lack of upskilling among and limited knowledge of blockchain among various professionals. Table 12.1 shows the demographics of the respondent, and the interview form and interview responses are attached at the end of this book chapter in Appendices 12.1, 12.2, 12.3, 12.4, 12.5, respectively.

12.6 Challenges

With our knowledge gained after reviewing of literature available, we found out following as we faced challenges when talking about blockchain technology in the healthcare industry:

1. Talent upskilling: for blockchain to be a success, we are lacking that talent and skills among the professionals of our country. When we had started to generate a database by cir-culating a form, then we found out that only a handful of people are working on this Blockchain technology, and out

of them, very few had an in-depth knowledge of blockchain, besides being IT professional, they do not have much idea about blockchain, which suggests an immediate need of knowledge upskilling. A study by Clohessy *et al.* [19] mentions talent upskilling as the biggest challenge among service providers across India and the world.

2. Laws & regulation: Legal laws and regulatory bodies can have a direct effect on blockchain applications. So, the role of laws and regulations cannot be neglected in this case. Every country has its firm regulatory approach. However, in India, there is a lack of implementation and monitoring of firm regulation. The government of India is planning to adopt blockchain in every sector but its preparation, regulation, and implementation are at a very slow pace.

3. Privacy: blockchain is at a high consideration for its application in every sector due to its privacy. However, as everything have some loophole, blockchain lacks at providing anonymity, since the transactions are shared, it makes it easy for third parties to reveal the true identities of the individuals. So, privacy is still a major challenge for blockchain applications.

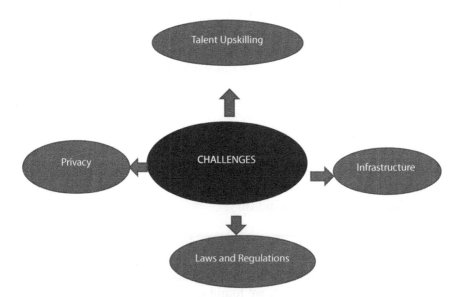

Figure 12.3 Major challenges of blockchain in healthcare sector.

4. Infrastructure: for blockchain to operate smoothly, highly efficient tools are required for storage, mining, processing, communication, and network administration or address management [20]. And sometimes, developing countries like India lack in providing these tools.

12.6.1   How to Overcome This Problem

When we started to collect information regarding blockchain in healthcare, we faced that there is lack of knowledge and a dearth of written literature regarding the same. The following points will suggest how we can fill those gaps for further references.

When we started to collect information regarding blockchain in healthcare, we faced that there is lack of knowledge and a dearth of written literature regarding the same. The following points will suggest how we can fill those gaps for further references.

Expand Blockchain Services: all companies should work on improving the quality of improving the services whatever they are serving in name of blockchain. There is a need for Indian healthcare providers to improve their proficiencies by implementing new applications across all major sectors.

Strengthen Blockchain Talent Development: There is a shortage of skilled blockchain talent in India, and the overall Blockchain system is on the verge to solve the problem effectively. Service providers have taken this task in designing and implementing blockchain training programs, both on their own and through collaborations with academic institutions.

Our review of the literature shows that the research field just started talking about blockchain, and there are only a few population groups who were aware of this technology. Therefore, more intensive researches are needed in this area to go into the depth of this technology. Along, with the theoretical research, some experimental studies focusing upon developing different protocols are needed for their applications in different sectors. Particularly, experimental studies using research protocols must ensure to study the various possible benefits of blockchain technology. Experimental studies will increase the reliability and validate the advantages and potential benefits of blockchain technology. This is applicable for the healthcare service providers, as well as the academic research.

12.7   Future Directions

According to researches and data available, it is believed that the market for Blockchain is expected to gain grow in the next 5 years. Data Bridge Market Research analyzes the market to account for USD 8362.01 million by 2027 growing at a CAGR of 72.0% in the abovementioned forecast period. This dependency on the blockchain is because of the data breaches that are occurring [20]. There is a surge in the adoption of blockchain technology because it is cost-effective and secure. In the blockchain, there is more transparency of the records, and the increase in technology like tracing and tracking has given acceleration to this growth of the blockchain for the healthcare market. On the other hand, an increase in new ideas of the organizations and investments for the development of the industry will open new and more opportunities for the growth of blockchain for the healthcare market in the next 5 to 7 years [21].

The report gives us details of recent developments, which has occurred in last few years, and provides the details of guidelines, which are to be followed. Analysis of the production, its impact on various levels in the market, details about the various opportunities available, details about regulations of market and changes being done, details of growth happening in the market, new product launches, developments, and various technical inventions in the market [22]. One of the main problems, researchers faced during the COVID-19 crisis, that when they were trying to analyze the data, they found that there is a lack of substantiated data sources that can be reproduced for research. While most of the data was taken from trustworthy sources like the Centre for Disease Control and the World Health Organization, and most of the data being linked from hospitals and various public and private agencies [22].

Reports suggest that one of the most relevant blockchain applications during the current pandemic is the Aarogya Setu app, which is a centralized app that helps for early detection and prevention of COVID-19. However, the world needs to be ready for such a pandemic like crisis and for that we need to come up with a decentralized database like blockchain that will not serve only the purpose of early detection and prevention but also help our scientists and researchers to be prepared with the solution of these crises with the help of proper data. Implementation of blockchain in healthcare will bring a revolution in the healthcare industry and it will help the industries to go interdisciplinary. It will provide real-time data to doctors, and it will be cost-effective for the patients as well. Employing blockchains in healthcare will help in clinical trials and medical research also, because as soon as a patient enrols in a study, complete collection of data will be available at once, due to availability on the distributed ledger, and hence the burden of data collection and its authorization will be reduced [24].

Gartner Hype Cycle 2020 Trend No. 2 talks about algorithmic trust, and it explains about using blockchain and its use for providing algorithmic trust. Gartner believes increased interest in blockchain will create increased digital authentication and verification options. Gartner also estimates that blockchain will generate $3.1 trillion in new business value by 2030. So, we can say that blockchain is the future for every sector [25].

12.8 Conclusion

Blockchain is now an established concept, and research and developments are increasing day by day contributing to the literature. This trend is also noticeable in the global healthcare industry sector, where the blockchain technology market is expected to cross $500 million by 2022 [26]. When we had started this chapter, we thought that we would get ample data to extract from the Internet, but when we went deep, we found that there is content available but when it comes to interpreting the data, then these data are not worthy. People who are closely working in this blockchain sector are hardly involved in the healthcare industry. With the responses from our survey form, we found that this field will be explored more shortly, which will help in improving the exchange of data about patients and will improve the healthcare sector.

References

1. Yli-Huumo, J., Ko, D., Choi, S., Park, S., Smolander, K., Where is current research on Blockchain technology? - A systematic review. *PloS One*, 11, 10, 1–27, 2016.
2. Carter, L. and Ubacht, J., Panel: Blockchain applications in government. *ACM Int. Conf. Proc. Ser.*, 2018 September.
3. Balsari, S., Sange, M., Udwadia, Z., COVID-19 care in India: The course to self-reliance. *Lancet Glob Heal [Internet]*, 8, 11, e1359–60, 2020, http://dx.doi.org/10.1016/S2214-109X(20)30384-3.
4. Agarwal, N., Jain, P., Pathak, R., Gupta, R., Telemedicine in India: A tool for transforming healthcare in the era of COVID-19 pandemic. *J. Educ. Health Promot. [Internet]*, 9, 190, 2020 Jul 28. https://pubmed.ncbi.nlm.nih.gov/32953916.

5. PwC India. Reimagining Health Information Exchange in India Using Blockchain. Pricewaterhousecoopers [Internet], 2019 April 28. https://www.pwc.in/assets/pdfs/consulting/technology/it-function-transformation/insights/reimagining-health-information-exchange-in-india-using-blockchain.pdf.

6. Health Policy, Programmes.

7. Dutta, P., 6 Biggest Ransomware Attacks that Happened in India [Internet], 2020. https://www.kratikal.com/blog/the-6-biggest-ransomware-attacks-that-happened-in-india/.

8. Hripcsak, G., Bloomrosen, M., FlatelyBrennan, P., Chute, C.G., Cimino, J., Detmer, D.E. *et al.*, Health data use, stewardship, and governance: Ongoing gaps and challenges: A report from AMIA's 2012 health policy meeting. *J. Am. Med. Inform. Assoc.*, 21, 2, 204–11, 2014.

9. Castaneda, C., Nalley, K., Mannion, C., Bhattacharyya, P., Blake, P., Pecora, A. *et al.*, Clinical decision support systems for improving diagnostic accuracy and achieving precision medicine. *J. Clin. Bioinform.*, 5, 1, 2015.

10. Nourie, C.E.N. and C. E., 2015, February. Retrieved March 01, 2018, from http://m.kidshealth.org/en/teens/medical--records.html [Internet]. Your Medical Records. https://kidshealth.org/en/teens/medical-records.html.

11. Bridged_patient_provider_centric_method_and_system.pdf.

12. Zhang, P., Schmidt, D.C., White, J., Lenz, G., Blockchain Technology Use Cases in Healthcare. *Adv. Comput.*, 111, 1–41, 2018.

13. SaiRam, R., Blockchain in Indian Healthcare System. Forbes [Internet]. https://www.forbesindia.com/article/great-lakes-institute-of-management/blockchain-in-indian-healthcare-system/57281/1.

14. Jani, S., *The Emergence of Blockchain Technology & its Adoption in India*, pp. 1–12, Universiy P, Systems MP, New Delhi, India, 2019 July.

15. Chaudhuri, B.R. and Roy, B.N., National health policy. *J. Indian Med. Assoc.*, 72, 6, 149–51, 1979.

16. Welfare M of H& F, Section) (eHealth. Digital Information Security in Healthcare, Act [Internet], 2018. https://www.nhp.gov.in/NHPfiles/R_4179_1521627488625_0.pdf.

17. Al MPK *et al.*, Strengthening health systems for universal health coverage and sustainable development [Internet], 2017. http://dx.doi.org/10.2471/BLT.16.187476.

18. Bogoeva, A., Blockchain in Healthcare: Opportunities and Challenges Blockchain Technology in Healthcare: Opportunities and Challenges as part of the degree program Master of Science Business Informatics, 2019 July.

19. Clohessy, T., Acton, T., Rogers, N., Blockchain Adoption: Technological, Organisational and Environmental Considerations, in: *Business Transformation through Blockchain*, vol. I, pp. 47–76, Springer International Publishing, Cham, 2019, https://doi.org/10.1007/978-3-319-98911-2_2.

20. Mohsin, A.H., Zaidan, A.A., Zaidan, B.B., Albahri, O.S., Albahri, A.S., Alsalem, M.A. *et al.*, Blockchain authentication of network applications:

Taxonomy, classification, capabilities, open challenges, motivations, recommendations and future directions. *Comput. Stand Interface. [Internet]*, 2019;64, 41–60, December 2018, https://doi.org/10.1016/j.csi.2018.12.002.

21. *Research DBM. Blockchain for healthcare market by 2027*, 2020, Internet blog resource, 2020. https://primefeed.in/news/4489835/blockchain-for-healthcare-market-by-2027-ibm-corporation-microsoft-guardtime-gem-hashed-health/.

22. *Research DBM. Blockchain for Healthcare Market Big Growth in 2020| IBM Corporation, Microsoft, Guardtime, PokitDok, Inc., Gem, Hashed Health, Chronicled, iSolve, LLC*, Internet blog resource, 2020. https://www.openpr.com/news/1916239/blockchain-for-healthcare-market-big-growth-in-2020-ibm.

23. Schlapkohl, K., Blockchain applications that are transforming the world. IBM [Internet], 2020. https://www.ibm.com/blogs/blockchain/2020/04/blockchain-applications-that-are-transforming-the-world/.

24. Siyal, A.A., Junejo, A.Z., Zawish, M., Ahmed, K., Khalil, A., Soursou, G., Applications of Blockchain Technology in Medicine and Healthcare: Challenges and Future Perspectives. *Cryptography*, 3, 13, 2019.

25. Panetta, K., 5 Trends Drive the Gartner Hype Cycle for Emerging Technologies, 2020 [Internet]. *Smarter Gartner*, 2020. https://www.gartner.com/smarterwithgartner/5-trends-drive-the-gartner-hype-cycle-for-emerging-technologies-2020/.

26. Hasselgren, A., Kralevska, K., Gligoroski, D., Pedersen, S.A., Faxvaag, A., Blockchain in healthcare and health sciences—A scoping review. *Int. J. Med. Inform.*, 134, 2020.

Appendix

Appendix 12.1

Interview Form

11/3/2020 Interview Form https://docs.google.com/forms/d/1cJBX3vZ WHM3nsaynBoGopDXczTjs7k5C42G_ifLtlmY/edit 1/5

Interview Form

I 'Dr. Sneha Chakraverty' and 'Dr. Sakshi Bansal' (Assistant professor, Galgotias University), is writing a book chapter on 'Research challenges and future directions in applying blockchain technology in the healthcare domain' and for this, we are interviewing people from IT sectors, data scientist, healthcare professionals, or anyone having any idea of blockchain. We, hereby declare that the data given by you will be kept confidential and we will only analyze the results from the data for academic purposes. None, of your personal information, will be shared with others. For any assistance or query, you can contact us at the following email id: sneha.chakraverty@galgotiasuniversity.edu.in or sakshi.bansal@galgotiasuniversity.edu.in

1. Email address
2. Name
3. Occupation
4. Designation
5. Organization
6. Do you give consent to take part in this study?
   Mark only one oval.
   Yes
   No
   Maybe
7. What is the status of blockchain in the healthcare industry?
8. What are the most prominent examples of implemented use cases/applications you have encountered?
9. How will the technology impact the healthcare industry in general? What potential benefits can result from the implementation?
10. What are prominent issues in the field of healthcare that can be positively impacted by the implementation of blockchain or technology in general?

11. Can blockchain coexist with existing regulations and processes?
Mark only one oval.
YES
No
MAYBE
Other:
11/3/2020 Interview Form https://docs.google.com/forms/d/1c-JBX3vZWHM3nsaynBoGopDXczTjs7k5C42G_ifLtlmY/edit 3/5

12. What are other regulatory implications of blockchain in the healthcare industry? What regulations need to be introduced or discarded or modified?

13. What are the success metrics for blockchain in general and in the healthcare industry?

14. What should healthcare companies and organizations do to successfully implement blockchain initiatives (organizational and technological change)?

15. What are the internal governance issues that healthcare organizations should consider?

16. What are the biggest hurdles/challenges the industry is currently facing that prevent the implementation and adoption of blockchain technology?

17. What is your prediction for the technology's development and adoption in the next year and 5years?

18. What variations of the technology you can envision that would be more widely adaptable than the Blockchain?

19. Additional remarks/insights on the topic?

Appendix 12.2: Response 1

11/3/2020 Interview Form https://docs.google.com/forms/d/1cJBX3vZW HM3nsaynBoGopDXczTjs7k5C42G_ifLtlmY/edit#response=ACYDBN-jeMM8D2lIlGnd78pTuun9b8yJ... 1/4

Interview Form

I 'Dr. Sneha Chakraverty' and 'Dr. Sakshi Bansal' (Assistant professor, Galgotias University), is writing a book chapter on 'Research challenges and future directions in applying blockchain technology in the healthcare domain' and for this, we are interviewing people from IT sectors, data scientist, healthcare professionals, or anyone having any idea of blockchain.

We, hereby declare that the data given by you will be kept confidential and we will only analyze the results from the data for academic purposes. None, of your personal information, will be shared with others. For any assistance or query, you can contact us at the following email id: sneha.chakraverty@galgotiasuniversity.edu.in or sakshi.bansal@galgotiasuniversity.edu.in

Name
Occupation *
IT
Designation *
Blockchain Developer
Organization *
Accenture private limited
Do you give consent to take part in this study? *
Yes√
No
Maybe

What is the status of blockchain in the healthcare industry? *
I have not worked in healthcare

What are the most prominent examples of implemented use cases/ applications you have encountered? *
Supply chain management

How will the technology impact the healthcare industry in general? What potential benefits can result from the implementation? *

1. Medicine that are defective can be traced and revoked only that particular batch not the whole batch. Track the source of medicine.
2. Organ donor and receiver can be put on blockchain to keep a track and be donor be available in case of needed.

What are prominent issues in the field of healthcare that can be positively impacted by the implementation of blockchain or technology in general? *
Customer health history can be tracked.

Can blockchain coexist with existing regulations and processes? *
YES√
No

MAYBE
Other:

What are other regulatory implications of blockchain in the healthcare industry? What regulations need to be introduced or discarded or modified?
There are no past records of any individual in emergency care.

What are the success metrics for blockchain in general and in the healthcare industry? *
It is really great even satisfactory customer reviews

What should healthcare companies and organizations do to successfully implement blockchain initiatives (organizational and technological change)? *
Start making pilot with limited nodes and then go to production and then slowly try to onboard other nodes.

What are the internal governance issues that healthcare organizations should consider? *
Any healthcare practitioner's degree is genuine or background check takes lot of time and dependent on third party for the same.

What are the biggest hurdles/challenges the industry is currently facing that prevent the implementation and adoption of blockchain technology? *
It is still new so people are not willing to go full onboard on production.

What is your prediction for the technology's development and adoption in the next year and 5years? *
Everything is going digital and using the next gen technology.

What variations of the technology you can envision that would be more widely adaptable than the Blockchain? *
Machine learning to predict the diagnosis of patients considering the history of patient.

Additional remarks/insights on the topic?
People will help from having blockchain and machine learning used in healthcare services.

Appendix 12.3: Response 2

11/3/2020 Interview Form https://docs.google.com/forms/d/1cJBX3vZW
HM3nsaynBoGopDXczTjs7k5C42G_ifLtlmY/edit#response=ACYDB-
NiLfaswBBTxD8u2JlKmMWnkF... 1/4

Interview Form

I 'Dr. Sneha Chakraverty' and 'Dr. Sakshi Bansal' (Assistant professor,
Galgotias University), is writing a book chapter on 'Research challenges
and future directions in applying blockchain technology in the healthcare
domain' and for this, we are interviewing people from IT sectors, data scientist, healthcare professionals, or anyone having any idea of blockchain.
We, hereby declare that the data given by you will be kept confidential and
we will only analyze the results from the data for academic purposes. None,
of your personal information, will be shared with others. For any assistance
or query, you can contact us at the following email id :sneha.chakraverty@
galgotiasuniversity.edu.in or sakshi.bansal@galgotiasuniversity.edu.in

Occupation *
Software Engineer
Designation *
Sr. Software Engineer
Organization *
Sophos Technology pvt. Ltd.
Do you give consent to take part in this study? *
Yes√
No
Maybe

What is the status of blockchain in the healthcare industry? *
Not many innovations coming up

**What are the most prominent examples of implemented use cases/
applications you have encountered?** *
None that i know of

**How will the technology impact the healthcare industry in general?
What potential benefits can result from the implementation?** *
Better impact on overall health of society. Better understanding of
human health

What are prominent issues in the field of healthcare that can be positively impacted by the implementation of blockchain or technology in general? *
Predicting diseases due to lifestyle and age at which an individual maybe impacted

Can blockchain coexist with existing regulations and processes? *
YES
No
MAYBE√
Other:

What are other regulatory implications of blockchain in the healthcare industry? What regulations need to be introduced or discarded or modified?
What are the success metrics for blockchain in general and in the healthcare industry? *
NA

What should healthcare companies and organizations do to successfully implement blockchain initiatives (organizational and technological change)? *
Invest in RnD and getter an understanding of what blockchain is and focus less on making profit and improving health of individuals

What are the internal governance issues that healthcare organizations should consider? *
Customer over business

What are the biggest hurdles/challenges the industry is currently facing that prevent the implementation and adoption of blockchain technology? *
Lack of knowledge and maybe will to implement it

What is your prediction for the technology's development and adoption in the next year and 5years? *
High scale rapid development going in the health sector

What variations of the technology you can envision that would be more widely adaptable than the Blockchain? *
NA

Additional remarks/insights on the topic?

Appendix 12.4: Response 3

11/3/2020 Interview Form https://docs.google.com/forms/d/1cJBX3vZW
HM3nsaynBoGopDXczTjs7k5C42G_ifLtlmY/edit#response=ACYDBN-
jk8Mfa4iidrYPTew3ZlmXiftCfi2... 1/4

Interview Form

I 'Dr. Sneha Chakraverty' and 'Dr. Sakshi Bansal' (Assistant professor,
Galgotias University), is writing a book chapter on 'Research challenges
and future directions in applying blockchain technology in the healthcare
domain' and for this, we are interviewing people from IT sectors, data scientist, healthcare professionals, or anyone having any idea of blockchain.
We, hereby declare that the data given by you will be kept confidential and
we will only analyze the results from the data for academic purposes. None,
of your personal information, will be shared with others. For any assistance
or query, you can contact us at the following email id :sneha.chakraverty@
galgotiasuniversity.edu.in or sakshi.bansal@galgotiasuniversity.edu.in

Occupation *
Software Engineer Mobility
Designation *
Tech Lead
Organization *
1Tab
Do you give consent to take part in this study? *
Yes√
No
Maybe
What is the status of blockchain in the healthcare industry? *
NA

**What are the most prominent examples of implemented use cases/
applications you have encountered?** *
Prescription reading via a OCR, it helps us to place an order fast mode.

**How will the technology impact the healthcare industry in general?
What potential benefits can result from the implementation?** *
Door stop solution, time consuming, better option

What are prominent issues in the field of healthcare that can be positively impacted by the implementation of blockchain or technology in general?*

Customer service

Can blockchain coexist with existing regulations and processes? *

YES

No

MAYBE√

Other:

What are other regulatory implications of blockchain in the healthcare industry? What regulations need to be introduced or discarded or modified?

Authentication

What are the success metrics for blockchain in general and in the healthcare industry? *

50-50

What should healthcare companies and organizations do to successfully implement blockchain initiatives (organizational and technological change)? *

Analysis, Discussion and Conclusion

What are the internal governance issues that healthcare organizations should consider? *

Authentic

What are the biggest hurdles/challenges the industry is currently facing that prevent the implementation and adoption of blockchain technology? *

Policy

What is your prediction for the technology's development and adoption in the next year and 5years? *

High

What variations of the technology you can envision that would be more widely adaptable than the Blockchain? *

Na

Additional remarks/insights on the topic?

Appendix 12.5: Response 4

11/3/2020 Interview Form https://docs.google.com/forms/d/1cJBX3vZW HM3nsaynBoGopDXczTjs7k5C42G_ifLtlmY/edit#response=ACYDBN-h61dapU5-Uy1k9Vr4xmXnMQ... 1/5

Interview Form

I 'Dr. Sneha Chakraverty' and 'Dr. Sakshi Bansal' (Assistant professor, Galgotias University), is writing a book chapter on 'Research challenges and future directions in applying blockchain technology in the healthcare domain' and for this, we are interviewing people from IT sectors, data scientist, healthcare professionals, or anyone having any idea of blockchain. We, hereby declare that the data given by you will be kept confidential and we will only analyze the results from the data for academic purposes. None, of your personal information, will be shared with others. For any assistance or query, you can contact us at the following email id :sneha.chakraverty@ galgotiasuniversity.edu.in or sakshi.bansal@galgotiasuniversity.edu.in

Occupation *
Student (PGDIS)
Designation *
Independent Researcher
Organization *
IGNOU
Do you give consent to take part in this study? *
Yes√
No
Maybe

What is the status of blockchain in the healthcare industry? *
Around 10% of the total BCT initiatives in India are in healthcare sector. It has only been a couple of years time since the healthcare industry started blockchain adoption. The healthcare industry is included in 'followers" category, as compared to early adaptors & innovators category. Most of the projects have not yet entered the production stage & are in the Proof of Concept (POC) & Pilot Stages.

What are the most prominent examples of implemented use cases/ applications you have encountered? *
Cold chain tracking, Drug Provenance, Organ Registry, Pharma track and trace, Physician Recertification, Medical Record maintenance & sharing, providing insurance & medical loans, identify & prevent counterfeit medicines are some of the applications for BCT in healthcare.

How will the technology impact the healthcare industry in general? What potential benefits can result from the implementation? *
Impact: increase trust in healthcare, provide confidentiality, create universal lifetime medical history, reduce per capita cost of healthcare, reduce clinician & staff burnout. Potential Benefits: improve the patient experience of care, providing insurance & medical loans, pharma traceability, real-time analysis, hassle free medical records, compare effectiveness of various treatments & procedures, increase in quality of service, compliance with best practices guidelines.

What are prominent issues in the field of healthcare that can be positively impacted by the implementation of blockchain or technology in general? *
1. Elimination of fake drugs, 2. Professional Accountability, 3. Professional Registration & Recertification, 4. Secured healthcare data sharing, Integration with Insurance companies and patients, 5. Medical Record maintenance, 6. Medical supply chain including medical waste management.

Can blockchain coexist with existing regulations and processes? *
YES√
No
MAYBE
Other:

What are other regulatory implications of blockchain in the healthcare industry? What regulations need to be introduced or discarded or modified?
For governing the standards for Blockchain Technology, it would be better to have a National Blockchain Association (NBA), with representatives from industry & government. Besides developing the BCT

standards, it shall provide a Integrated Blockchain Information Platform for various industries. As far as discarding or modifying regulations is concerned, BCT can always co-exist with the existing regulations, as BCT is only a means (like internet) & not a product in itself. One can easily implement/program the "EHR/EMR standards for India" on a Blockchain platform.

What are the success metrics for blockchain in general and in the healthcare industry? *

In general, success metrics after BCT adoption are Transparency, Trust, Decentralization, & Immutability. In specific to Healthcare industry, lower readmission rates(high effectiveness of care), efficient use of medical imaging & records, decrease in medication errors, easy patient follow-up, patient confidentiality, reduced average insurance claim processing time & cost, as well as, claims denial rate are some key success metrics after BCT adoption.

What should healthcare companies and organizations do to successfully implement blockchain initiatives (organizational and technological change)? *

Business Process Re-engineering using BCT, Strengthen Blockchain Talent Development, Invest in Patents & IP, Strategic R&D investment, Developing POCs on BCT, & Change Management.

What are the internal governance issues that healthcare organizations should consider? *

1. Integration Issue: Some BCT solutions require significant changes in existing systems. So Healthcare institutions must strategize the transition. 2. Cultural/Adoption Issues: For complete shift it requires buy-in of its users & operators. 3. Nascent/Experimental Stage: Most projects in POC or Pilot stage, besides an acute shortage of skilled BCT professionals. 4. Initial Costs.

What are the biggest hurdles/challenges the industry is currently facing that prevent the implementation and adoption of blockchain technology? *

Besides the uncertain regulatory status, the Control, Security, & Privacy are some of the technical challenges in the adoption of BCT. Other than that there is a high initial cost as the technology is in its nascent/initial stage. Moreover the current pandemic scenario has overburdened the healthcare industry which might delay the BCT adoption.

What is your prediction for the technology's development and adoption in the next year and 5years? *

With the current market size of BCT initiatives estimated to be USD 3 Billion in 2020, it is predicted to reach USD 30 Billion by 2025. There has been a tremendous growth in BCT especially over the last few years. Besides the surge in investment, the value demonstration through POCs & pilot engagement has helped in building a momentum towards enterprise adoption. Having said that we must not be surprised if the investments in BCT initiatives in the upcoming year, exceeds the total value of investments in the past years.

What variations of the technology you can envision that would be more widely adaptable than the Blockchain? *

Other than BCT there are some emerging technologies that could revolutionise the healthcare industry, like, Artificial Intelligence (to store medical records, design treatment plans, create drugs faster) and Virtual Reality & Augmented Reality (in training & performing surgery). Some other fascinating technologies are 3D printing, nanomedicine, robotics, healthcare wearables, trackers & sensors.

Additional remarks/insights on the topic?

Every invention is aimed at bridging some GAP that exists in the society & as a by-product gives rise to some new companies. Like the Steam Engine (1800s) & Internet (1900s) which bridged the POWER GAP & DISTANCE GAP respectively, gave rise to the manufacturing companies & online companies. The Blockchain Technology bridges the TRUST GAP, giving rise to a new kind of companies which will change the way we trust in business & commerce.

Index

Also of Interest

Check out these published and forthcoming titles in the "Next-Generation Computing and Communication Engineering" series from Scrivener Publishing

Role of Edge Analytics on Sustainable Smart City Development
Edited by G.R. Kanagachidambaresan
Published 2020. ISBN 9781119681281

www.scrivenerpublishing.com

Printed and bound by CPI Group (UK) Ltd, Croydon, CR0 4YY

27/10/2024

14580175-0002